Macmillan/McGraw-Hill Edition

McGRAW-HILL READING

**McGraw-Hill
School Division**

New York   Farmington

Contributors

The Princeton Review, Time Magazine

The Princeton Review is not
affiliated with Princeton
University or ETS.

McGraw-Hill School Division

A Division of The McGraw-Hill Companies

McGraw-Hill School Division
Two Penn Plaza
New York, New York 10121

Printed in the United States of America

ISBN 0-02-184744-4/K, U.4

2 3 4 5 6 7 8 9 043/073 04 03 02 01 00 99

McGraw-Hill
School Division

New York   Farmington

McGraw-Hill Reading

Authors
Make the Difference...

Dr. James Flood

Ms. Angela Shelf Medearis

Dr. Jan E. Hasbrouck

Dr. Scott Paris

Dr. James V. Hoffman

Dr. Steven Stahl

Dr. Diane Lapp

Dr. Josefina Villamil Tinajero

Dr. Karen D. Wood

Contributing
Authors

Dr. Barbara Coulter

Ms. Frankie Dungan

Dr. Joseph B. Rubin

Dr. Carl B. Smith

Dr. Shirley Wright

iv

Part 1
START TOGETHER
Focus on Reading and Skills

All students start with the SAME:
- Read Aloud
- Pretaught Skills
  Phonics
  Comprehension
- Build Background
- Selection Vocabulary

...Never hold a child back. Never leave a child behind.

Part 2
MEET INDIVIDUAL NEEDS
Read the Literature

Core Selection

Pupil Selection

Leveled Books

How Kittens Grow

Easy

The World of Cats

Freedom CAT

Independent/On-Level

Authentic/Challenge

Leveled Practice

RETEACH

PRACTICE

EXTEND

Easy

On-Level

Challenge

Examples Taken From Grade 2

Part 3
FINISH TOGETHER
Build Skills

All students finish with the SAME:
- Phonics
- Comprehension
- Vocabulary
- Study Skills
- Assessment

McGraw-Hill Reading
Applying the Research

Phonological Awareness

Phonological awareness is the ability to hear the sounds in spoken language. It includes the ability to separate spoken words into discrete sounds as well as the ability to blend sounds together to make words. A child with good phonological awareness can identify rhyming words, hear the separate syllables in a word, separate the first sound in a word (onset) from the rest of the word (rime), and blend sounds together to make words.

Recent research findings have strongly concluded that children with good phonological awareness skills are more likely to learn to read well. These skills can be improved through systematic, explicit instruction involving auditory practice. McGraw-Hill Reading develops these key skills by providing an explicit Phonological Awareness lesson in every selection at grades K-2. Motivating activities such as blending, segmenting, and rhyming help to develop children's awareness of the sounds in our language.

Guided Instruction/ Guided Reading

Research on reading shows that guided instruction enables students to develop as independent, strategic readers. The *reciprocal-teaching model* of Anne-Marie Palincsar encourages teachers to model strategic-thinking, questioning, clarifying, and problem-solving strategies for students as students read together with the teacher. In McGraw-Hill Reading, guided instruction for all Pupil Edition selections incorporates the Palincsar model by providing interactive questioning prompts. The *guided-reading model* of Gay Su Pinnell is also incorporated into the McGraw-Hill Reading program. Through the guided-reading lessons provided for the leveled books offered with the program, teachers can work with small groups of students of different ability levels, closely observing them as they read and providing support specific to their needs.

By adapting instruction to include successful models of teaching and the appropriate materials to deliver instruction, McGraw-Hill Reading enables teachers to offer the appropriate type of instruction for all students in the classroom.

Phonics

Our language system uses an alphabetic code to communicate meaning from writing. Phonics involves learning the phonemes or sounds that letters make and the symbols or letters that represent those sounds. Children learn to blend the sounds of letters to decode unknown or unfamiliar words. The goal of good phonics instruction is to enable students to read words accurately and automatically.

Research has clearly identified the critical role of phonics in the ability of readers to read fluently and with good understanding, as well as to write and spell. Effective phonics instruction requires carefully sequenced lessons that teach the sounds of letters and how to use these sounds to read words. The McGraw-Hill program provides daily explicit and systematic phonics instruction to teach the letter sounds and blending. There are three explicit Phonics and Decoding lessons for every selection. Daily Phonics Routines are provided for quick reinforcement, in addition to activities in the Phonics Workbook and technology components. This combination of direct skills instruction and applied practice leads to reading success.

Curriculum Connections

As in the child's real-world environment, boundaries between disciplines must be dissolved. Recent research emphasizes the need to make connections between and across subject areas. McGraw-Hill Reading is committed to this approach. Each reading selection offers activities that tie in with social studies, language arts, geography, science, mathematics, art, music, health, and physical education. The program threads numerous research and inquiry activities that encourage the child to use the library and the Internet to seek out information. Reading and language skills are applied to a variety of genres, balancing fiction and nonfiction.

Integrated Language Arts

Success in developing communication skills is greatly enhanced by integrating the language arts in connected and purposeful ways. This allows students to understand the need for proper writing, grammar, and spelling. McGraw-Hill Reading sets the stage for meaningful learning. Each week a full writing-process lesson is provided. This lesson is supported by a 5-day spelling plan, emphasizing spelling patterns and spelling rules, and a 5-day grammar plan, focusing on proper grammar, mechanics, and usage.

Meeting Individual Needs

Every classroom is a microcosm of a world composed of diverse individuals with unique needs and abilities. Research points out that such needs must be addressed with frequent intensive opportunities to learn with engaging materials. McGraw-Hill Reading makes reading a successful experience for every child by providing a rich collection of leveled books for easy, independent, and challenging reading. Leveled practice is provided in Reteach, Practice, and Extend skills books. To address various learning styles and language needs, the program offers alternative teaching strategies, prevention/intervention techniques, language support activities, and ESL teaching suggestions.

Assessment

Frequent assessment in the classroom makes it easier for teachers to identify problems and to find remedies for them. McGraw-Hill Reading makes assessment an important component of instruction. Formal and informal opportunities are a part of each lesson. Minilessons, prevention/intervention strategies, and informal checklists, as well as student self-assessments, provide many informal assessment opportunities. Formal assessments, such as weekly selection tests and criterion-referenced unit tests, help to monitor students' knowledge of important skills and concepts. McGraw-Hill Reading also addresses how to adapt instruction based on student performance with resources such as the Alternate Teaching Strategies. Weekly lessons on test preparation, including test preparation practice books, help students to transfer skills to new contexts and to become better test takers.

McGraw-Hill School
TECHNOLOGY

*inter*NET
CONNECTION
For information on research that supports this program, visit
www.mhschool.com/reading

McGraw-Hill Reading

Theme Chart

MULTI-AGE Classroom

Using the same global themes at each grade level facilitates the use of materials in multi-age classrooms.

GRADE LEVEL	Experience Experiences can tell us about ourselves and our world.	Connections Making connections develops new understandings.
Kindergarten	**My World** We learn a lot from all the things we see and do at home and in school.	**All Kinds of Friends** When we work and play together, we learn more about ourselves.
Subtheme 1	At Home	Working Together
Subtheme 2	School Days	Playing Together
1	**Day by Day** Each day brings new experiences.	**Together Is Better** We like to share ideas and experiences with others.
2	**What's New?** With each day, we learn something new.	**Just Between Us** Family and friends help us see the world in new ways.
3	**Great Adventures** Life is made up of big and small experiences.	**Nature Links** Nature can give us new ideas.
4	**Reflections** Stories let us share the experiences of others.	**Something in Common** Sharing ideas can lead to meaningful cooperation.
5	**Time of My Life** We sometimes find memorable experiences in unexpected places.	**Building Bridges** Knowing what we have in common helps us appreciate our differences.
6	**Pathways** Reflecting on life's experiences can lead to new understandings.	**A Common Thread** A look beneath the surface may uncover hidden connections.

Themes: Kindergarten – Grade 6

Six Units IN EVERY GRADE

Expression	Inquiry	Problem Solving	Making Decisions
There are many styles and forms for expressing ourselves.	By exploring and asking questions, we make discoveries.	Analyzing information can help us solve problems.	Using what we know helps us evaluate situations.
Time to Shine We can use our ideas and our imagination to do many wonderful things.	**I Wonder** We can make discoveries about the wonders of nature in our own backyard.	**Let's Work It Out** Working as part of a team can help me find a way to solve problems.	**Choices** We can make many good choices and decisions every day.
Great Ideas	In My Backyard	Try and Try Again	Good Choices
Let's Pretend	Wonders of Nature	Teamwork	Let's Decide
Stories to Tell Each one of us has a different story to tell.	**Let's Find Out!** Looking for answers is an adventure.	**Think About It!** It takes time to solve problems.	**Many Paths** Each decision opens the door to a new path.
Express Yourself We share our ideas in many ways.	**Look Around** There are surprises all around us.	**Figure It Out** We can solve problems by working together.	**Starting Now** Unexpected events can lead to new decisions.
Be Creative! We can all express ourselves in creative, wonderful ways.	**Tell Me More** Looking and listening closely will help us find out the facts.	**Think It Through** Solutions come in many shapes and sizes.	**Turning Points** We make new judgments based on our experiences.
Our Voices We can each use our talents to communicate ideas.	**Just Curious** We can find answers in surprising places.	**Make a Plan** Often we have to think carefully about a problem in order to solve it.	**Sorting It Out** We make decisions that can lead to new ideas and discoveries.
Imagine That The way we express our thoughts and feelings can take different forms.	**Investigate!** We never know where the search for answers might lead us.	**Bright Ideas** Some problems require unusual approaches.	**Crossroads** Decisions cause changes that can enrich our lives.
With Flying Colors Creative people help us see the world from different perspectives.	**Seek and Discover** To make new discoveries, we must observe and explore.	**Brainstorms** We can meet any challenge with determination and ingenuity.	**All Things Considered** Encountering new places and people can help us make decisions.

UNIT 4

I Wonder

Contents

*We can make discoveries about
the wonders of nature in our own backyard.*

 "The Little Turtle" a poem by *Vachel Lindsay*

Subtheme: In My Backyard

You Are IT!

SKILLS			
Phonics	**Comprehension**	**Vocabulary**	**Beginning Reading Concepts**
• **Introduce** Initial /r/r	• **Introduce** Main Idea	• **Introduce** High-Frequency Words: *to*	• **Introduce** On, Off
• **Review** /r/r, /f/f; Blending with Short *a, i, o*	• **Review** Main Idea	• **Review** *to, the, that*	

Tap the Sap

SKILLS			
Phonics	**Comprehension**	**Vocabulary**	**Beginning Reading Concepts**
• **Introduce** Initial /p/p	• **Introduce** Compare and Contrast	• **Introduce** High-Frequency Words: *me*	• **Introduce** Inside, Outside
• **Introduce** Final /p/p	• **Review** Compare and Contrast	• **Review** *me, to, you*	
• **Review** /p/p; Blending with Short *a, i, o*			

Unit Planner

You Are IT!

Tap the Sap

	WEEK 1 You Are IT!	**WEEK 2** Tap the Sap
📖 **Leveled Books**	Patterned Book: *Ron's Radishes*	Patterned Book: *The Picnic*
☑ **Tested Skills**	☑ **Phonics and Decoding** Initial /r/r, 186W–186, 188C–188, 190C–190 Initial /f/f, 190C–190 Blending with Short *a, i, o,* 192C–192, 196C–196 ☑ **Comprehension** Main Idea, 189C–189, 195A–195 ☑ **Vocabulary** High-Frequency Word: *to,* 191C–191 *to, the, that,* 197C–197 ☑ **Beginning Reading Concepts** On, Off, 187C–187	☑ **Phonics and Decoding** Initial /p/p, 198I–198, 202C–202 Final /p/p, 200C–200, 202C–202 Blending with Short *a, i, o,* 204C–204, 208C–208 ☑ **Comprehension** Compare and Contrast 201C–201, 207A–207 ☑ **Vocabulary** High-Frequency Word: *me,* 203C–203 *me, to, you,* 209C–209 ☑ **Beginning Reading Concepts** Inside, Outside, 199C–199
Language Arts	✏ **Writing:** Letter Formation, 186W–186 Interactive Writing, 198A–198B	✏ **Writing:** Letter Formation, 198I–198, 200C–200 Interactive Writing, 210A–210B

CENTER Activities

Curriculum Connections		
Social Studies	Language Arts: Name That Cat, 187B	Language Arts: Dot To Dot, 199B
Mathematics	Science: Apple I.D., 189B	Language Arts: Giving Art, 205/206D
Science	Social Studies: Safety First, 193/194D	Science: 209B
Music	Science: Watch It Grow! 197B	
Art		
Drama		
Language Arts		
🖐 CULTURAL PERSPECTIVES	After School, 191A	Seasons, 201B Pottery, 203A

Nap in a Lap

Mud Fun

Fun in the Sun

WEEK 3 — Nap in a Lap

Patterned Book: *Let's Go*

☑ **Phonics and Decoding**
Initial /l/l, 210I–210, 212C–212, 214C–214
Initial and Final /p/p, 214C–214
Review Blending with Short *a, i, o,* 216C–216, 220C–220

☑ **Comprehension**
Main Idea, 213C–213, 219A–219

☑ **Vocabulary**
High-Frequency Word: *go,* 215C–215
go, to, me, you, 221C–221

☑ **Beginning Reading Concepts**
Over, Under, 211C–211

 Writing: Letter Formation, 210I–210
Interactive Writing, 222A–222B

Language Arts: Animal Alphabet, 211B

Science: Nature Up Close, 213B

Math: Fair Share, 217/218D

Social Studies: Safety Signs, 221B

Camouflage, 215A

WEEK 4 — Mud Fun

Patterned Book: *Fun on the Farm*

☑ **Phonics and Decoding**
Initial /u/u, 222I–222, 226C–226
Medial /u/u, 224C–224, 226C–226
Blending with Short *u, o,* 228C–228, 232C–232

☑ **Comprehension**
Compare and Contrast, 225C–225, 231A–231

☑ **Vocabulary**
High-Frequency Word: *do,* 227C–227
do, go, I, and, me, 233C–233

☑ **Beginning Reading Concepts**
Up, Down, 223C–223

 **Writing:** Letter Formation, 222I–222, 224C–224
Interactive Writing, 234A–234B

Language Arts: Picture This! 223B

Math: Pour It On, 229/230D

Math: Cats of a Different Color, 233B

Nature, 225B
Counting, 227A

WEEK 5 — Fun in the Sun

Self–Selected Reading of Patterned Books

☑ **Phonics and Decoding**
Initial /r/r, /p/p, /l/l, 234I–234, 238C–238
Final /p/p, 236C–236
Blending with Short *u, o, i,* 240C–240, 244C–244

☑ **Comprehension**
Main Idea, 237C–237
Compare and Contrast, 243A–243

☑ **Vocabulary**
High-Frequency Words: *to, me, go, do,* 239C–239, 245C–245

☑ **Beginning Reading Concepts**
On, Off; Inside, Outside; Over, Under; Up, Down, 235C–235

Writing: Interactive Writing, 246A–246B

Language Arts: Stuck On Letters, 235B

Science: Our Five Senses, 237B

Social Studies: Our Town, 239A

Science: Sun Spots, 241/242D

Science: Kinder-Garden, 245B

WEEK 6 — Review, Assessment

Self-Selected Reading

☑ **Assess Skills**

Phonics and Decoding
Initial /r/r, /f/f, /p/p, /l/l, /u/u
Final /p/p,
Medial /u/u
Blending with Short *a, i, o, u*

Comprehension
Main Idea
Compare and Contrast

Vocabulary
High-Frequency Words: *to, me, go, do, the, that, you, I,* and

Beginning Reading Concepts
On, Off
Inside, Outside
Over, Under
Up, Down

☑ **Unit 4 Assessment**

☑ **Standardized Test Preparation**

Unit Resources

LITERATURE

DECODABLE STORIES These four-color stories in the Pupil Edition consist of words containing the phonetic elements that have been taught, as well as the high-frequency words. The stories reinforce the comprehension and concepts of print skills.

LEVELED BOOKS These engaging stories include the high-frequency words and words with the phonetic elements that are focused on. They reinforce the comprehension skills and correlate to the unit themes.

📖 **Patterned**
- *Ron's Radishes*
- *The Picnic*
- *Let's Go*
- *Fun on the Farm*

ABC BIG BOOK Children build alphabetic knowledge and letter identification as they enjoy a shared reading of this story that correlates to the theme.
- *Allie's Adventure from A to Z*

LITERATURE BIG BOOKS Shared readings of the highest-quality literature reinforce comprehension skills and introduce children to a variety of genres.
- *The Apple Pie Tree*
- *Nature Spy*

READ ALOUDS Traditional folk tales, fables, fairy tales, and stories from around the world can be shared with children as they develop their oral comprehension skills and learn about other cultures.
- *Every Time I Climb a Tree*
- *Hill of Fire*
- *The Clever Turtle*
- *How Many Spots Does a Leopard Have?*

🎧 **STUDENT LISTENING LIBRARY**
Recordings of the Big Books, Patterned Books, and Unit Opener and Closer Poetry.

SKILLS

PUPIL EDITION Colorful practice pages help you to assess children's progress as they learn and review each skill, including phonics, high-frequency words, readiness, comprehension, and letter formation.

PRACTICE BOOK Practice pages in alternative formats provide additional reinforcement of each skill as well as extra handwriting practice.

BIG BOOK OF PHONICS RHYMES AND POEMS Traditional and contemporary poems emphasize phonics and rhyme and allow children to develop oral comprehension skills.

BIG BOOK OF REAL-LIFE READING This lively big book, which introduces children to important study skills, focuses on maps in this unit. The context for the teaching is the Read Aloud selection children have just heard.

WORD BUILDING BOOK
Letter and word cards to utilize phonics and build children's vocabulary. Includes high-frequency word cards.

LANGUAGE SUPPORT BOOK
Parallel teaching and practice activities for children needing language support.

McGraw-Hill School
TECHNOLOGY

Phonics CD-ROM Provides interactive lessons for additional phonics support.

interNET CONNECTION Extend lessons through Research and Inquiry Ideas.

Visit www.mhschool.com

Resources for Meeting Individual Needs

	EASY	ON-LEVEL	CHALLENGE	LANGUAGE SUPPORT

UNIT 4

You Are IT!

You Are IT!

EASY
You Are IT!
Teaching Strategies 186, 187, 188, 189, 190, 191, 192, 195, 196, 197
Alternate Teaching Strategy T24–T27
 **Writing** 198B

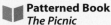 CD-ROM

ON-LEVEL
You Are IT!
Teaching Strategies 186–192, 195–197
Alternate Teaching Strategy T24–T27
 **Writing** 198B

Patterned Book *Ron's Radishes*
 CD-ROM

CHALLENGE
 Patterned Book *Ron's Radishes*
Teaching Strategies 186, 187, 188, 189, 190, 191, 192, 195, 196, 197
 Writing 198B

CD-ROM

LANGUAGE SUPPORT
Teaching Strategies 186, 187, 188, 189, 190, 191, 192, 195, 196, 197
Alternate Teaching Strategy T24–T27
Writing 198B

CD-ROM

Tap the Sap

Tap the Sap

EASY
Tap the Sap
Teaching Strategies 198, 199, 200, 201, 202, 203, 204, 207, 208, 209
Alternate Teaching Strategy T27–T30
Writing 210B

CD-ROM

ON-LEVEL
Tap the Sap
Teaching Strategies 198–204, 207–209
Alternate Teaching Strategy T27–T30
Writing 210B

Patterned Book *The Picnic*
CD-ROM

CHALLENGE
Patterned Book *The Picnic*
Teaching Strategies 198, 199, 200, 201, 202, 203, 204, 207, 208, 209
Writing 210B

CD-ROM

LANGUAGE SUPPORT
Teaching Strategies 198, 199, 200, 201, 202, 203, 204, 207, 208, 209
Alternate Teaching Strategy T27–T30
Writing 210B

CD-ROM

Nap in a Lap

Nap in a Lap

EASY
Nap in a Lap
Teaching Strategies 210, 211, 212, 213, 214, 215, 216, 219, 220, 221
Alternate Teaching Strategy T26–T28, T31, T33
 **Writing** 222B

CD-ROM

ON-LEVEL
Nap in a Lap
Teaching Strategies 210–216, 219–221
Alternate Teaching Strategy T26–T28, T31, T33
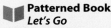 **Writing** 222B

Patterned Book *Let's Go*
CD-ROM

CHALLENGE
Patterned Book *Let's Go*
Teaching Strategies 210, 211, 212, 213, 214, 215, 216, 219, 220, 221
Writing 222B

CD-ROM

LANGUAGE SUPPORT
Teaching Strategies 210, 211, 212, 213, 214, 215, 216, 219, 220, 221
Alternate Teaching Strategy T26–T28, T31, T33
Writing 222B

CD-ROM

Mud Fun

Mud Fun

EASY
Mud Fun
Teaching Strategies 222, 223, 224, 225, 226, 227, 228, 231, 232, 233
Alternate Teaching Strategy T27, T30, T32, T33
Writing 234B

CD-ROM

ON-LEVEL
Mud Fun
Teaching Strategies 222–228, 231–233
Alternate Teaching Strategy T27, T30, T32, T33
Writing 234B

Patterned Book *Fun on the Farm*
CD-ROM

CHALLENGE
Patterned Book *Fun on the Farm*
Teaching Strategies 222, 223, 224, 225, 226, 227, 228, 231, 232, 233
Writing 234B

CD-ROM

LANGUAGE SUPPORT
Teaching Strategies 222, 223, 224, 225, 226, 227, 228, 231, 232, 233
Alternate Teaching Strategy T27, T30, T32, T33
Writing 234B

CD-ROM

Fun in the Sun

Fun in the Sun

EASY
Fun in the Sun
Teaching Strategies 234, 235, 236, 237, 238, 239, 240, 243, 244, 245
Alternate Teaching Strategy T24–T32
Writing 246B

CD-ROM

ON-LEVEL
Fun in the Sun
Teaching Strategies 234–240, 243–245
Alternate Teaching Strategy T24–T32
Writing 246B

Patterned Book *Patterned Book Choice*
CD-ROM

CHALLENGE
Patterned Book *Patterned Book Choice*
Teaching Strategies 234, 235, 236, 237, 238, 239, 240, 243, 244, 245
 Writing 246B

 CD-ROM

LANGUAGE SUPPORT
Teaching Strategies 234, 235, 236, 237, 238, 239, 240, 243, 244, 245
Alternate Teaching Strategy T24–T32
Writing 246B

CD-ROM

INFORMAL

Informal Assessment
- Phonics and Decoding, 186W, 188C, 190C, 192C, 196C, 198I, 200C, 202C, 204C, 208C, 210I, 212C, 214C, 216C, 220C, 222I, 224C, 226C, 228C, 232C, 234I, 236C, 238C, 240C, 244C
- Comprehension, 187B, 189B, 189C, 195A, 197A, 199B, 201B, 201C, 207A, 209A, 211B, 213B, 213C, 219A, 221A, 223B, 225B, 225C, 231A, 233A, 235B, 237B, 237C, 243A, 245A
- High-Frequency Words, 191C, 197C, 203C, 209C, 215C, 221C, 227C, 233C, 239C, 245C
- Beginning Reading Concepts, 187C, 199C, 211C, 223C, 235C

Performance Assessment
- Research and Inquiry Project, 186O, 246C
- Interactive Writing, 198A–198B, 210A–210B, 222A–222B, 234A–234B, 246A–246B
- Listening, Speaking, Viewing Activities, 186U, 188A, 190A, 192A, 196A, 198B, 198G, 200A, 202A, 204A, 208A, 210B, 210G, 212A, 214A, 216A, 220A, 222B, 222G, 224A, 226A, 228A, 232A, 234B, 234G, 236A, 238A, 240A, 244A, 246B
- Portfolio
  Writing, 198A–198B, 210A–210B, 222A–222B, 234A–234B, 246A–246B
  Cross-Curricular Activities, 187B, 189B, 191B, 193/194D, 197B, 199B, 201B, 203B, 205/206D, 209B, 211B, 213B, 215B, 217/218D, 221B, 223B, 225B, 227B, 229/230D, 233B, 235B, 237B, 239B, 241/242D, 245B

Practice
- **Phonics and Decoding**
  /r/r, 186, 188, 190, 234, 238; /f/f, 190; /p/p, 198, 200, 202, 214, 234, 236, 238; /l/l, 210, 212, 214, 234, 238; /u/u, 222, 224, 226
  Blending with Short *a, i, o, u,* 192, 196, 204, 208, 216, 220, 228, 232, 240, 244
- **Comprehension**
  Main Idea, 189, 195, 213, 219, 237
  Compare and Contrast, 201, 207, 225, 231, 243
- **High-Frequency Words**
  to, me, go, do, 191, 197, 203, 209, 215, 221, 227, 233, 239, 245
- **Beginning Reading Concepts**
  On, Off, 187; Inside, Outside, 199; Over, Under, 211; Up, Down, 223

FORMAL

Unit 4 Assessment
- **Phonics and Decoding**
  Initial /r/r
  Initial /f/f
  Initial and Final /p/p
  Initial /l/l
  Initial and Medial /u/u
  Blending with Short *a, i, o, u*
- **Comprehension**
  Main Idea
  Compare and Contrast
- **High-Frequency Words**
  to, me, go, do
- **Beginning Reading Concepts**
  On, Off
  Inside, Outside
  Over, Under
  Up, Down

Diagnostic/Placement Evaluation
- Individual Reading Inventory
- Running Record
- Phonics and Decoding Inventory
- Grade K Diagnostic/Evaluation
- Grade 1 Diagnostic/Evaluation
- Grade 2 Diagnostic/Evaluation
- Grade 3 Diagnostic/Evaluation

Test Preparation
- Standardized Test Preparation Practice Book

Assessment Checklist

	You Are IT!	Tap the Sap	Nap in a Lap	Mud Fun	Fun in the Sun	Assessment Summary
Student .... **Grade**						
Teacher						

Student .... **Grade** ....

Teacher ....

LISTENING/SPEAKING

	You Are IT!	Tap the Sap	Nap in a Lap	Mud Fun	Fun in the Sun	Assessment Summary
Participates in oral language experiences						
Listens and speaks to gain knowledge of culture						
Speaks appropriately to audiences for different purposes						
Communicates clearly (gains increasing control of grammar)						

READING

Demonstrates knowledge of concepts of print						
Uses phonological awareness strategies, including						
• Identifying, segmenting, and combining syllables						
• Producing rhyming words						
• Identifying and isolating initial and final sounds						
Uses letter/sound knowledge, including						
• Applying letter-sound correspondences to begin to read						
• Phonics and Decoding: initial /r/ *R,r*						
• Phonics and Decoding: initial, final /p/ *P,p*						
• Phonics and Decoding: initial /l/ *L,l*						
• Phonics and Decoding: initial, medial /u/ *U,u*						
• Blending with *a, i, o, u*						
Develops an extensive vocabulary, including						
• High-frequency words: *to, me, go, do*						
Uses a variety of strategies to comprehend selections						
• Main Idea						
• Compare and Contrast						
Responds to various texts						
Recognizes characteristics of various types of texts						
Conducts research using various sources						
Reads to increase knowledge						

WRITING

Writes his/her own name						
Writes each letter of the alphabet						
Uses phonological knowledge to write messages						
Gains increasing control of penmanship						
Composes original texts						
Uses writing as a tool for learning and research						

+ Observed   − Not Observed

Unit Opener

Introducing the Theme

I Wonder
We can make discoveries about the wonders of nature in our own backyard.

PRESENT THE THEME Read the theme statement to children. Begin a discussion about animals, plants, and other things children have found in their yards and in parks.

READ THE POEM Read the poem, "The Little Turtle" aloud. Ask children if they have ever watched animals in the outdoors. Invite volunteers to share their observations. Discuss why animals act in certain ways.

THE LITTLE TURTLE

There was a little turtle.
He lived in a box.
He swam in a puddle.
He climbed on the rocks.

He snapped at a mosquito.
He snapped at a flea.
He snapped at a minnow.
And he snapped at me.

He caught the mosquito.
He caught the flea.
He caught the minnow.
But he didn't catch me.

Vachel Lindsay

Student Listening Library
AUDIO

DISCUSS THE POEM After children listen to "The Little Turtle," ask them to tell things they learned about turtles. Ask how they think the poet learned these things about turtles.

THEME SUMMARY Each lesson relates to the unit theme *I Wonder* as well as to the global theme *Inquiry*. These thematic links will help children to make connections from their experiences with nature to the literature of the unit.

Literature selections presented within the first two lessons are also related to the subtheme *In My Backyard*. These stories include experiences with nature that are familiar to many children.

Selections for the third and fourth lessons are more closely tied to the subtheme *Wonders of Nature*. These stories enable children to expand their knowledge as they make discoveries about nature beyond their local world.

The fifth lesson gives children the opportunity to reread their favorite literature selections and discuss the main theme of *I Wonder*.

Research and Inquiry

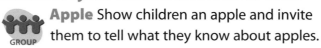

Theme Project: The Life and Travels of an Apple Show children an apple and invite them to tell what they know about apples. Then ask: "How did this apple get here?"

GROUP

List What They Know Assist children in creating a "We know" list. For example:
• *We know that Miss Tyler brought the apple from home.*
• *We know that the apple grew on a tree.*

Ask Questions and Identify Resources Next, help children identify things that they do not know about the apple and help them to determine resources for finding information, such as a supermarket produce manager, Internet sites, and so on.

Create a Presentation Using information they found, children can paint a mural to show "The Life and Travels of the Apple."

Setting Up the Centers

Independent Learning Centers will help to reinforce children's skills across all areas of the curriculum. Here's what you will need to help you set up the centers in this unit.

Reading/Language Arts Center

- cat-face templates, animal pictures, pictures of simple objects
- drawing paper, construction paper, posterboard
- pencils, markers, string
- scissors, hole punch
- The Giving Tree by Shel Silverstein
- audiocassette recorder, blank audiocassette
- Student Listening Library Audiocassette

For suggested activities, see pages 187B, 199B, 205/206D, 211B, 223B, 235B.

Math Center

- cups, measuring cups
- small pot, large bowl
- dry rice, counters
- cat-face cut-outs

For suggested activities, see pages 217/218D, 229/230D, 233B.

Science Center

- apple, knife, watering can, planting trays
- empty milk containers, seed packets
- potting soil
- laminated food cards
- nature tray, index cards, paper plates
- drawing paper, markers, crayons, magazines
- scissors, paste, dark construction paper
- erasers, cubes, paper clips

For suggested activities, see pages 189B, 197B, 209B, 213B, 237B, 241/242D, 245B.

Social Studies/Cultural Perspectives Center

- index cards, posterboard, markers
- safety signs
- mural paper, crayons, pencils
- clay, craft sticks, paint, paintbrushes
- circles of white paper
- beans, abacus, calculator
- paper, pens

For suggested activities, see pages 191B, 193/194D, 201B, 203B, 215B, 221B, 225B, 227B.

Managing the Centers

MANAGEMENT TIP Just before you begin center activities, tell children which center you will be working at. If children in other groups have questions, suggest that they ask someone in their group first, then ask you. Rotate the centers and the children with whom you work.

ORGANIZATIONAL TIP Gather divided boxes, such as those in which bottles are shipped. They make great "cubbies" for storing center materials. Help children label the cubbies with words and pictures.

ASSESSMENT TIP Check children's work to make sure they are following instructions for completing the project. Provide assistance for those who are experiencing difficulties.

CLEAN-UP TIP Put a small amount of shaving cream on art or writing center tables. Allow children to use it as finger paint. When children are finished, let them wipe off tables with paper towels. This will rid tables of crayon and pencil marks.

You Are IT!

Children will read and listen to stories about explorations with nature.

You Are IT!

**Decodable Story,
pages 193–194 of the
Pupil Edition**

**Listening
Library
Audiocassette**

Ron's Radishes
by Ray Tanner
illustrated by Andrea Wallace

**Patterned Book,
page 197B**

Every Time I Climb
a Tree
by David McCord

**Teacher Read Aloud,
page 191A**

Allie's Adventure
From A to Z

Written by Ellen Dreyer   Illustrated by Jui Ishida

**ABC Big Book,
pages 187A–187B**

**Listening
Library
Audiocassette**

The
Apple Pie
Tree
BY Zoe Hall
ILLUSTRATED BY
Shari Halpern

**Literature Big Book,
pages 189A–189B**

**Listening
Library
Audiocassette**

**Pupil Edition,
pages 186–197**

**Big Book of Real-Life Reading,
page 24**

**Big Book of Phonics Rhymes and
Poems, pages 44, 45**

 **Listening
Library
Audiocassette**

**Practice Book,
pages 186–197**

- **Phonics Kit**
- **Language Support Book**
- **Alternate Teaching Strategies,**
  pages T24–T27

McGraw-Hill School
TECHNOLOGY

Phonics **CD-ROM** Provides
extra phonics support.

**interNET
CONNECTION** Research & Inquiry Ideas.

Visit www.mhschool.com

You Are IT!

Suggested Lesson Planner

READING AND LANGUAGE ARTS

- **Phonological Awareness**
- **Phonics** *initial /r/r*
- **Comprehension**
- **Vocabulary**
- **Beginning Reading Concepts**
- **Listening, Speaking, Viewing, Representing**

DAY 1

Focus on Reading Skills

Develop Phonological Awareness,
186U–186V
"R is for Ribbon" *Big Book of Phonics Rhymes and Poems*, 45
**Introduce Initial /r/r**, 186W–186
Practice Book, 186
Phonics/Phonemic Awareness
Practice Book

 CD-ROM

Read the Literature

Read *Allie's Adventure from A to Z* **Big Book,** 187A–187B
Shared Reading

Build Skills
- ☑ On, Off, 187C–187
  Practice Book, 187

DAY 2

Focus on Reading Skills

Develop Phonological Awareness,
188A–188B
"Rainbow Riddle" *Big Book of Phonics Rhymes and Poems*, 44
Review Initial /r/r, 188C–188
Practice Book, 188
Phonics/Phonemic Awareness
Practice Book

CD-ROM

Read the Literature
Read *The Apple Pie Tree* **Big Book,** 189A–189B
Shared Reading

Build Skills
- ☑ Main Idea, 189C–189
  Practice Book, 189

- **Cross Curriculum**

 Language Arts, 187B

 Science, 189B

- **Writing**

 Writing Prompt: Write about what happens next to Allie and Zack.

Journal Writing, 187B
Letter Formation, 186W

 Writing Prompt: Write about what you learned about apple trees from the story.
Journal Writing, 189B
Letter Formation, 188C

DAY 3

Every Time I Climb a Tree

Focus on Reading Skills

Develop Phonological Awareness, 190A–190B
"R is for Ribbon" and "Rainbow Riddle" *Big Book of Phonics Rhymes and Poems,* 44–45

 **Review /r/r, /f/f,** 190C–190
Practice Book, 190
Phonics/Phonemic Awareness Practice Book

 **CD-ROM**

Read the Literature

Read "Every Time I Climb a Tree" Teacher Read Aloud, 191A–191B
Shared Reading
Read the Big Book of Real-Life Reading, 24–25
☑ Maps

Build Skills

☑ High-Frequency Word: *to* 191C–191
Practice Book, 191

 Cultural Perspectives, 191B

 Writing Prompt: What is your favorite kind of tree? Draw it and explain what you like about it.

DAY 4

You Are IT!

Focus on Reading Skills

Develop Phonological Awareness, 192A–192B
"Ron the Cat"
 **Review Blending with Short *a, i, o,*** 192C–192
Practice Book, 192
Phonics/Phonemic Awareness Practice Book

 **CD-ROM**

Read the Literature

Read "You Are IT!" Decodable Story, 193/194A–193/194D

☑ Initial /r/r; Blending
☑ Main Idea
☑ High-Frequency Word: *to*
☑ Concepts of Print

Build Skills

☑ Main Idea, 195A–195
Practice Book, 195

 Social Studies, 193/194D

 Writing Prompt: What game do you like to play with your friends? Write about it.

Letter Formation Practice Book, 193–194

DAY 5

You Are IT!

Ron's Radishes
by Ray Tanner
illustrated by Andrea Wallace

Focus on Reading Skills

Develop Phonological Awareness, 196A–196B
"Ron the Cat"
Review Blending with Short *a, i, o,* 196C–196
Practice Book, 172
Phonics/Phonemic Awareness Practice Book

 **CD-ROM**

Read the Literature

Reread "You Are IT!" Decodable Story, 197A
Read "Ron's Radishes" Patterned Book, 197B
Guided Reading
☑ Initial /r/r; Blending
☑ Main Idea
☑ High-Frequency Word: *to*
☑ Concepts of Print

Build Skills

☑ High-Frequency Words: *to, the, that,* 197C–197
Practice Book, 197

Science, 197B

Writing Prompt: Write about your favorite thing in your neighborhood.

Interactive Writing, 198A–198B

Develop Phonological Awareness

Listen

R is for Ribbon
a poem

R is for ribbon,
   a rose
   and a ring,
   a ruby,
   a raindrop
   and a robin in spring!
Margaret and John Travers Moore

Big Book of Phonics Rhymes and Poems, page 45

Objective: Listen for Rhyming Words

LISTEN TO THE POEM Gather children in a circle. Read the title and the poem aloud. Emphasize the /r/ sound. Ask children to say the words from the poem that have the /r/ sound.

> ribbon   rose   ring
> ruby   raindrop   robin

LISTEN FOR RHYMING WORDS Reread the poem and have children listen for the rhyming words. Ask a volunteer to name the rhyming words. Have children think of other words that rhyme with *ring*.

> ring   spring   thing
> wing   king   sing

Say the word *rose*, emphasizing the /r/ sound. Have children think of other words that rhyme with *rose*.

> rose   hose   toes   nose   dose

REMEMBER WORDS IN SEQUENCE Say a sequence of three words that begin with /r/ from the poem. Ask children to repeat the sequence after you. Repeat a few times. Then repeat the activity with four words.

> ribbon   rose   ring   ruby

IDENTIFY RHYMING WORDS Say the words *ring, ruby, king*. Ask a volunteer to identify and repeat the words that rhyme. Repeat this activity with the words *nose, ball, toes*. Then continue with other rhyming words.

Objective: Listen for /r/

NAME WORDS WITH /r/ Reread the poem, encouraging children to say it along with you. As you read, emphasize words with the initial /r/ sound. Then read the poem one line at a time and have children repeat the words that begin with /r/.

> ribbon   rose   ring   ruby
> raindrop   robin

SAY WORDS WITH INITIAL /r/ Say the following words, one at a time. Have children wiggle their fingers like rain if the word begins with /r/.

> rainbow   cloud   rabbit
> dog   rhino   race

Then have volunteers lead the group by saying any word. Have the class continue to wiggle their fingers if the word begins with /r/. Encourage children to think of words that begin with /r/.

ADD THE /r/ SOUND Say the word ending *–ing*. Then tell children you will put the /r/ sound at the beginning of the word. Say *r-ing*. Ask a volunteer to tell you what word you made. Continue saying word endings and have children add the /r/ sound to make words.

> r-un   r-ain   r-ope   r-oll
> r-ake   r-at   r-ace

ROAR FOR THE /r/ SOUND Say the word rake, emphasizing the /r/ sound. Ask children to roar if they heard the /r/ sound. Repeat this activity with the following words.

> ball   rainbow   fan
> root   real   sun

From Phonemic Awareness to Phonics

Objective: Identify /r/R,r

IDENTIFY THE LETTER FOR THE SOUND Explain to children that the letters *R,r* stand for the sound /r/. Ask children to say the sound with you.

Display the Big Book of Phonics Rhymes and Poems, page 45. Point to the letters in the corner and identify them. Have children make the /r/ sound as you point to the letters.

REREAD THE POEM Reread the poem, pointing to each word. Ask children to raise a finger when you point to and say a word that begins with /r/.

FIND WORDS WITH R,r Have children find words that begin with R, r and put self-stick notes under them.

SOLVE THE RIDDLE Tell children you are going to play a game with words that begin with R, r from the poem. Then say the sentence: *I'd like to smell a ____ (rose).* Ask a volunteer to say the word to finish the sentence. Repeat with the following sentences.

> The present had a <u>(ribbon)</u>.
> I have a <u>(ring)</u> on my finger.

R is for ribbon,
a rose
and a ring,
a ruby,
a raindrop
and a robin in spring!
Margaret and John Travers Moore

Big Book of Phonics Rhymes and Poems, p. 45

OBJECTIVES

Children will:

- identify the letters *R, r*
- identify /r/*R,r*

....

MATERIALS

- letter cards and word cards from the Word Building Book

TEACHING TIP

INSTRUCTIONAL As you introduce new letters, add labels to objects in your classroom whose names begin with the sound the letter stands for. Ask children to suggest objects to label.

ALTERNATE TEACHING STRATEGY
....

INITIAL /r/r

For a different approach to teaching this skill, see page T24.

▶ **Visual/Auditory/ Kinesthetic**

Introduce Initial /r/r

TEACH

Identify /r/ R, r Write the letters *R,r* on the chalkboard, identify them, and have children make the sound. Ask them to name objects they have in their homes that begin with /r/, such as: *ruler, ring, rake, room, radio, rug,* and *rice.* Write the words on the chalkboard using *R* or *r*. Call on volunteers to underline the *R* or *r* as you say each word aloud.

Form R, r Display letters *R, r,* and trace the letters with your fingers. Then, ask children to do the same. Then show them pictures and have them write *R* if the picture shows an animal and *r* if it shows a thing. Display pictures such as the following: *rabbit, rock, raccoon, rake,* and *ring.*

PRACTICE

Complete the Pupil Edition Page Read the directions on page 186 of the Pupil Edition, and make sure children clearly understand what they are being asked to do. Identify each picture, and complete the first item together. Then work through the page with children or have them complete the page independently.

ASSESS/CLOSE

Identify and Use R, r Mix the initial *r* picture cards used in the Teach activity with picture cards showing objects and animals that do not begin with *r*. Have children name each object and hold up their *R, r* letter cards if the picture name begins with the /r/ sound.

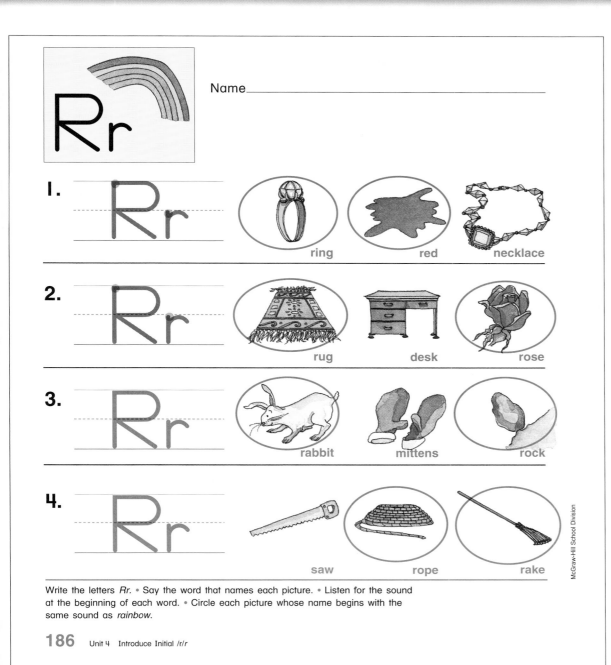

R r

Name

1. R r — ring · red · necklace

2. R r — rug · desk · rose

3. R r — rabbit · mittens · rock

4. R r — saw · rope · rake

Write the letters *Rr.* • Say the word that names each picture. • Listen for the sound at the beginning of each word. • Circle each picture whose name begins with the same sound as *rainbow.*

McGraw-Hill School Division

186 Unit 4 Introduce Initial /r/r

Pupil Edition, page 186

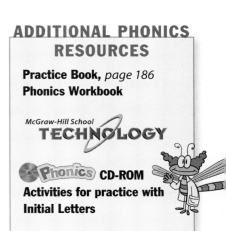

R r Name

Practice **186**

1. R r — rake · pony

2. R r — moon · rocket

3. R r — rabbit · dog

4. R r — dolphin · ring

Trace and write the letters *Rr.* Say the word that names each picture. Color the picture whose name begins with the same sound as *rope.*

At Home: Play "I'm Going to Rio Grande."
Take turns naming things you will pack. Each thing must begin with *r.*

186

Unit 4
Introduce Initial /r/r

PRACTICE BOOK, page 186

Meeting Individual Needs for Phonics

EASY	ON-LEVEL	CHALLENGE	LANGUAGE SUPPORT
Give children modeling clay, and demonstrate how to roll it into long rolls. Have children use the pieces to form the letters *R* and *r.* Ask them to talk about the shapes they made to show the letters, and have them say the sound /r/.	**Tell** children you are thinking of a word that begins with *r.* Give them clues, such as: *This is a color. This is another name for bunny. This is a kind of weather.* Write the answers on the chalkboard, leaving blank spaces for *r.* Ask children to fill in the blanks by writing *r.*	**Say** the following words: *man, cat, bed, sun, bag.* Ask children to make rhyming words by changing the beginning letter to *r.* (*ran, rat, red, run, rag*) Have them write each word on their papers, and then use one of the words in a sentence.	**Ask** children to pantomime the following action words that begin with the letter *r: run, roll, rip, rake.* Repeat the words, and have children trace the letter *r* in the air with their fingers. Invite children to suggest more *r* action words that begin with the sound *r.*

186

OBJECTIVES

Children will:

- recognize the ABC story structure
- understand the main idea of the story

 ELLEN DREYER lives in New York City. She has written many books for young readers. She says, "My cat Dixie loves having adventures and then curling up on her special pillow."

 JUI ISHIDA grew up in Japan and now lives in California. She had a cat just like Allie in Japan, and misses her very much.

TEACHING TIP

INSTRUCTIONAL

Provide different types of alphabet books in your library corner. Talk about how they are organized and how they are alike and how they are different. Take picture walks through a few of the books and help children identify the letters of the alphabet on each page.

Read the Big Book

Before Reading

Build Background

EVALUATE PRIOR KNOWLEDGE Hold up a picture of a cat or a stuffed animal. Ask if any children have cats as pets. Talk about what their cats do during the day.

MAKE A MURAL Have children draw or cut out pictures of different types of cats. Talk about how they are alike and how they are different.

Preview and Predict

DISCUSS AUTHOR AND ILLUSTRATOR Display the Big Book cover and read the title. Identify the author and the illustrator, and give some background information. Ask children to tell you who wrote the story and who drew the pictures.

TAKE A PICTURE WALK Take a picture walk through several spreads of the book. Ask whether the book is a real-life story or a fantasy. Discuss what children see and how the alphabet is a part of the story.

MAKE PREDICTIONS Ask them to predict what might happen in the story.

Set Purposes

Ask children what they want to find out about the kitten. Explain how they can name the letter on each page, and use the picture and the letter to say the words.

Allie's Adventure from A to Z, pages 2–3

During Reading

Read Together

- Point to the capital and lowercase letters at the top of each page as you name the letter. Make sure children connect the initial sound of the highlighted word with the letter. *Concepts of Print*

- Before you begin to read, point to the first word in the first sentence. Explain that this is where you will begin to read. Continue to track print as you read the story. *Tracking Print*

- Make the /r/ sound and have children make it with you. After you read page 21, have children say the word with initial /r/. (rest) *Phonics*

- After reading page 32, ask children to tell what the story was about. Help children summarize the events to tell the main idea. *Main Idea*

Allie needs a **rest**!

Allie's Adventure from A to Z, page 21

After Reading

Return to Predictions and Purposes

Ask children if they found out what they wanted to know about Allie.

Literary Response

JOURNAL WRITING Ask children to write about and draw something that Allie did during the day.

ORAL RESPONSE Ask:
- *Would you likew to have Allie as a pet? Why or why not?*
- *How would you take care of a kitten?*

ABC Activity

Say four or five letters of the alphabet in sequence, but reverse two of the letters: *c, d, e, g, f.* Children say the letters that are reversed.

CENTER Activity

Cross Curricular: Language Arts

NAME THAT CAT Provide templates of cat faces. Have children trace and cut out cat faces. Then ask children to name their cats, printing the first initial on the back. Children may then choose to put the cats in ABC order.

▶ **Spatial/Intrapersonal**

OBJECTIVES

Children will:
- identify on and off

MATERIALS
- *Allie's Adventure from A to Z*

TEACHING TIP

INSTRUCTIONAL Be aware of when you use directional terms during the day. Help children to review their meanings by asking questions, such as: *Is the cap on the marker or off the marker?*

Introduce On, Off

PREPARE

Act Out On and Off
Take a book off the shelf and ask children what you just did. Then ask a child to put the book on the shelf. Next, put on a hat, and have children describe what you just did. Then take the hat off and say, *The hat is off my head.*

TEACH

Describe On and Off
Display the Big Book *Allie's Adventure from A to Z* and have children recall the story. Then turn to page 11 and ask where the beetle is. Then turn to page 6 and ask where the hen is sitting. (on Allie's nose, on her eggs) Then have children find other examples in the classroom that illustrate on and off.

PRACTICE

Show On and Off
Read the directions on page 187 to the children, and make sure they clearly understand what they are asked to do. Identify each picture, and complete the first item. Then work through the page with children, or have them complete the page independently.

ASSESS/CLOSE

Review the Page
Check children's work on the Pupil Edition page. Note areas where children need extra help.

Name_____

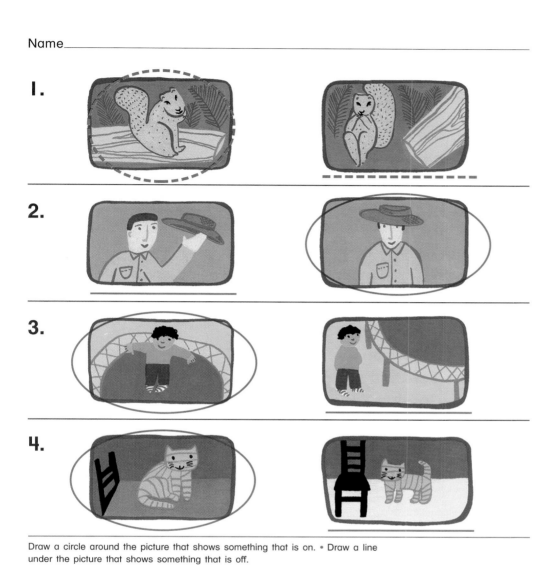

1.

2.

3.

4.

Draw a circle around the picture that shows something that is on. • Draw a line under the picture that shows something that is off.

Unit 4   Introduce On, Off   **187**

Pupil Edition, page 187

ALTERNATE TEACHING STRATEGY
....

ON, OFF

For a different approach to teaching this skill, see page T25.

▶ **Visual/Auditory/ Kinesthetic**

Practice **187**

Name_____

Look at the picture. Color the items that are *on* the tree. Draw a circle around the things that are *off* the tree.

9 Unit 4
Introduce On, Off

At Home: Place common objects on a table and on the floor. Together, talk about the items that are on the table and those that are off.

187

PRACTICE BOOK, page 187

Meeting Individual Needs for Beginning Reading Concepts

EASY	ON-LEVEL	CHALLENGE	LANGUAGE SUPPORT
Play a game of "Musical Chairs" with a small group. Explain that when they hear music they get off the chairs and walk. When the music stops, they find a chair to sit on.	**Take** a walk around the classroom and have partners make a picture or a word list of things whose positions could be described using on or off. Have children compare their lists.	**Help** children fold a sheet of drawing paper in half. Ask them to draw a snowman with a hat on in the first section. In the second section, the hat is off. Continue on the back showing the snowman with a scarf and a jacket both on and off.	**Give** children opportunities to follow your directions: *Put the block on the table. Take the hat off her head. Put the book on the shelf.* If necessary, perform the action yourself and then have children do the same.

187

Develop Phonological Awareness

Listen

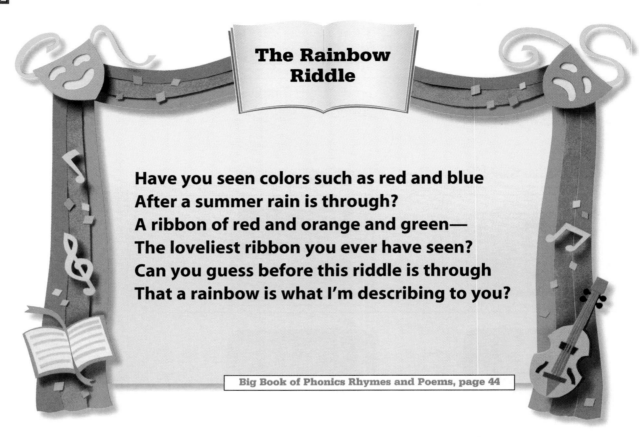

The Rainbow Riddle

Have you seen colors such as red and blue
After a summer rain is through?
A ribbon of red and orange and green—
The loveliest ribbon you ever have seen?
Can you guess before this riddle is through
That a rainbow is what I'm describing to you?

Big Book of Phonics Rhymes and Poems, page 44

Objective: Listen for Matching Sounds

LISTEN TO THE POEM

- Read the title and the poem aloud. Emphasize the /r/ sound.
- Ask children to listen as you say three words. Explain that two of the words will begin with the same sound.

> rock   ring   song

- Ask which two words begin with the same sound.
- Continue with these words: *boat, car, bottle; ribbon, fiddle, riddle; lion, tiger, tap.*

LISTEN FOR THE WORD THAT DOESN'T BELONG

- Say these words: *rain, red, sun*. Ask which word does not begin with the same sound as the other two.
- Continue with similar groups of words.

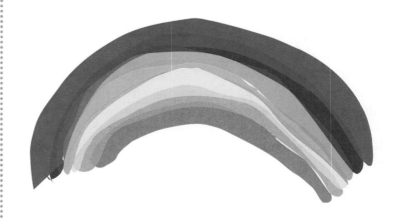

Objective: Listen for Initial /r/

USE WORDS FROM THE POEM

- Say the /r/ sound and have children repeat it after you. Say the title of the poem, emphasizing the words with initial /r/.
- Say the poem, one line at a time. Ask children to say a word in each line that begins with /r/.
- Slowly read the poem again. Have children run in place when they hear a word with initial /r/.

IDENTIFY WORDS WITH INITIAL /r/

- Say the following sentence: *Ron has a red ribbon.*
- Invite children to substitute other words that begin with /r/ for the word *ribbon: ring, rose, rug, rabbit, racer,* and so on.

Read Together

From Phonemic Awareness to Phonics

Objective: Identify /r/ R, r

IDENTIFY THE LETTER FOR THE SOUND

- Explain to children that the letters *R, r* stand for the sound /r/. Ask children to say the sound with you.
- Display the Big Book of Phonics Rhymes and Poems, page 44. Point to the letters in the corner and identify them. Have children make the /r/ sound as you point to the letters.

REREAD THE POEM

- Reread the poem, pointing to each word. Ask children to raise a finger when you point to and say a word that begins with /r/.

LOOK FOR WORDS

- Tell children that one line in the poem has two words that begin with *r*. Have them find the words and the line in the poem.

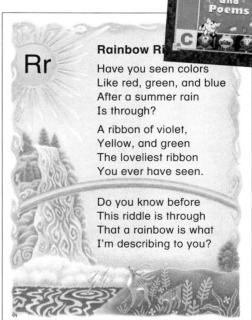

Rr

Rainbow Ri[...]

Have you seen colors
Like red, green, and blue
After a summer rain
Is through?

A ribbon of violet,
Yellow, and green
The loveliest ribbon
You ever have seen.

Do you know before
This riddle is through
That a rainbow is what
I'm describing to you?

Big Book of Phonics Rhymes and Poems, page 44

OBJECTIVES

Children will:

- identify /r/ *R,r*
- write and use letters *R,r*

....

MATERIALS

- letter cards from the Word Building Book

TEACHING TIP

INSTRUCTIONAL Invite children to join you in creating gestures to pantomime action words that begin with *r* such as: *ride, row, read, raise, rinse, rush.* Invite children to suggest additional initial *r* action words.

ALTERNATE TEACHING STRATEGY
....

INITIAL /r/r

For a different approach to teaching this skill, see page T24.

▶ **Visual/Auditory/ Kinesthetic**

Review Initial /r/r

TEACH

Identify /r/ R, r   Tell children they will review the sound /r/ and write the letters *R, r*. Write the letters, identify them, and make the /r/ sound together. Write incomplete sentences on the chalkboard, such as: *He has a ___ cap. His dog can ___ beside him.* Ask children to think of words that begin with /r/ to complete the sentences. Write the words *red* and *run* and ask volunteers to draw a circle around each initial *r*.

Form R, r   Write *R* on one part of the chalkboard and *r* on another part of the chalkboard. Display the following word cards on the ledge, and ask children to identify which form of *r* to place them beneath. For example: *Ron, Ruth, ran, rod, Rick, rim, rid.*

PRACTICE

Complete the Pupil Edition Page   Read the directions on page 188 to the children, and make sure they clearly understand what they are being asked to do. Identify each picture, and complete the first item together. Then work through the page with children or have them complete the page independently.

ASSESS/CLOSE

Identify and Use R, r   Tell this story: *Ron ran to the river. He wanted to ride in his new boat.* As you read the sentences again, ask children to hold up their *r* letter card each time you say a word that begins with the sound /r/.

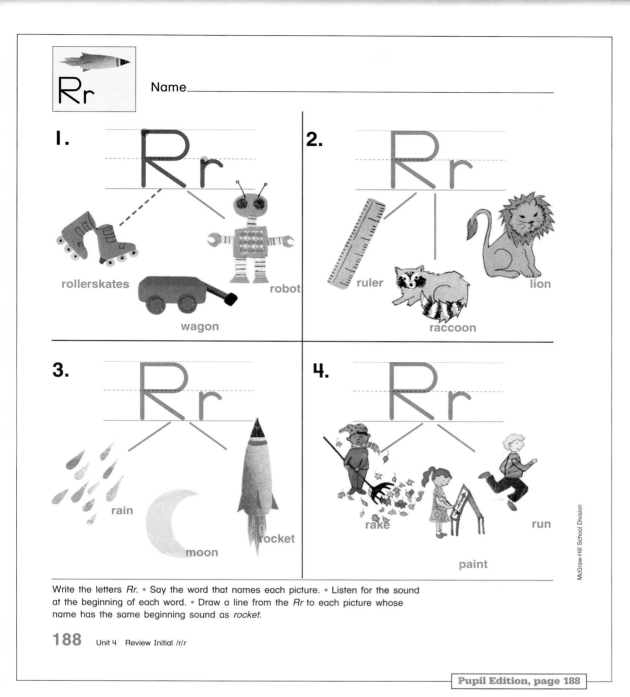

Rr Name_____

1. Rr

rollerskates robot wagon

2. Rr

ruler raccoon lion

3. Rr

rain moon rocket

4. Rr

rake paint run

Write the letters *Rr*. • Say the word that names each picture. • Listen for the sound at the beginning of each word. • Draw a line from the *Rr* to each picture whose name has the same beginning sound as *rocket*.

188 Unit 4 Review Initial /r/r

McGraw-Hill School Division

Pupil Edition, page 188

ADDITIONAL PHONICS RESOURCES

Practice Book, *page 188*
Phonics Workbook

McGraw-Hill School
TECHNOLOGY

Phonics CD-ROM
Activities for practice with Initial Letters

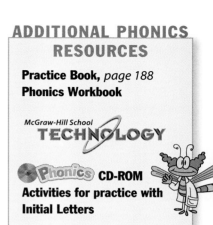

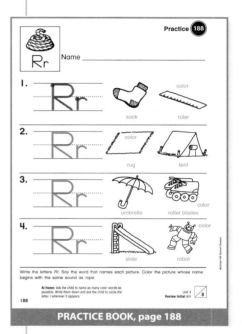

Practice 188

Rr Name_____

1. Rr
sock ruler color

2. Rr
rug color tent

3. Rr
umbrella roller blades color

4. Rr
slide robot color

Write the letters *Rr*. Say the word that names each picture. Color the picture whose name begins with the same sound as *rope*.

At Home: Ask the child to name as many color words as possible. Write them down and ask the child to circle the letter *r* wherever it appears.

188

Unit 4
Review Initial /r/r

PRACTICE BOOK, page 188

Meeting Individual Needs for Phonics

EASY	ON-LEVEL	CHALLENGE	LANGUAGE SUPPORT
Give children a selection of tactile letters *R* and *r*, and ask them to sort for capital and lowercase letters. Invite them to think of a name that begins with *R* and an object or animal whose name begins with *r*.	**Ask** children to name objects or animals whose names begin with *r*, such as: *raccoon, rug, rain, rainbow, rabbit*. Have them write the letter *r* each time they hear a word that begins with /r/.	**Ask** children to listen to what you say and write the letter *R* or *r* on a sheet of paper covered with a thin layer of fingerpaint. Remind children of the rules of capitalization. Say words that begin in *r* such as *Roy, river, rent, Rita, really, ride*.	**Help** ESL children recognize initial *R,r* by having them write or trace the letter forms on self-stick labels and label things in the classroom, such as *ruler, raincoat, ring, rug, red, raisins*.

188

OBJECTIVES

- recognize words with initial /r/
- understand the main idea of the story

ZOE HALL loves to bake pies and used her own recipe in this book. Her first book "It's Pumpkin Time!" won several major awards.

SHARI HALPERN grew up in Massachusetts and used one of her mother's apple pies as a model for the art in this book. She lives in New Jersey with her husband Paul, who is a puppet maker, and her cats.

TEACHING TIP

INSTRUCTIONAL

Encourage children to observe trees in your neighborhood. Talk about how they change during the seasons. You may wish to encourage children to choose a tree and draw how it looks during each season.

Read the Big Book

Before Reading

Build Background

EVALUATE PRIOR KNOWLEDGE Hold up an apple or a picture of an apple, and talk about where they come from. Discuss where children get apples, such as apple trees, farm stands, and grocery stores. Ask if they have ever seen an apple tree.

WHAT DO YOU SEE WHEN YOU LOOK AT A TREE? Draw the bark and branches of a simple apple tree on chart paper. Invite volunteers to point to and identify the bark and the branches. Have children draw leaves and apples.

Preview and Predict

Read the title of the book and talk about the cover. Name the author and illustrator and share some information about them.

TAKE A PICTURE WALK Invite children to take a picture walk with you through half of the book. Invite children to talk about how the tree changes during the story.

MAKE PREDICTIONS Then ask them to predict what the children might do in the story.

Set Purposes

Tell children you will read to find out what happens to the Apple Pie Tree.

But in spring, leaves grow on every branch.

Look! Two robins are building a nest in our tree.

Apple Pie Tree, pages 6–7

During Reading

Read Together

- Before you begin to read, point to the first word in the first sentence. Explain that this is where you will begin to read. Continue to track print as you read the story. *Tracking Print*

- Have children look at the pictures of the tree on pages 5–7. Have them describe how the tree changes from winter to spring. *Use Illustrations*

- Reread pages 16–17. Ask children to *raise* their hands when they hear words that begin with /r/. (rains, robins) *Phonics and Decoding*

- After you finish reading the story, ask children to describe how the tree changes during the year. *Understand Main Idea*

Apple Pie Tree, page 27

After Reading

Return to Predictions and Purposes

Discuss the purposes and predictions that children made before reading the story. Ask if their questions were answered. If not, revisit sections of the story. Ask whether the story could really happen or if it is a fantasy.

Literary Response

JOURNAL WRITING Help children draw the apple tree during one season. Invite them to write about the tree. Then have them compare their pictures.

ORAL RESPONSE Engage children in a discussion of the story by asking questions such as:

- *How does the tree look during the spring?*

- *What appears on the branches?*

- *How do the buds change?*

CENTER Activity

Cross-Curricular: Science

APPLE I.D. Cut an apple in half. Invite children to describe the texture, colors, and smell of the apple. Then identify the parts of an apple: stem, skin, seeds, core, and pulp. Provide a picture of an apple, and have children color each part a different color.

OBJECTIVES

Children will:

- use story details to determine the main idea

MATERIALS

- *The Apple Pie Tree*

TEACHING TIP

INSTRUCTIONAL If children have difficulty with the concept of a main idea, focus on very familiar stories. Have one child give the name of a story and then have a partner state the main idea. Partners switch roles and repeat.

Introduce Main Idea

PREPARE

Warm-Up: Recall a Story
Invite volunteers to use one sentence to tell the Big Book story *The Apple Pie Tree*. Explain that the main idea tells the important idea in the story. Help children decide which child did the best job of telling the main idea.

TEACH

Decide Upon the Main Theme
Reread *The Apple Pie Tree,* taking time to talk about the story. Then ask: *What do you think the author was trying to tell us about the apple tree? What is the book mainly about?*

PRACTICE

Find the Main Idea
Read the directions on page 189 to the children, and make sure they clearly understand what they are asked to do. Identify each picture, and complete the first item together. Then work through the page with children or have them complete the page independently.

ASSESS/CLOSE

Review the Page
Review children's work on the Pupil Edition page, and note children who are experiencing difficulty.

Name_____

1.

The cat sat on a mat.

The cat ran to Mom.

_____

2.

Nan is mad.

Sam is sad.

_____

Look at each picture. • Then read the sentences. • Draw a line under the sentence that tells what the picture is all about.

Unit 4 Introduce Main Idea   **189**

Pupil Edition, page 189

ALTERNATE TEACHING STRATEGY

MAIN IDEA
For a different approach to teaching this skill, see page T26.

▶ **Visual/Auditory/Kinesthetic**

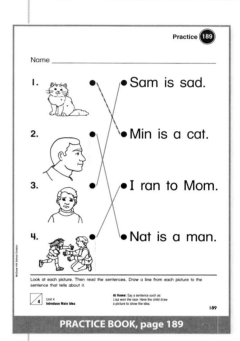

PRACTICE BOOK, page 189

Meeting Individual Needs for Comprehension

EASY	ON-LEVEL	CHALLENGE	LANGUAGE SUPPORT
Ask children to name the seasons, beginning with spring. Ask how the tree in the story changed during each season. Then complete the sentence: This story is mainly about how a tree _____.	**Invite** children to choose a book from your classroom library. Reread it together, and then work together to complete the sentence: This story is mainly about ____.	**Identify** the main idea of the story with the children. Then work together to compose a letter to the author. Include any questions children might have about the story or the author.	**Tell** children that the story is mainly about an apple tree that changes during the seasons. Have them talk about how the tree changes, using illustrations from the book.

189

Develop Phonological Awareness

Listen

Rainbow Riddle
a poem
Ferris Wheel Fun
a poem

Have you seen colors
Like red, green, and blue
After a summer rain
Is through?
A ribbon of violet,
Yellow, and green
The loveliest ribbon
You ever have seen.
Do you know before
This riddle is through
That a rainbow is what
I'm describing to you?

Fasten my seat belt.
This feels fun!
I'm on the Ferris wheel
For ride number one!
It's going fast!
And faster still.
Ferris wheel fun
Is such a thrill!

Big Book of Phonics Rhymes and Poems, pages 44, 13

Objective: Listen for Everyday Sounds

READ THE POEM Read the poem "Rainbow Riddle." Invite children to echo read the poem, line by line. Talk about times when children have walked in a summer rain. Have them close their eyes and describe what rain looks and feels like.

DESCRIBE THE SOUNDS OF RAIN Invite children to describe what rain sounds like as it falls in a puddle, hits an umbrella, or splashes against a window pane. Encourage children to use words that tell what rain sounds like. You may want to get them started with several examples.

| drip drop | pitter patter | splat |
| splish splash | dot-a-dot-dot | squish |

DESCRIBE OTHER WEATHER SOUNDS Suggest other types of weather sounds for children to describe, such as a powerful wind, thunder and lightning, or hail.

190A *You Are IT!*

Objective: Listen for /r/ and /f/

LISTEN FOR INITIAL /R/ Read the poem "Rainbow Riddle," emphasizing words that begin with /r/.

Have children repeat words that begin with /r/.

> **rainbow riddle red**
> **rain ribbon**

GUESS THE ACTION Tell children that you will whisper something to act out in a volunteer's ear. Explain that the group will guess what the person is doing. Point out that the answers will be words that begin with the /r/ sound.

> **rowing a boat running**
> **reading a book raking leaves**

LISTEN FOR INITIAL /F/ As you read the poem "Ferris Wheel Fun" aloud to children, stress words that begin with /f/. Have children repeat the words.

GUESS THE WORD Provide clues to help children guess the word. The first clue is always the initial sound. Say: *I am thinking of something whose name begins with /f/. It lives in the water.*

> **fish farm food fan**

From Phonemic Awareness to Phonics

Read Together

Objective: Identify /r/ R, r and /f/ F, f

IDENTIFY THE LETTERS Display the Big Book of Phonics Rhymes and Poems, pages 19 and 44. On each page, point to the letters, identify them, and say the sounds they stand for.

REREAD THE POEMS Reread the poems, tracking the print and emphasizing the words with initial /r/ or /f/. Have children repeat the words after you.

FIND WORDS WITH R, r, F, f Have children use their fingers to frame words in the poems that begin with R, r, F, or f.

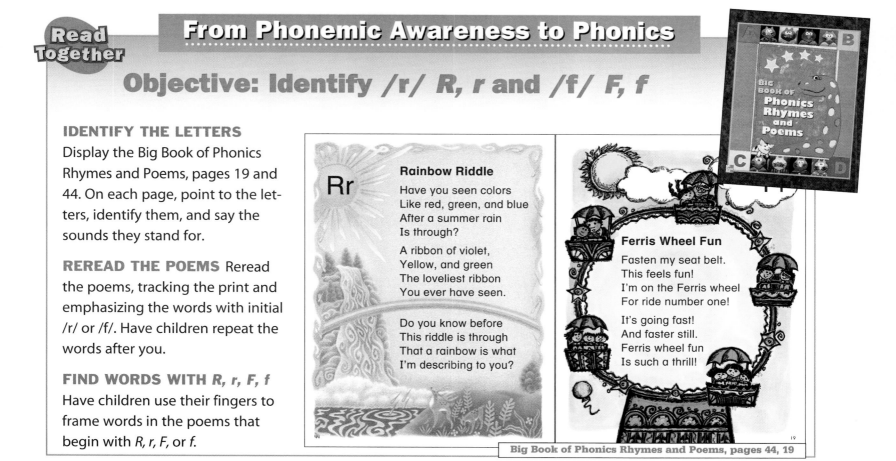

Rr

Rainbow Riddle

Have you seen colors
Like red, green, and blue
After a summer rain
Is through?

A ribbon of violet,
Yellow, and green
The loveliest ribbon
You ever have seen.

Do you know before
This riddle is through
That a rainbow is what
I'm describing to you?

Ferris Wheel Fun

Fasten my seat belt.
This feels fun!
I'm on the Ferris wheel
For ride number one!

It's going fast!
And faster still.
Ferris wheel fun
Is such a thrill!

Big Book of Phonics Rhymes and Poems, pages 44, 19

OBJECTIVES

Children will:

- identify and discriminate between /r/R,r and /f/F,f
- write and use letters R,r and F,f

....

MATERIALS

- letter cards from the Word Play Book

┌─────────────────────────────┐

TEACHING TIP

INSTRUCTIONAL Children will enjoy pantomiming action words such as *run, rip, fan*. Invite children to think of other actions that begin with /r/ or /f/ that they can pantomime.

└─────────────────────────────┘

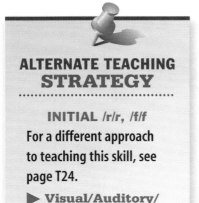

ALTERNATE TEACHING STRATEGY
....

INITIAL /r/r, /f/f

For a different approach to teaching this skill, see page T24.

▶ **Visual/Auditory/ Kinesthetic**

Review Initial r/r, /f/f

TEACH

Identify and Discriminate Between /r/ R,r and /f/ F,f

Tell children they will review the sounds /r/ and /f/ and write letters R,r and F,f. Write the letters R,r on one side of the chalkboard and F,f on the other side. Say, "Rod had fun." Repeat the sentence, asking children to point to one of the letters if a word begins with that letter's sound. Then write the words beneath the letters.

Write and Use R,r and F,f

Display letter cards R,r and F,f. Have children write each of the letter forms on four index cards. Then ask them to exchange cards with a partner and write the missing form of each letter on the reverse side of every card.

PRACTICE

Complete the Pupil Edition Page

Read the directions on page 190 to children, and make sure they clearly understand what they are being asked to do. Identify each picture and complete the first item together. Then work through the page with children, or have them complete the page independently.

ASSESS/CLOSE

Identify and Use R,r and F,f

Have children use the letter cards they completed in the Teach activity, and give them several blank cards. Write the following words on the chalkboard: *rot, Ron, rat, fit, fin, fan*. Ask children to show the pattern of *r* and *f* with their letter cards and to write more letter cards as they need them.

Name_____

feather

rollercoaster

family

f

r

f

rooster

fire

finger

r

f

f

Say the name of each picture. • Then write the letter for the sound you hear at the beginning of the picture name.

McGraw-Hill School Division

190   Unit 4   Review /r/r, /f/f

Pupil Edition, page 190

ADDITIONAL PHONICS
RESOURCES

Practice Book, *page 190*
Phonics Workbook

McGraw-Hill School
TECHNOLOGY

Phonics CD-ROM
Activities for practice with Initial Letters

PRACTICE BOOK, page 190

Meeting Individual Needs for Phonics

EASY	ON-LEVEL	CHALLENGE	LANGUAGE SUPPORT
Give children letter cards *r* and *f* and pictures such as the following: *rope, rug, rain, face, family, farm.* Ask them to name the pictures and to sort the pictures, placing each with the letter card that shows the sound the picture's name begins with.	**Show** pictures such as the following: *fox, fan, fish, ring, rake, rabbit.* Have children name the objects in the pictures. Ask them to write *r* or *f* on self-stick labels and place them on the pictures to show the letter each object's name begins with.	**Show** two pictures at a time, for example: *rabbit, ring; ring, fan; fan, fork.* Ask children if both objects begin with the same letter. If not, show more pictures until there is a match. In each case, ask children to write the object and its initial letter.	**Give** ESL children extra practice with initial *f* and *r* words. Write and say sentences, and have children identify initial /f/ and /r/: *Run to the fox. A rabbit can run fast.*

190

Teacher Read Aloud

Every Time I Climb a Tree
by David McCord

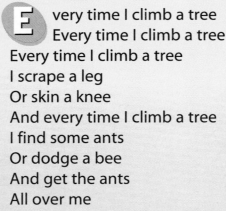

Every time I climb a tree
Every time I climb a tree
Every time I climb a tree
I scrape a leg
Or skin a knee
And every time I climb a tree
I find some ants
Or dodge a bee
And get the ants
All over me

And every time I climb a tree
Where have you been?
They say to me
But don't they know that I
   am free
Every time I climb a tree?
I like it best

To spot a nest
That has an egg
Or maybe three

And then I skin
The other leg
But every time I climb a tree
I see a lot of things to see
Swallows rooftops and TV
And all the fields and farms
   there be
Every time I climb a tree
Though climbing may be good
   for ants
It isn't awfully good for pants
But still it's pretty good for me
Every time I climb a tree

Oral Comprehension

LISTENING AND SPEAKING Ask children if they have ever climbed a tree, and why someone might like to climb a tree. Explain to children that they will hear a poem about a child who climbs a tree. Encourage children to think about the main idea of the poem by asking them to listen to the story that the poem tells.

After children hear the poem, ask: *What is the poem mainly about?* Then ask them to recall details of the poem that they remember.

Activity Ask children to pretend that they have climbed a tree near your school. Have them describe what they might see. You may wish to make a class list of their ideas.

▶ **Linguistic**

Real-Life Reading

Can you follow the footsteps?
Start at **X**.

24   25

Big Book of Real-Life Reading, pages 24–25

Objective: Read a Map

READ THE PAGE Ask children what they like to do after school and where they go to play. Then ask children to recall the poem "Every Time I Climb a Tree." Have them retell the events described in the poem. Explain to children that you will look at a map that shows what the boy did one day. Then discuss the map.

ANSWER THE QUESTION Establish that the children begin at the *X*, and have them locate it. Have a volunteer move her or his finger and ask: *Where did the boy go first? Where did he go next?*

Provide a simple map of your classroom. Show the door, the windows, and your desk. Have children draw the remaining features of the room.

CULTURAL PERSPECTIVES

AFTER SCHOOL Share that children throughout the world do different things after school. In India, children might take care of their younger brothers and sisters. In the U.S., children might go to an after-school program until their parents finish work. In East Africa, children might play the flute or drums and help their parents with little tasks.

Activity Help children interview each other to find out what they most like to do after school. Make a mural tally to show the information.

▶ **Logical/Interpersonal**

TESTED OBJECTIVES

Children will:

- identify and read the high-frequency word *to*

....

MATERIALS

- word cards from the Word Play Book
- *You Are IT!*

TEACHING TIP

MANAGEMENT Continue to have children work in pairs if they are not ready to complete worksheets independently. You may also wish to provide frames to help children isolate specific items they are working on.

Introduce High-Frequency Words: *to*

PREPARE

Listen to Words
Explain to the children that they will be learning a new word: *to*. Say the following sentence: *Run to the tree.* Say the sentence again, and ask children to raise a hand when they hear the word *to*. Repeat with the sentence: *I like to play.*

TEACH

Model Reading the Word in Context
Give a word card to each child, and read the word. Reread the sentences, and have children raise their word cards when they hear the word.

Identify the Word
Write the sentences above on the chalkboard. Track print and read each sentence. Children hold up their word card when they hear the word *to*. Then ask volunteers to point to and circle the word *to* in the sentences.

Write the Word
Review how to write the letters *t* and *o*. Then have children practice tracing the word on their word card.

PRACTICE

Complete the Pupil Edition Page
Read the directions on page 191 to the children, and make sure they clearly understand what they are asked to do. Complete the first item together. Then work through the page with children or have them complete the page independently.

ASSESS/CLOSE

Review the Page
Review children's work, and note children who are experiencing difficulty or need additional practice.

Name_____

1.

Nan ran to Dad.

_____

2.

Dad ran to Ron.

_____

3.

Ron ran to Mom.

_____

4.

Mom ran to Min.

_____

Read the sentence. • Draw a line under the word *to* in the sentence.

Unit 4   Introduce High-Frequency Words: *to*   **191**

Pupil Edition, page 191

ALTERNATE TEACHING STRATEGY

HIGH-FREQUENCY WORDS
For a different approach to teaching this skill, see page T27.

▶ **Visual/Auditory/ Kinesthetic**

Practice **191**

Name _____

1.

Tom ran <u>to</u> the cat.

2.

The cat ran <u>to</u> Nan.

3.

Nan ran <u>to</u> the mat.

4. The cat ran <u>to</u> the mat.

Read the sentence. Draw a line under the word *to* in the sentence.

4 Unit 4 Introduce High-Frequency Words: *to*   **At Home:** Tell about something you need, such as "I need a snack." The child answers, using the word *to*, such as "I will go to the kitchen."   191

PRACTICE BOOK, page 191

Meeting Individual Needs for Vocabulary

EASY	ON-LEVEL	CHALLENGE	LANGUAGE SUPPORT
Give children the word card: *to*. Have children practice writing the word in a sand/salt tray. Then have children make their own word card on an index card to take home.	**Provide** classroom picture books and have children find the word *to*. Have partners work together, and keep a tally to show how many times they find the word.	**Reread** the lines from the poem: *I like it best / To spot a nest.* Have children rewrite the last line by filling in the last three words. (To _____ _____ _____.). Explain that the lines do not need to rhyme. Invite children to share their ideas.	**Make** a simple board game with squares. Write the word *to* in some of the squares. Children roll a number cube and move a marker around the board. When they land on a square with *to*, they read the word and score a point. You may also put other words to read in the boxes.

Develop Phonological Awareness

Listen

Ron the Cat
a poem

Ron the Cat ran to my cup.
He ran up to the rim.
Dip the cup; tip the cup.
Give a sip to him.
Then Ron the Cat ran to the cot,
And curled up in my hat.
He took a nap and snored a lot,
That funny little cat!

Objective: Listen for Everyday Sounds

READ THE POEM Read the poem, "Ron the Cat." Encourage children to listen carefully to find out what Ron the Cat does when he naps.

snores

IMITATE SOUNDS Invite children to demonstrate how Ron sounded as he napped in the hat. Then have children demonstrate other sounds, such as a sneeze, a cough, and a hearty laugh.

PLAY A SOUND GAME Tell children that you will make a sound and they have to guess what was used to create the sound. Ask them to close their eyes. You might ring a bell, crumple paper, slam the desk drawer closed, or clap the chalkboard erasers together.

Objective: Blending with Short *a*, *i*, and *o* with /r/

MAKE A CAT Use an empty tissue box that opens at the top to make a cat head. The opening will be the cat's mouth. Add eyes, nose, and whiskers with a marker.

LISTEN AND BLEND Read the poem, "Ron the Cat." Tell children that Ron the Cat likes to speak slowly. Point out that if Ron the Cat says /r/-/a/-/n/, they can figure out what Ron the Cat is saying by blending the sounds together. Model and have children repeat after you.

> /r/-/a/-/n/ ran

MORE BLENDING Say: /r/-/i/-/m/. Invite children to repeat the segmented word and then blend the sounds together to say the word *rim*. Continue with other words.

> /r/-/a/-/m/
> /r/-/i/-/d/
> /r/-/o/-/d/

STEP AND BLEND Invite children to creep like Ron the Cat as they repeat each sound of a segmented word you say, one step for each sound. Then have children stop and blend the sounds together to say the word.

> /r/-/a/-/t/   /r/-/o/-/t/

From Phonemic Awareness to Phonics

Read Together

Objective: Focus on Print

LISTEN FOR SOUNDS Read the poem "Ron the Cat." To help children recall that the word *ran* has three sounds, say the word aloud, segmenting the sounds.

> /r/ - /a/ - /n/

IDENTIFY THE LETTERS Write the word *ran* on the chalkboard. Point to the letters, one at a time, and have children identify them and say the sounds they stand for. Repeat for the word *rat*.

COMPARE WORDS Ask children to look closely at the words on the chalkboard and tell how they are the same and how they are different.

COUNT THE LETTERS Write the word *ran* on the chalkboard in large print. Set out several sheets of colored paper and some tape. As you say the name of each letter in the word, have a volunteer cover the letter with a piece of colored paper. Have children count the number of colored papers to determine the number of letters in

the word. Repeat with the word *rat*.

LOOK AT MORE WORDS Write the words *rim* and *rid* on the chalkboard. Repeat the letter identification, comparison, and letter counting with this pair of words.

OBJECTIVES

Children will:

- identify /a/*a*, /i/*i*, and /o/*o*
- blend and read short *a, i,* and *o* words
- write short *a, i,* and *o* words
- review /r/*r*

MATERIALS

- letter cards from the Word Building Book

TEACHING TIP

INSTRUCTIONAL Have children use a mirror as they say /r/. Ask them to describe how their mouths look as they say the following words: *Ron, ran, rid.*

ALTERNATE TEACHING STRATEGY

BLENDING SHORT *a, i, o*

For a different approach to teaching this skill, see Unit 1, page T32; Unit 2, page T32; Unit 3, page T30.

▶ **Visual/Auditory/ Kinesthetic**

<u>Review</u> **Blending with**  **short *a, i, o***

TEACH

Identify *a, i, o* as the Symbols for /a/, /i/, /o/
Tell children they will continue to read words with *a, i,* and *o.*

- Display the *a* letter card and say /a/. Have children repeat the sound /a/ after you as you point to the *a* card.

BLENDING Model and Guide Practice
- Place the *r* card before the *a* card. Blend the sounds together and have children repeat after you.

- Place the *n* card after the *a* to show *ran.* Blend to read *ran.*

Use the Word in Context
- Use the word *ran* in a sentence, such as: *I ran to first base.* Have children use *ran* in a sentence.

Repeat the Procedure
- Use the following words to continue modeling and for guided practice with short *a, i, o: rot, Ron, ran, rat, rod, rid, ram.*

PRACTICE

Complete the Pupil Edition Page
Read aloud the directions on page 192. Identify each picture, and complete the first item together. Work through the page with children, or have them complete the page independently.

ASSESS/CLOSE

Write Short *a, i,* and *o* Words
Observe children as they complete page 192. Then have them write 3 words that begin with /r/*r*, one word each for short *a, i, o.* Write *t, m, d, n* for children to use as last letter choices.

Name_____

1. r a t   rat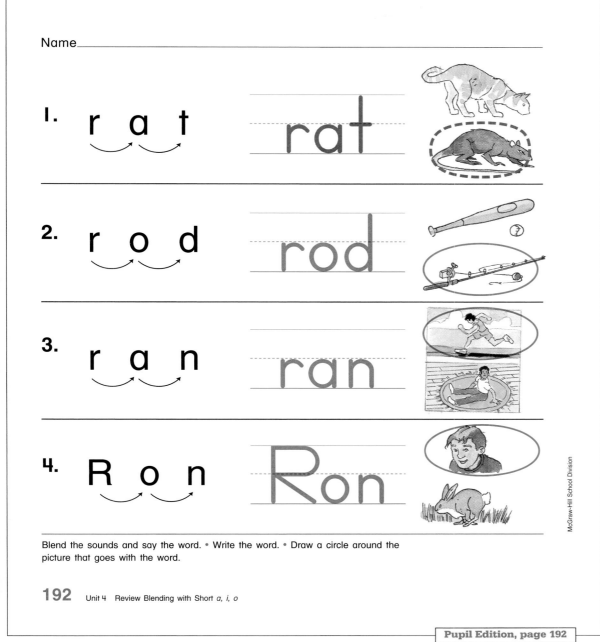

2. r o d   rod

3. r a n   ran

4. R o n   Ron

Blend the sounds and say the word. • Write the word. • Draw a circle around the
picture that goes with the word.

McGraw-Hill School Division

Pupil Edition, page 192

ADDITIONAL PHONICS
RESOURCES

Practice Book, *page 192*
Phonics Workbook

McGraw-Hill School
TECHNOLOGY

Phonics **CD-ROM**
**Activities for practice with
Blending and Segmenting**

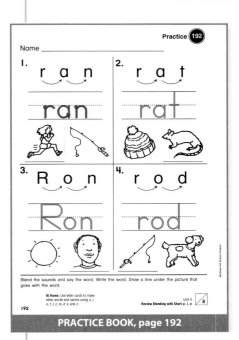

Practice 192

Name _____

1. r a n   2. r a t
   ran   rat

3. R o n   4. r o d
   Ron   rod

Blend the sounds and say the word. Write the word. Draw a line under the picture that
goes with the word.

At Home: Use letter cards to make
other words and names using *a, i,
o, t, l, c, m, d, s,* and *n*

192   Unit 4
                Review Blending with Short *a, i, o*

McGraw-Hill School Division

PRACTICE BOOK, page 192

Meeting Individual Needs for Phonics

EASY	ON-LEVEL	CHALLENGE	LANGUAGE SUPPORT
Write *rod, rot, rat, ran, Ron* on the chalkboard and blend sounds with children to read the words aloud. Ask children to use these words to complete sentences you say, such as: *When I go fishing, I take a (rod). The food was so old it began to (rot). I (ran) fast in the race.*	**Place** the following word cards on the chalkboard ledge or on a table: *rot, ran, rid.* Give children a variety of word cards, and have them identify words that rhyme with *rot, ran,* and *rid.* Suggestions: *cot, not ,dot, tot; Nan, Dan, man, can; did, Sid.*	**Write** *r* on the left side of the chalkboard; *a, i, o* in the middle; and *t, m, d, n* on the right side. Ask children to select a middle letter to follow first letter *r* and then select a last letter. Write the word, then blend sounds with children to read the words.	**Give** children additional opportunities to discriminate among short vowels *a, i,* and *o* by writing, and then blending to read aloud with children the following initial *r* words: *rat, ran, rim, rot, rod, rid.* Be sure children understand the meaning of each word.

192

Guided Instruction

BEFORE READING

PREVIEW AND PREDICT Take a brief **picture walk** through the book, focusing on the illustrations. Ask children:

- *Who is the story about? Where is it taking place?*

- *What do you think will happen in the story?*

- *Do you think the story will be realistic or make-believe? Why?*

SET PURPOSES Discuss with children what they would like to find out about as they read. For example, they might want to know what game the children are playing.

TEACHING **TIP**

To put book together:
1. Tear out the story page.
2. Cut along dotted line.
3. Fold each section on fold line.
4. Assemble book.

INSTRUCTIONAL Continue to point out and review punctuation marks when you are reading books from your classroom library. When you are reading aloud, note when the text uses question marks and exclamation points.

You Are IT!

"You are IT!" said Ron.

3

Ron ran to Tom.

2

Tom ran to Nan.

4

McGraw-Hill School Division

Guided Instruction

DURING READING

☑ **Concepts of Print**

☑ **Phonics**

☑ **High-Frequency Words:** *to*

☑ **Use Illustrations**

① **CONCEPTS OF PRINT** Point to the first letter in each word of the title on the title page. Explain that the first letters of words in a title are always capital letters.

② **PHONICS** After you read page 2, ask children to point to the two words that begin with the letter *r*. Ask which word uses a lowercase letter and which word uses an capital letter.

③ **CONCEPTS OF PRINT** After you read page 3, point to the word *IT*, and talk about why it is written with capital letters. Frame the exclamation point. Have volunteers read the sentence with excitement.

LANGUAGE SUPPORT

ESL Talk to the children about the game of tag. Many different cultures have this game or a similar one. Invite ESL students to describe or act out games they know how to play.

Guided Instruction

DURING READING

4 HIGH-FREQUENCY WORDS Ask children to point to the word *to* on page 4. Read the word as you track print. Then have children do the same.

5 USE ILLUSTRATIONS After you read page 5, ask who is "it" now. (Nan) Ask what Nan needs to do. (Run and tag someone else.)

6 MAKE PREDICTIONS After you read page 7, ask: *Who is "it" now? What do you think Dad will do now?*

7 MAIN IDEA After children read page 8, ask them what the story is mainly about. (*children who play a game of tag with Dad*)

ASSESSMENT

PHONICS

HOW TO ASSESS Have several pictures of simple objects, some of which begin with the initial *r* sound. Ask children to identify the pictures that have this sound.

FOLLOW UP Have children say the name of each picture aloud. Ask them to listen for the initial sound.

"You are IT!" said Tom.

5

"You are IT!" said Nan.

7

Nan ran to Dad.

6

Ron, Tom, and Nan
ran and ran.

8

Guided Instruction

AFTER READING

RETURN TO PREDICTIONS AND PURPOSES
Remind children of their predictions about the story. Ask if they found out what game the children were playing. Revisit the story if necessary.

RETELL THE STORY Hold up the book so that children can see the first picture, but cover the sentence with your hand. Ask a volunteer to tell you what happened first, using the illustration as a clue. Continue through the story.

LITERARY RESPONSE Ask children to think about other games they like to play outside with friends. Have them write and draw about it in their journals.

CENTER Activity

Cross Curricular: Social Studies

SAFETY FIRST Talk about safe and fair play. Ask children to make a set of rules that they can use outside to ensure safe, fair play. Children can write or draw on index cards, or they may choose to make a poster.

Rules For Playing
1. Don't throw any objects if there are people nearby.
2. Take Turns.

▶ **Interpersonal**

OBJECTIVES

Children will:

- identify the main idea of a story

MATERIALS

- *You Are IT!*

TEACHING TIP

INSTRUCTIONAL Ask children to explain how to play tag. Point out that some children may play by different rules. Discuss what the label "IT" means in the game of tag.

Introduce Main Idea

PREPARE

Tell About a Favorite Show
Ask children to think of a favorite television show or movie. Have volunteers take turns telling what the show or movie was about with one sentence.

TEACH

Identify the Main Idea
Reread the story together. Then ask children how the story begins, what happens, and how the story ends. Explain that the main idea briefly tells what the story is about. Ask volunteers to state in one sentence what the story is about. (children playing tag)

PRACTICE

Complete the Pupil Edition Page
Read the directions on page 195 to the children, and make sure they clearly understand what they are asked to do. Identify each picture, and complete the first item together. Then work through the page with children or have them complete the page independently.

ASSESS/CLOSE

Review the Page
Review children's pages, and note children who are experiencing difficulty.

Name_____

1.

A cat is on the cot.

Ron and Nan sat on the cot.

2.

Ron ran to Dad and Nan.

Mom and Dad sat.

Look at each picture. • Then read the sentences. • Draw a line under the sentence
that tells what the picture is all about.

Pupil Edition, page 195

ALTERNATE TEACHING
STRATEGY

IDENTIFY MAIN IDEA
For a different approach to
teaching this skill, see
page T26.

▶ **Visual/Auditory/
Kinesthetic**

PRACTICE BOOK, page 195

Meeting Individual Needs for Comprehension

EASY	ON-LEVEL	CHALLENGE	LANGUAGE SUPPORT
Reread the story together. Remind children what the story is mainly about. Have children draw a picture to record their answers.	**Help** children fold a sheet of drawing paper into fourths. Have them draw pictures to show a story about something they like to play with their parents. Then ask children to say the main idea of the story.	**Have** children write a different ending to the story. Children can illustrate their endings. Then have them tell the main idea of the new story.	**Ask** children to name familiar games, such as "hide-and-seek" and "duck, duck, goose." Have children explain the rules to you.

Develop Phonological Awareness

Listen

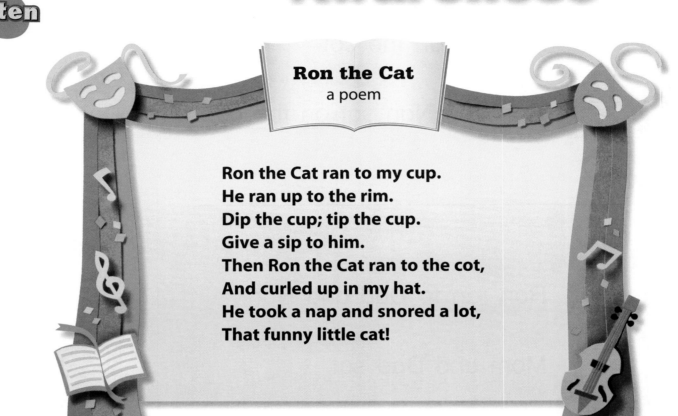

Ron the Cat
a poem

Ron the Cat ran to my cup.
He ran up to the rim.
Dip the cup; tip the cup.
Give a sip to him.
Then Ron the Cat ran to the cot,
And curled up in my hat.
He took a nap and snored a lot,
That funny little cat!

Objective: Focus on Words

READ THE POEM Encourage children to listen carefully as you read the poem "Ron the Cat." Recite the poem again, clapping once for each word. Then reread the poem and invite children to clap the words with you.

COUNTING WORDS Give each child eight blocks, interlocking cubes, or squares of heavy paper. Repeat the first line in the poem. Model for children how to use the blocks to represent the words. Use one block for each word, arranging the blocks from left to right.

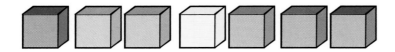
Ron the Cat ran to my cup.

Continue reading the poem, line by line. Encourage children to use their blocks to keep track of the number of words. After each line, have children count the blocks to determine the number of words.

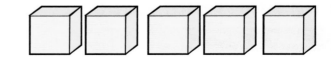

Objective: Blend Sounds to Form Words

LISTEN TO WORDS IN A POEM Have children listen to the words as you read the poem "Ron the Cat." Tell children that Ron the Cat likes to take things apart, especially words. Invite children to put the words that Ron the Cat takes apart back together again.

LISTEN AND BLEND Say the following word aloud slowly, segmenting each of the three sounds: /k/-/o/-/t/. Have children repeat the segmented sounds after you. Then challenge children to put the word together by blending the sounds. Repeat the activity with other words.

> ran   rim   not   dam   rod   fit

BLEND AND GUESS Place in a bag the following items: a can, a stick-on dot, and a tin. Say the sounds that make up the name of each object, one at a time. Have children blend the sounds together. When they say the word, display the object.

> can   tin   dot

Read Together

From Phonemic Awareness to Phonics

Objective: Identify Words with the Same Word Endings

LISTEN FOR FINAL SOUNDS
Read the fifth and sixth lines of the poem "Ron the Cat." Ask children where Ron curled up.

> in   a   hat

Write the word *in* on the board. Tell children that you think that Ron the Cat eats from a tin. Write the word *tin* on the board. Encourage children to tell how the two words on the board are alike. Say the words again, emphasizing the final two sounds.

> /i/-/n/

NAME RHYMING WORDS
Invite children to name other words that rhyme with *in* and *tin*. Write their responses on the board, framing the letters *i* and *n*.

PLAY A GAME Write the words listed on the board on index cards, using one card for each word. Add a few other word cards with words that do not rhyme with *in* and *tin*. Place all the cards in a box or bag.

Invite volunteers to pull out a card and place it in a hat if it ends with the same letters as *in* and *tin*.

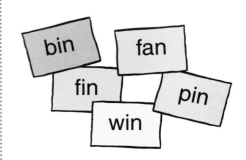

196B

OBJECTIVES

Children will:

- identify /a/*a*, /i/*i*, and /o/*o*
- blend and read short *a, i,* and *o* words
- write short *a, i,* and *o* words
- review /r/*r*, /f/*f*, /k/*c*, /t/*t*, /m/*m*, /s/*s*, /d/*d*, and /n/*n*

MATERIALS

- letter cards from the Word Building Book

TEACHING TIP

INSTRUCTIONAL Give each child on one side of the room the letter card *r, f, c,* or *t*. Give each child on the other side an *a, i,* or *o* card. On the chalkboard write: *rat, cot, fit*. Blend and read the words. Then ask children to find others who have the letters to make the words on the chalkboard.

ALTERNATE TEACHING STRATEGY

BLENDING SHORT *a, i, o*
For a different approach to teaching this skill, see Unit 1, page T32; Unit 2, page T32; Unit 3 page T30.
▶ **Visual/Auditory/ Kinesthetic**

196C *You Are IT!*

Review Blending with short *a, i, o*

TEACH

Identify *a, i, o* as the Symbols for /a/, /i/, /o/

Tell children they will continue to read words with *a, i,* and *o*.

- Display the *i* letter card and say /i/. Have children repeat the sound /i/ as you point to the *i* card.

BLENDING Model and Guide Practice

- Place the *r* card before the *i* card. Blend the sounds together and have children repeat after you.

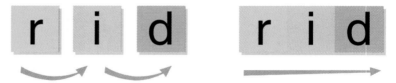

- Place a *d* card after the *i* to show *rid*. Blend to read *rid*.

Use the Word in Context

- Say *I would like to get rid of some extra toys in my room*. Ask children to name one thing they would like to get *rid* of.

Repeat the Procedure

- Use the following words to continue modeling and for guided practice with short *a, i, o*: *rod, Ron, fan, tin, rat, dim, nod*.

PRACTICE

Complete the Pupil Edition Page

Read aloud the directions on page 196. Identify each picture, and complete the first item together. Then work through the page with children, or have them complete the page independently.

ASSESS/CLOSE

Build Short *a, i, o* Words

Observe children as they complete page 196. Then have them use *r, f, c, t, m, s, d,* and *n* letter cards to build words that have medial *a, i, o*.

Name _____

1. cat mat

    cat

2. ran rod

    rod

3. Mom Dad

    Dad

4. fin fan

    fin

Draw a circle around the word that names the picture. • Say the word. • Then write the word.

McGraw-Hill School Division

Pupil Edition, page 196

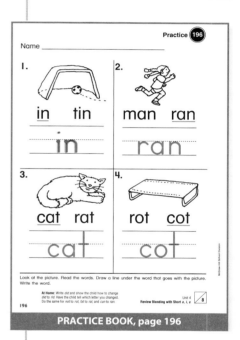

ADDITIONAL PHONICS RESOURCES

Practice Book, *page 196*
Phonics Workbook

McGraw-Hill School
TECHNOLOGY

Phonics CD-ROM
Activities for practice with Blending and Segmenting

Practice 196

Name _____

1. in tin   2. man ran
    in   ran

3. cat rat   4. rot cot
    cat   cot

Look at the picture. Read the words. Draw a line under the word that goes with the picture. Write the word.

At Home: Write *did* and show the child how to change *did* to *rid.* Have the child tell which letter you changed. Do the same for *rot* to *rat, fat* to *rat,* and *can* to *ran*

196   Review Blending with Short *A, I, o*   Unit 4   8

PRACTICE BOOK, page 196

Meeting Individual Needs for Phonics

EASY	ON-LEVEL	CHALLENGE	LANGUAGE SUPPORT
Display these word cards on the chalkboard ledge: *rat, rot, dim, dam, rid, rod.* Ask children to sort words by short /a/, /i/, and /o/. Then have them blend the sounds together to read each word aloud.	**Write** *can* on the chalkboard, and ask children to read the word aloud. Then ask them to write a word that rhymes with *can* but begins with *r.* Ask them to read the word aloud. When children say *ran,* write it next to *can.* Continue the activity with *nod, did, cot, mat, Don, dim.*	**Pass** around a *can* that contains strips of paper with the letters *r, f, c, t, m, s, d,* and *n* on one side and *a, i,* or *o* on the other side. Children must say a word that begins or ends with the consonant and has the vowel *a, i,* or *o* in the middle.	**Have** children sort these words by first letter and ask them to name that letter: *rot, cot, fan, man, sit, did.* Give each child a word card and ask them to listen for the word you say. Call out words one at a time and if a child is holding that word card, he or she stands up.

Reread the Decodable Story

You Are IT!

☑ **Initial /r/ R, r**
☑ **Use Illustrations**
☑ **Concepts of Print**
☑ **High-Frequency Word:** *to*

You Are IT!

TEACHING TIP

MANAGEMENT You may wish to reread the story with a small group of children who had difficulties during the first reading. Use visual and physical prompts to help children understand the story better.

USE ILLUSTRATIONS

HOW TO ASSESS Ask children to use illustrations in the story to answer questions, such as: *What are Ron, Tom, and Nan doing on page 8?* (running)

FOLLOW UP If children have difficulty, point to picture clues in the story to help them answer the questions.

Guided Reading

SET PURPOSES Tell children that when they read the story again, they can find out more about what happened. Explain that you also want them to look for and read the words that begin with *r*. Remind them that they know the word *to* and will see it again in this story.

REREAD THE BOOK As you guide children through the story, address specific problems they may have had during the first read. Use the following prompts to guide the lesson:

• **CONCEPTS OF PRINT** Ask children to frame the quotation marks and to explain what they mean. Ask who is speaking. (Ron)

• **USE ILLUSTRATIONS** Ask children to show you how the children responded after being tagged. (they pointed to themselves)

RETURN TO PURPOSES Ask children if they found out more about what happened in the story. Find out if children found words that begin with *r*. Ask if anyone found the word *to*.

LITERARY RESPONSE Ask children to write and draw a different ending to the story. Share the endings.

Read the Patterned Book

Ron's Radishes

☑ **Initial /r/r**
☑ **Main Idea**
☑ **High-Frequency Word:** *to*
☑ **Concepts of Print**

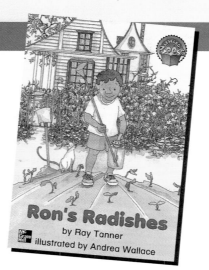

Ron's Radishes
by Ray Tanner
illustrated by Andrea Wallace

Guided Reading

PREVIEW AND PREDICT Read the title, and make sure children understand what a radish is. Read the author's and the illustrator's name, and remind children how each person contributed to the book. Take a **picture walk** through pages 2–4, and have children describe what the boy is doing. Have children make predictions about what will happen next in the story.

SET PURPOSES Have children decide what they want to find out from the story and predict what the boy might do. Tell them that the story contains words with initial *r*.

READ THE BOOK Use the following prompts while the children are reading or after they have read independently. Remind them to run their fingers under each word as they read.

PAGES 2–3: *Let's point to the word that begins with* t *and read it together:* to. *High-Frequency Words*

PAGES 4–5: Model: *I can use what I know about initial r to read the word that begins with r. Each letter makes its own sound. Let's blend these sounds together. R-o-n.* Have the children repeat the word with you. *Phonics and Decoding*

PAGES 6–7: *Who can find two words that are the same on these two pages?* (Ron, likes, to) *Concepts of Print*

PAGE 8: *What is the story about?* (a boy who grows radishes in his garden). *Main Idea*

RETURN TO PREDICTIONS AND PURPOSES Ask children if they found out what they needed to know from the story. See if they have any unanswered questions.

LITERARY RESPONSE The following questions will help focus children's responses:

• What do the seeds need to grow?

• What would you like to grow in a garden? Draw a picture and write about it in your journal.

CENTER Activity

Cross Curricular: Science

WATCH IT GROW Make direction cards that show children how to plant seeds in empty milk containers. Then have children place the containers in different areas of the room. Establish a watering schedule, and have children compare the seeds over a period of several weeks. Children can draw and write to compare the plants.

Children will:

- identify and read the high-frequency word *to*

MATERIALS

- word cards from the Word Building Book
- *You Are IT!*

TEACHING TIP

INSTRUCTIONAL Write the word *two* on the chalkboard. Point out that some words sound the same, but are spelled differently. Write the number *2* and the word *two*.

Review *to, the, that*

PREPARE

Listen to Words Explain to the children that they will review the word *to*. Say the word together. Then ask children to say words that rhyme: *do, coo, moo.*

TEACH

Model Reading the Word in Context Have children reread the decodable book. Ask children to listen for the word *to.*

Identify the Word Ask children to look at their word cards, and then ask them to say the word: *to.* Have children read the sentences and track print. Have volunteers put a stick-on note below the word. Have children move the stick-on note from page to page.

Write the Word Review how to write the letters *t* and *o.* Then children practice writing the word.

Review High-Frequency Words Hold up word cards for the following words: *a, my, I, and, you, said, we, are, is, have, the, that.* Have children say the words.

PRACTICE

Complete the Pupil Edition Page Read the directions on page 197 to the children, and make sure they clearly understand what they are being asked to do. Complete the first item together. Then work through the page with children or have them complete the page independently.

ASSESS/CLOSE

Review the Page Review children's work, and note children who are experiencing difficulty or need additional practice.

Name_____

I.

Nan and Sam ran (to) Dad.

2.

Nan said, "Is (that) the cat?"

3.

(The) cat ran to Sam.

4.

Dad said, "(That) is the cat."

Read the sentences. **I.** Draw a circle around the word *to*. **2.** Draw a circle around the word *that*. **3.** Draw a circle around the word *the*. **4.** Draw a circle around the word *that*. Draw a line under the word *the*.

Unit 4   Review *to, the, that*   **197**

Pupil Edition, page 197

ALTERNATE TEACHING STRATEGY

HIGH-FREQUENCY WORDS: *to*

For a different approach to teaching this skill, see page T27.

▶ **Visual/Auditory/ Kinesthetic**

Practice 197

Name _____

I. "Is (the) cat on (the) mat?" said Mom.

2. The cat ran (to) Mom.

3. "Is (that) my cat?" said Nat.

4. Nat ran (to) the cat.

Read the sentences. **I.** Draw a circle around the word *the*. **2.** Draw a circle around the word *to*. **3.** Draw a circle around the word *that*. **4.** Draw a circle around the word *to*. Draw a line under the word *the*.

At Home: Look for titles of books or movies that contain these words.

6   Unit 4
Review *to, the, that*   197

PRACTICE BOOK, page 197

Meeting Individual Needs for Vocabulary

EASY	ON-LEVEL	CHALLENGE	LANGUAGE SUPPORT
Place ten cutout or magnetic letters (including letters *t* and *o*) in a bag. Have children use their sense of touch to find the letters *t* and *o*.	**Gather** four shoeboxes and label them with these letters: *t, o, b, i.* Children take turns throwing a beanbag and trying to have it land in the boxes with *t* and *o*. Then they use the word in a sentence.	**Write** the following words on index cards: *the, a, my, that, and, to, we, are.* Make two sets. Then place the cards facedown in a grid. Children play a game of concentration, matching cards and reading the words.	**Have** children complete this sentence: *I like to ___.* Have them circle the word *to* and illustrate the sentence.

Interactive Writing

Write a Poem

GRAMMAR/SPELLING CONNECTIONS
Model subject-verb agreement, complete sentences, and correct tense so that students may gain increasing control of grammar when speaking and writing.

Prewrite

LOOK AT THE STORY PATTERN Reread the story *The Apple Pie Tree*. Talk about the sequence of the story, and how the story follows the seasons of the year. Have children help you to make a list of short phrases that explain how the apple tree changes during the seasons.

Draft

WRITE A CLASS POEM Explain to children that you will work together to write a poem about apples. Point out that poems do not always have to rhyme. Decide as a class if the poem will or will not rhyme.

- Begin by supplying the first line of the poem, such as: *Apples are red*. Invite children to use words from the list to think of the next line.

- Continue in the same manner, writing lines as children dictate.

Publish

CREATE THE POEM Reread the poem, and have children make any final changes or revisions. Have volunteers help you rewrite the final version of the poem on chart paper.

Apples are red.
Apples are green.
Apples are sometimes yellow, too.
Apples are crunchy.
Apples are juicy.
I like to eat them all year long.

Presentation Ideas

ILLUSTRATE THE POEM Have each child draw a picture to illustrate the poem. Make a display of the pictures and the poem.

▶ **Representing/Viewing**

DO A CHORAL READING Have the children read the poem together. Track print, and invite children to join in on words they can read or remember.

▶ **Representing/Speaking**

COMMUNICATION TIPS

- **Speaking** When children read together, remind them to listen to others. Establish a rhythm, and track print as you read.

TECHNOLOGY TIP

Have volunteers help you input the poem on the computer. Print out copies of the poem for children to take home and share.

LANGUAGE SUPPORT

ESL Bring in apples and slice them for children to eat. Have them describe the taste, texture, color, and so on. Make a list of descriptive words.

Meeting Individual Needs for Writing

EASY	ON-LEVEL	CHALLENGE
Find Letters Make another copy of the poem and have children find letters that you name. Then have them practice writing the letters.	**Write a Book** Invite children to write a book about apples. Children can complete the phrase: *Apples are* ___. Children illustrate each page and combine them to make the book.	**Write Descriptive Words** Draw large apple shapes on drawing paper. Have children cut out the shapes and write words that describe apples. Help as necessary.

Tap the Sap

The variety of literature in this lesson will offer children opportunities to read and listen to stories about backyard nature discoveries and experiences.

Tap the Sap

**Listening
Library
Audiocassette**

**Decodable Story,
pages 205–206 of the
Pupil Edition**

**Patterned Book,
page 209B**

Hill of Fire

**Teacher Read Aloud,
page 203A**

**Listening
Library
Audiocassette**

**ABC Big Book,
pages 199A–199B**

**Listening
Library
Audiocassette**

**Literature Big Book,
pages 201A–201B**

**Pupil Edition,
pages 198–209**

**Big Book of Real-Life Reading,
page 26**

**Big Book of Phonics Rhymes and
Poems, pages 41, 42**

 **Listening
Library
Audiocassette**

ADDITIONAL RESOURCES

**Practice Book,
pages 198–209**

- **Phonics Kit**
- **Language Support Book**
- **Alternate Teaching Strategies,**
  pages T27–T30

McGraw-Hill School
TECHNOLOGY

Phonics **CD-ROM** Provides
extra phonics support.

interNET
CONNECTION Research & Inquiry Ideas.

Visit www.mhschool.com

Tap the Sap

READING AND LANGUAGE ARTS	DAY 1	DAY 2

- Phonological Awareness

- Phonics *initial and final /p/p*

- Comprehension

- Vocabulary

- Beginning Reading Concepts

- Listening, Speaking, Viewing, Representing

Focus on Reading Skills

Develop Phonological Awareness, 198G–198H
"Pease Porridge Hot" *Big Book of Phonics Rhymes and Poems,* 41

 Introduce Initial /p/p, 198I–198
Practice Book, 198
Phonics/Phonemic Awareness Practice Book

 **Phonics** CD-ROM

Focus on Reading Skills

Develop Phonological Awareness, 200A–200B
"Chicken Soup" *Big Book of Phonics Rhymes and Poems,* 42

Introduce Final /p/p, 200C–200
Practice Book, 200
Phonics/Phonemic Awareness Practice Book

Phonics CD-ROM

Read the Literature

 Read *Allie's Adventure from A to Z* **Big Book,** 199A–199B
Shared Reading

Read the Literature

Read *The Apple Pie Tree* **Big Book,** 201A–201B
Shared Reading

Build Skills

☑ Inside, Outside, 199C–199
Practice Book, 199

Build Skills

☑ Compare and Contrast, 201C–201
Practice Book, 201

- **Cross Curriculum**

 Activity Language Arts, 199B

Activity Cultural Perspectives, 201B

- **Writing**

 Writing Prompt: Write about Allie having a new adventure.

 Journal Writing, 199B
Letter Formation, 198I

 Writing Prompt: Write about your favorite food. Describe how it tastes.

 Journal Writing, 201B
Letter Formation, 200C

☑ = **Skill Assessed in Unit Test**

DAY 3

BIG BOOK OF
REAL LIFE
READING
Door
Funnel
Engine
Hill of Fire

Focus on Reading Skills

Develop Phonological Awareness,
202A–202B
"Pease Porridge Hot" and "Chicken Soup" *Big Book of Phonics Rhymes and Poems,* 41–42

Review /p/*p*, 202C–202
Practice Book, 202
Phonics/Phonemic Awareness Practice Book

Phonics **CD-ROM**

Read the Literature

Read "Hill of Fire" Teacher Read Aloud,
203A–203B
Shared Reading

Read the Big Book of Real-Life Reading, 26–27
☑ Maps

Build Skills

☑ High-Frequency Word: *me*
203C–203
Practice Book, 203

Activity **Cultural Perspectives,** 203B

Writing Prompt: How did the volcano change the man's life? Write about how his life changed after the volcano.

DAY 4

Tap the Sap

Focus on Reading Skills

Develop Phonological Awareness,
204A–204B
"Yes, I Did!"

Review Blending with Short *a, i, o,*
204C–204
Practice Book, 204
Phonics/Phonemic Awareness Practice Book

Phonics **CD-ROM**

Read the Literature

Read "Tap the Sap" Decodable Story,
205/206A–205/206D

☑ Initial and Final /p/*p;* Blending
☑ Compare and Contrast
☑ High-Frequency Words: *me*
☑ Concepts of Print

Build Skills

☑ Compare and Contrast,
207A–207
Practice Book, 207

Activity **Language Arts,** 205/206D

Writing Prompt: Have children write about their favorite breakfast food.

Letter Formation Practice Book, 205–206

DAY 5

Tap the Sap
The Picnic
by Anne Miranda
strated by Carol Nicklaus

Focus on Reading Skills

Develop Phonological Awareness,
208A–208B
"Yes, I Did!"

Review Blending with Short *a, i, o,*
208C–208
Practice Book, 208
Phonics/Phonemic Awareness Practice Book

Phonics **CD-ROM**

Read the Literature

Reread "Tap the Sap" Decodable Story,
209A

Read "The Picnic" Patterned Book,
209B
Guided Reading
☑ Initial and Final /p/*p;* Blending
☑ Compare and Contrast
☑ High-Frequency Words: *me*
☑ Concepts of Print

Build Skills

☑ High-Frequency Words: *me, to, you,* 209C–209
Practice Book, 209

Activity **Science,** 209B

Writing Prompt: Write about your favorite thing to do in your neighborhood.

Interactive Writing, 210A–210B

Develop Phonological Awareness

Listen

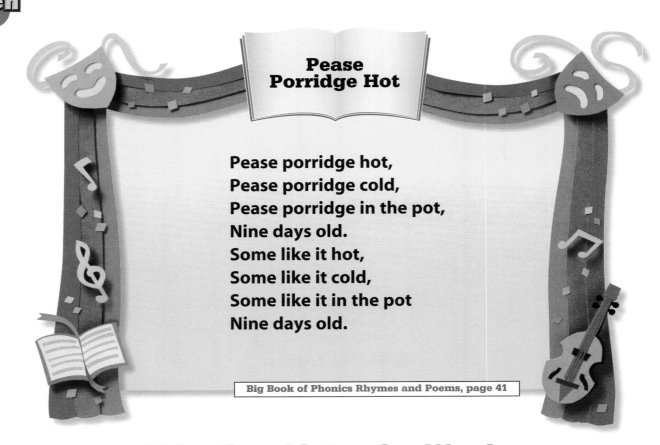

Pease Porridge Hot

Pease porridge hot,
Pease porridge cold,
Pease porridge in the pot,
Nine days old.
Some like it hot,
Some like it cold,
Some like it in the pot
Nine days old.

Big Book of Phonics Rhymes and Poems, page 41

Objective: Listen for Words

LISTEN TO THE POEM

- Reread the first four lines of "Pease Porridge Hot" several times, having children join in when they are ready. Repeat until children are familiar with the chant.

- Then say the first sentence, *Pease porridge hot*. Place one block in front of you as you say the word: *pease*. Do the same for the other two words. Determine there are three words in that line.

- Then say the line: *Some like it hot*. Have children place one block in front of them to represent each word. Determine there are four words in that line.

- Continue with other lines from the poem.

REPEAT LAST WORD

- Tell children you will say the poem again. This time you will not say the last word in each line. Have children say the last word.

- Discuss the rhyming words in the poem.

Objective: Listen for Initial /p/

USE WORDS FROM THE POEM
SEGMENTING

- Say the word *pease* and emphasize the initial /p/ sound. Have children repeat the sound after you.

- Then read each line of the poem slowly. Children hold up fingers to show how many times they hear a word that begins with /p/.

RECOGNIZE THE SOUND

- Say the following foods. Children raise a hand if the word begins with /p/.

> **pudding   stew   nuts**
> **peas   potato**

SEGMENT THE SOUND

- Say the word *pease.* Then segment the initial /p/ sound. (p-ease)

- Then say *ease* and have the children add the /p/ sound to make the word *pease.*

- Say the remaining words that begin with *p*, leaving out the /p/ sound. Have children add the /p/ sound.

> **porridge   pot**

Read Together

From Phonemic Awareness to Phonics

Objective: Identify Initial /p/ *p*, P

IDENTIFY THE LETTER FOR THE SOUND

- Explain to children the letter *p* stands for the sound /p/. Say the sound and have children repeat it.

- Then display page 41 in the Big Book of Phonics Rhymes and Poems. Point to the letters in the corner of the page and identify them. Have children repeat the sound after you.

REREAD THE POEM

- Read the poem again. Explain that you will point to the words that begin with *p*, *P* as you read.

LOOK FOR P, p

- Write the letters *P*, *p* on small pieces of paper.

- Volunteers take a letter and find a word in the poem that begins with *P* or *p*.

- After he or she finds a word, say the word together. Then child *puts* the *piece* of *paper* in a *pot*. Emphasize the initial /p/ in each word.

- Afterward, count the pieces of each to determine how many *p* words are in the poem.

Pease Porridge Hot

Pease porridge hot,
    Pease porridge cold,
Pease porridge in the pot,
    Nine days old.
Some like it hot,
    Some like it cold,
Some like it in the pot,
    Nine days old.

Big Book of Phonics Rhymes and Poems, page 41

 OBJECTIVES

Children will:

- identify the letters *P,p*
- identify /p/ *P,p*
- form the letters *P,p*

....

MATERIALS

- letter cards and picture cards from the Word Building Book

TEACHING TIP

MANAGEMENT Many children will recognize that the form of uppercase and lower case *p* is the same but may have difficulty understanding where to begin to write. Provide handwriting paper with beginning dots to help.

ALTERNATE TEACHING STRATEGY

....

INITIAL /p/p

For a different approach to teaching this skill, see page T28.

▶ **Visual/Auditory/ Kinesthetic**

Introduce Initial /o/ o

TEACH

Identify /p/ P,p   Tell children they will learn to write the /p/ with the letters *P,p*. Write the letters on the chalkboard, identify them, and make the /p/ sound. Hold up a *pencil,* and ask children to name the object. Have them repeat the /p/ sound. Invite children to identify other objects in the room that begin with *p,* such as: *paper, picture, pen, paint, puzzle.* Show picture cards of similar objects, mixed with ones showing objects whose names do not begin with *p.* Ask children to point to the pictures whose names begin with *p* as each picture name is correctly identified.

Form P,p   Display the letters *P,p* and, with your back to the children, trace them in the air. Ask children to do to do the same. Then give each child a sheet of paper. Help them fold the paper so that there are four boxes. The have them write capital *P* on one side of the paper and lowercase *p* on the other side. Encourage children to fill their pages with *p*'s.

PRACTICE

Complete the Pupil Edition Page   Read the directions on page 198 of the Pupil Edition, and make sure children clearly understand what they are being asked to do. Identify each picture, and complete the first item together. Then work through the page with children or have them complete the page independently.

ASSESS/CLOSE

Identify and Use N,n   Say the following words. Have children hold up their *P* letter cards when they hear a word that begins with /p/: *book, pail, penny, nest, dog, pack, pond, hat.*

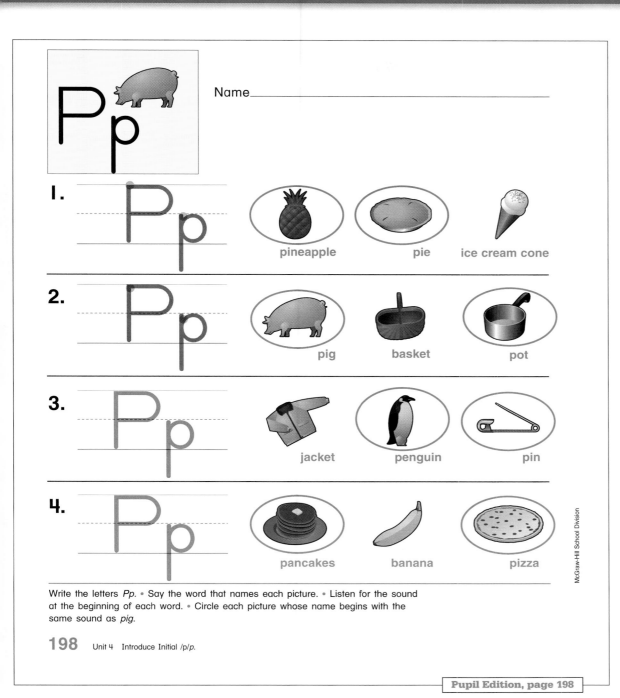

P p

Name_____

1. **P p** — pineapple, pie, ice cream cone

2. **P p** — pig, basket, pot

3. **P p** — jacket, penguin, pin

4. **P p** — pancakes, banana, pizza

Write the letters *Pp*. • Say the word that names each picture. • Listen for the sound at the beginning of each word. • Circle each picture whose name begins with the same sound as *pig*.

198   Unit 4   Introduce Initial /p/p.

McGraw-Hill School Division

Pupil Edition, page 198

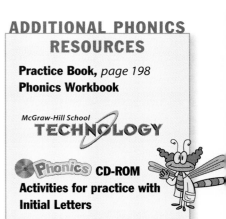

ADDITIONAL PHONICS RESOURCES

Practice Book, *page 198*
Phonics Workbook

McGraw-Hill School
TECHNOLOGY

Phonics CD-ROM
Activities for practice with Initial Letters

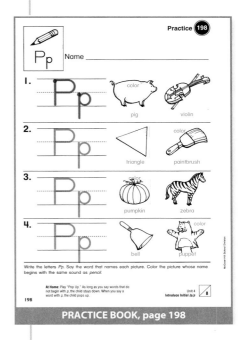

Practice **198**

P p Name_____

1. **P p** — pig, violin — color

2. **P p** — triangle, paintbrush — color

3. **P p** — pumpkin, zebra — color

4. **P p** — bell, puppet — color

Write the letters *Pp*. Say the word that names each picture. Color the picture whose name begins with the same sound as *pencil*.

At Home: Play "Pop Up." As long as you say words that do not begin with *p*, the child stays down. When you say a word with *p*, the child pops up.

198   Introduce Initial /p/p   Unit 4   8

PRACTICE BOOK, page 198

Meeting Individual Needs for Phonics

EASY	ON-LEVEL	CHALLENGE	LANGUAGE SUPPORT
Give children a selection of tactile letters *P* and *p*, such as sandpaper and rigid foam cutouts, bent pipe cleaners and bendable straws. Ask them to talk about the shapes and to describe how *p* and *P* are alike and how they are different. invite lchildren to paint *P*'s and *p*'s.	**Write** the following passage on chart paper. Ask children to listen for words that begin with /p/ as you read the passage aloud. Have volunteers circle the *P*'s and *p*'s in the passage.	**Have** children form a circle to play the game "I'm going on a Picnic." Invite children to think of foods that begin with *p*, such as: *peanut butter, pizza, popcorn, pears, peaches, pie, potatoes, pickles, peas*. Have them pass the letter *p* around as they "pack" for the picnic.	**Help** ESL children learn important action words. Model gestures for words that being with *p*, such as: *push, pull, pat, pick, point, pour*. Have children repeat each word after you and then act out the word with you.

OBJECTIVES

Children will:

- recognize words with initial *p*
- compare and contrast how the main character feels

TEACHING TIP

INSTRUCTIONAL Use the alphabet during daily activities, such as lining up. Ask children whose first names begin with *T* to line up, then *S,* and so on.

Read the Big Book

Before Reading

Develop Oral Language

Sing "The Alphabet Song" together. The song is on page 2 of the Big Book of Phonics Rhymes and Poems. Then distribute letter cards. Ask children to hold up the appropriate card as you sing the song again. Remind children that they read a story about a kitten. Ask them to recall some of the places Allie went.

Set Purposes

Remind children that when they read the story the first time, they read about a kitten who had adventures. When children read the story for the second time, have children think about the following:

Model: *When we read the story today, let's think about the order of places Allie goes.*

Model: *Let's look for the words on each page that begin with the same letters.*

Allie sees some **eggs.**

Allie sees lots of **feathers.**

Allie's Adventure from A to Z, pages 6–7

During Reading

Read Together

- Before you begin to read, point to the first word in the first sentence. Explain that this is where you will begin to read. Continue to track print as you read the story. *Tracking Print*

- Before you read page 2, ask a volunteer to locate the letter on the page and identify it. Then have him or her find the word that begins with the same letter. Continue through the story. *Phonics*

- After you read pages 2–3, ask where Allie is and where she is going. Continue to ask children to follow the sequence of events as you read the story. *Story Sequence*

- Make the /p/ sound, and have children say the sound with you. After you read pages 18–19, ask children which words begin with that sound. *Phonics*

Allie sees a **hole**.

Allie's Adventure from A to Z, page 10

After Reading

Return to Purposes

Ask children to recall where Allie was when the story started, and where she went next. Help them remember the sequence of the story.

Retell the Story

Invite children to retell the story, focusing on where Allie went and what she saw.

Literary Response

JOURNAL WRITING Ask children to draw a picture of another place that Allie could visit. Ask them to write about it.

ORAL RESPONSE Ask questions, such as:
- *Where is Allie going?*
- *What might she see there?*

ABC Activity

Distribute capital and lowercase letter cards to each child. Children mingle and find other children with cards to make matches.

INFORMAL ASSESSMENT

LETTER IDENTIFICATION

HOW TO ASSESS Place several capital and lowercase letter cards on the table. Ask children to point to the letters you call out.

FOLLOW UP Have children choose several letter cards from the table. Have them trace the letters with their fingers as you say the sound with them.

CENTER Activity

Cross Curricular: Language Arts

DOT TO DOT Make dot-to-dot pictures, using letters of the alphabet instead of numbers. Children follow the order of the letters to create a picture of a simple scene from the story.

▶ **Linguistic/Logical**

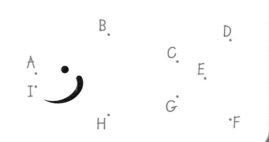

Children will:

• identify inside and outside

MATERIALS

• *The Apple Pie Tree*

TEACHING TIP

MANAGEMENT Picture cards can be of great benefit when children are working on individual activities. Ask parents to help you collect old magazines and catalogs. Cut out pictures and mount them on tagboard and laminate. Store the cards by topic.

Introduce Inside, Outside

PREPARE

Discuss Inside and Outside
Ask children what they like to do when they play inside. Point out that you are referring to children playing inside the house. Then ask what they like to do when they play outside.

TEACH

Identify Inside and Outside
Display the Big Book *The Apple Pie Tree* and recall the story. Ask what the children in the story like to do when they are outside. (watch the robins, watch the tree change, play, pick apples) *What do they like to do when they are inside the house?* (bake a pie) Then use a box or a bag and a classroom object. Put the object inside and ask, *Where is the book?* Then take it out and ask, *Is the book inside or outside the bag?*

PRACTICE

Show Inside and Outside
Read the directions on page 199 to the children, and make sure they clearly understand what they are asked to do. Identify each picture, and complete the first item. Then work through the page with the children, or have them complete the page independently.

ASSESS/CLOSE

Review the Page
Check children's work on the Pupil Edition page. Note areas where children need extra help.

Name_____

Draw a circle around the items in the picture that are inside. • Draw a line under the items in the picture that are outside. • Tell more about what you see in the picture.

Pupil Edition, page 199

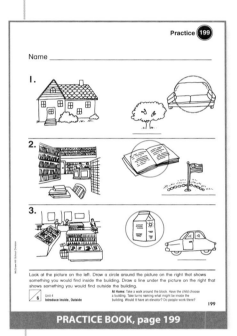

PRACTICE BOOK, page 199

Meeting Individual Needs for Beginning Reading Concepts

EASY	ON-LEVEL	CHALLENGE	LANGUAGE SUPPORT
Make a ring on a table with yarn or string. Give each child two connecting cubes. Give directions such as: *Put the red cube inside the ring. Put the blue cube outside the ring. Now put both cubes inside the ring.*	**Use** picture cards of people doing different activities. Have children sort the cards to show activities usually done inside and activities usually done outside. Talk about activities that can be done both inside *and* outside.	**Help** children draw a large circle on drawing paper. Then give these directions: *Draw a flower inside the ring. Draw a bird outside the ring. Draw an apple inside the ring. Draw a nest outside the ring.* Have children compare their drawings.	**Use** a box and small classroom objects, such as a pencil, crayon, shell, book, and so on. Give directions such as: *Put the pencil inside the box. Put the crayon outside the box.* Then have children give you similar directions to follow.

Develop Phonological Awareness

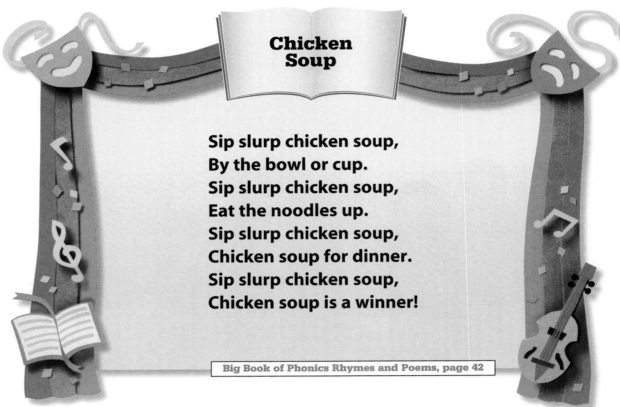

Chicken Soup

Sip slurp chicken soup,
By the bowl or cup.
Sip slurp chicken soup,
Eat the noodles up.
Sip slurp chicken soup,
Chicken soup for dinner.
Sip slurp chicken soup,
Chicken soup is a winner!

Big Book of Phonics Rhymes and Poems, page 42

Objective: Name Words that Rhyme

LISTEN TO THE POEM

- Have children sit in a circle. Read the poem "Chicken Soup."
- Say the word *cup*. Point out that the word *up* in the poem rhymes with *cup*.
- Roll a can of chicken soup to a child, who then says a word that rhymes with *cup*.

> **cup   pup**

- That child then rolls the can to another child, who says a word that rhymes with *cup*.

CONTINUE WITH RHYMING WORDS

- Continue until children run out of words that rhyme with *cup*. Then repeat with the words *for* and *sip*.

Objective: Listen for Final /p/

USE WORDS FROM THE POEM

- Read the title of the poem "Chicken Soup." Make the /p/ sound and have children repeat it after you. Ask which word in the title ends with /p/.
- Read the poem line by line. Stop and have children repeat words that end with /p/.

REPEAT THE WORDS

- Point to different parts of your body: head, neck, lip, arm, hip. Have children say each word. If the word ends with /p/, children clap and make the /p/ sound.

Read Together

From Phonemic Awareness to Phonics

Objective: Identify /p/p

IDENTIFY THE LETTER FOR THE SOUND

- Explain to children that the letter *p* stands for the sound /p/. Have children repeat the sound after you.
- Display page 42 in the Big Book of Phonics Rhymes and Poems. Point to the letters in the corner and identify them. Have children repeat the sound after you.

REREAD THE POEM

- Read the poem again as you point to each word. Emphasize words with the final sound of /p/.

- Invite volunteers to find words that end with *p*. Children frame the letter using their index fingers.

ACT OUT THE WORDS

- Write the letter *p* on the chalkboard, and have children make the /p/ sound.
- Then say action words. If the word ends with *p*, volunteers point to the letter and act out the word.

> clap snap slip jump
> sit hop run

Pp

Chicken Soup

Sip slurp chicken soup,
By the bowl or cup.
Sip slurp chicken soup,
Eat the noodles up.

Sip slurp chicken soup,
Chicken soup for dinner.
Sip slurp chicken soup,
Chicken soup is a winner!

42

Big Book of Phonics Rhymes and Poems, page 42

OBJECTIVES

Children will:

- identify the letters *P,p*
- identify /p/ *P,p*
- form the letters *P,p*

....

MATERIALS

- letter cards and word cards from the Word Play Book

TEACHING TIP

INSTRUCTIONAL To help distinguish between the /p/ and /b/ sounds have children hold two fingers in front of their mouths and say *tap-p-p* after you. Repeat for *tub-b-b*. Discuss how the /p/ sound creates a puff of air, while the /b/ sound does not. In addition, display tactile letters for *p* and *b,* and talk about how they are alike and how they are different.

ALTERNATE TEACHING
STRATEGY

....

FINAL /p/p

For a different approach to teaching this skill, see page T28.

▶ **Visual/Auditory/ Kinesthetic**

Introduce Final /p/ p

TEACH

Identify Final /p/ p   Tell children they will find and write the letter *p* at the end of words. Write the letter on the chalkboard, identify it, and say the /p/ sound. Have children repeat the /p/ sound after you. Then say, "tap, tap, tap," and ask children where the /p/ sound is. Write the word *tap* on the chalkboard, and underline the *p.* Then say the following words: *fan, top, bug, skip, cap, tub, hop.* Have children tap on the table when they hear a word that ends in /p/.

Form *p*   Tell children that they are going to make new words by using /p/ to replace the ending sound in each word you say. For example, if you say *cat,* children are to say *cap.* Use these words: *hit, dig, hot, man, rat, tan.* Then, write each word, leaving a blank space for the letter *p.* Have children write *p* to complete each word.

PRACTICE

Complete the Pupil Edition Page   Read the directions on page 200 of the Pupil Edition, and make sure children clearly understand what they are being asked to do. Identify each picture, and complete the first item together. Then work through the page with children or have them complete the page independently.

ASSESS/CLOSE

Identify and Use *p*   Write the following list of words on the chalkboard. Ask children to hold up their *p* letter cards when they recognize a word that ends in *p*: *cap, top, lap, lid, hat, cup.* Say the words aloud, and ask children to clap when they hear a word that ends in /p/.

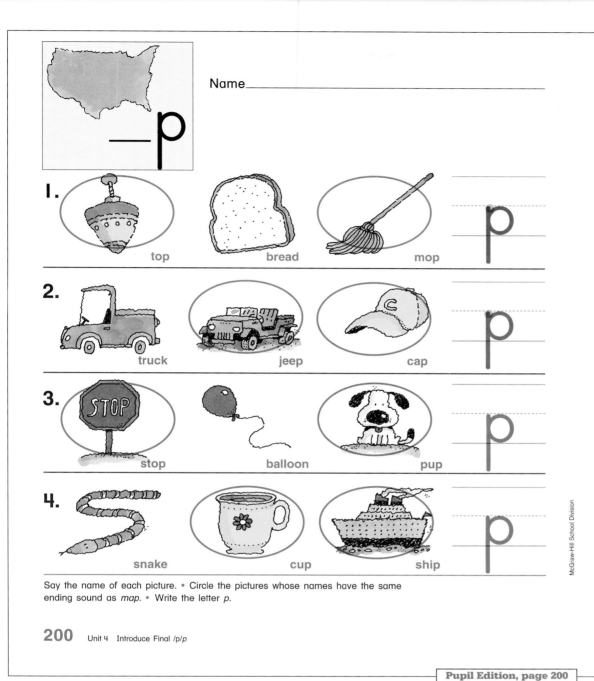

Name_____

_p

1. top   bread   mop   p

2. truck   jeep   cap   p

3. stop   balloon   pup   p

4. snake   cup   ship   p

Say the name of each picture. • Circle the pictures whose names have the same ending sound as *map*. • Write the letter *p*.

McGraw-Hill School Division

200   Unit 4   Introduce Final /p/*p*

Pupil Edition, page 200

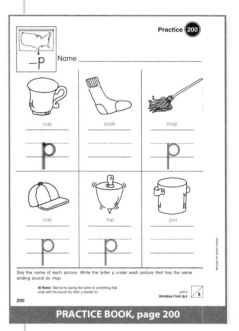

ADDITIONAL PHONICS RESOURCES

Practice Book, *page 200*
Phonics Workbook

McGraw-Hill School
TECHNOLOGY

Phonics CD-ROM
**Activities for practice with
Final Letters**

Practice 200

Name_____

_p

cup   sock   mop

p   p

cap   top   pot

p   p

Say the name of each picture. Write the letter *p* under each picture that has the same ending sound as *map*.

At Home: Take turns saying the name of something that ends with the sound the letter *p* stands for.

200

Unit 4
Introduce Final /p/*p*   6

McGraw-Hill School Division

PRACTICE BOOK, page 200

Meeting Individual Needs for Phonics

EASY	ON-LEVEL	CHALLENGE	LANGUAGE SUPPORT
Have children form a circle and perform actions that you call out, one at a time. Use action words that end in *p,* such as: *hop, skip, jump, leap, flap, snap.* Between actions, call out "stop." Each time children stop, ask them to trace the letter *p* in the air with their fingers.	**Play** "Simon Says." Tell children that in this version of the game, they are to do what Simon says only if the direction includes a word with /p/ at the end. Say, for example: "Hop on one foot. Raise your hand. Clap your hands. Stamp your feet. Touch your nose. Take a step."	**Play** "Step Up." Draw a set of steps on the chalkboard, and place a self-stick note with the letter *p* at the bottom. Each time someone says a word that ends in *p,* that child may move the *p* up a step. If you wish, draw two sets of steps and have children play in teams.	**To** help children identify confusable letters, show them words that end in *p, b,* and *d.* Read each word aloud, and have children find the words that end in *p.* To help children write *p,* tell them to **p**ull straight down for *p,* and then make a half-circle at the to**p**.

200

- recognize words with final /p/
- understand compare and contrast

TEACHING TIP

INSTRUCTIONAL Hold up a picture of a robin, or use an illustration from the book. Ask if children have ever seen this bird. Talk about places where birds live.

Read the Big Book

Before Reading

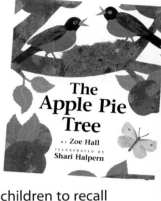

Develop Oral Language   Teach children the following finger play.

Two Little Apples

Way up high in the apple tree,
Two little apples smiled at me.
I shook that tree as hard as I could.
Down came the apples.
Mmm! They were good!

Have children do simple actions to the finger play.
Then display a copy of "The Apple Pie Tree" and ask children to recall the main idea of the story.

Set Purposes   *Model: We know that the story is mainly about how the apple tree changes during the seasons. When we read the story today, let's think about the robins who live in the tree. Let's find out what the robins do first.*

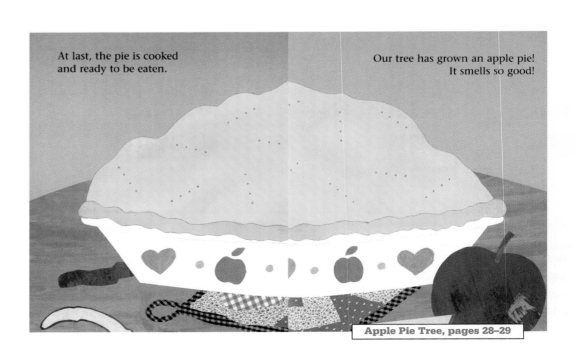

At last, the pie is cooked and ready to be eaten.

Our tree has grown an apple pie! It smells so good!

Apple Pie Tree, pages 28–29

During Reading

Read Together

- Before you begin to read, point to the first word in the first sentence. Explain that this is where you will begin to read. Continue to track print as you read the story. *Tracking Print*

- Reread the second sentence on page 9. Ask children to say the word that ends with /p/. (chirp) Invite children to say other words that describe how the birds sound. *Phonics and Decoding*

- Ask children to look at the pictures of the baby robins on pages 10 and 17. Talk about how the robins have changed. *Compare and Contrast/Use Illustrations*

Apple Pie Tree, page 27

After Reading

Retell the Story

Ask children to recall how the baby robins changed during the story. Focus on how they grew, learned to fly and find food, and finally moved away.

Literary Response

JOURNAL WRITING Invite children to draw a picture showing the baby robins. On the back of their drawings, have them draw another picture showing how the robins looked when they got older. Have them write about the pictures.

ORAL RESPONSE Engage children in a discussion of the story by asking questions such as:

- *What do the baby robins look like when they are born?*

- *What do they grow on their bodies?*

CULTURAL PERSPECTIVES

SEASONS Explain what the four seasons are and that they appear differently depending on where you live. People who live in Northern Russia, for example, need to wear a jacket even on the hottest day of summer. People who live in Mexico need only a sweater or a raincoat during winter.

Activity Divide mural paper into four squares. Mark them SUMMER, FALL, WINTER, SPRING. Ask children to draw what they do during each season. Then compare what children in Alaska might do during each season. Discuss the differences and the children's preferences.

▶ Spatial

OBJECTIVES

Children will:

- compare and contrast information from a story

....

MATERIALS

- *The Apple Pie Tree*

TEACHING TIP

INSTRUCTIONAL

Include books about trees in your classroom library. Choose books with illustrations and photographs of different kinds of trees. Have volunteers compare and contrast their choice of trees.

Introduce Compare and Contrast

PREPARE

Recall a Story
Ask children to recall the Big Book story *The Apple Pie Tree*. Ask children to tell how the tree changes during the story.

TEACH

Compare Robins and Compare Trees
Reread *The Apple Pie Tree*. After you read page 16, return to page 8. Discuss ways in which the robins have changed. Then turn children's attention to the apple tree on these pages. Ask children to tell how it is the same and how it is different.

PRACTICE

Compare Ostriches on the Pupil Edition Page
Read the directions on page 201 to the children, and make sure they clearly understand what they are asked to do. Identify each picture, and complete the first item together. Then work through the page with children or have them complete the page independently.

ASSESS/CLOSE

Review the Page
Review children's work on the Pupil Edition page, and note any children who are experiencing difficulty.

Name_____

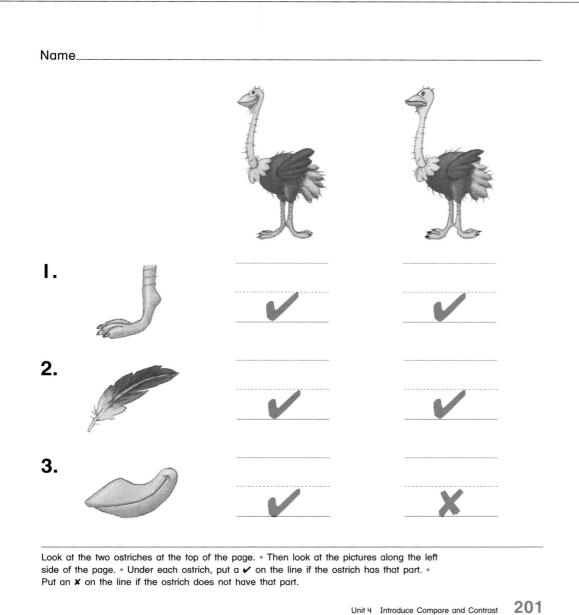

1.

2.

3.

Look at the two ostriches at the top of the page. • Then look at the pictures along the left side of the page. • Under each ostrich, put a ✔ on the line if the ostrich has that part. • Put an ✘ on the line if the ostrich does not have that part.

Pupil Edition, page 201

ALTERNATE TEACHING STRATEGY

COMPARE AND CONTRAST

For a different approach to teaching this skill, see page T30.

▶ **Visual/Auditory/ Kinesthetic**

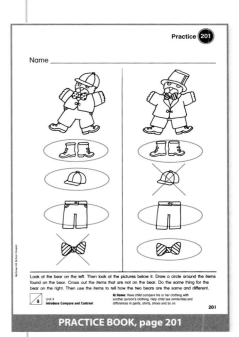

PRACTICE BOOK, page 201

Meeting Individual Needs for Comprehension

EASY	ON-LEVEL	CHALLENGE	LANGUAGE SUPPORT
Cut out pairs of paper apples. Have a large variety of matched pairs, such as by color, shape, and size. Mix up the apples, and have children find the pairs. Talk about how the pairs of apples are alike and how they are different.	**Bring** in a variety of different apples. Have children compare and contrast how the apples look. Then have them sample the different kinds of apples and compare how they taste. Record their findings.	**Bring** in books about apple trees and pine trees. Discuss the different types of trees. Then work with children to make a Venn diagram to show how the trees are different and how they are the same.	**Go** outside and find two trees that are near to each other. Have children describe how the trees are alike and how they are different.

Develop Phonological Awareness

Listen

Pease Porridge Hot
a poem
Chicken Soup
a poem

Pease porridge hot,
Pease porridge cold,
Pease porridge in the pot,
Nine days old.
Some like it hot,
Some like it cold,
Some like it in the pot,
Nine days old.

Sip slurp chicken soup,
By the bowl or cup.
Sip slurp chicken soup,
Eat the noodles up.

Sip slurp chicken soup,
Chicken soup for dinner.
Sip slurp chicken soup,
Chicken soup is a winner!

Big Book of Phonics Rhymes and Poems, pages 41–42

Objective: Focus on Words

READ THE POEM Encourage children to listen carefully as you read the poem "Chicken Soup" aloud. Invite children to talk about their favorite kinds of soup.

CLAP FOR THE WORDS Reread the poem line by line, pausing between words. Ask children to clap once for each word.

COUNT THE WORDS Provide each child with a cup and 10 small counters. Read the first two lines of the poem aloud and ask children to place one counter in the cup each time they hear a word.

CHECK YOUR NUMBER Reread the first two lines of the poem. This time have children remove a counter from the cup each time they hear a word. Continue the activity using other sentences from the poem.

Objective: Listen for /p/

LISTEN FOR INITIAL /P/ Read the poem "Pease Porridge Hot," emphasizing words with the initial /p/ sound. Say the /p/ sound and have children repeat it after you.

NAME THE PICTURE In advance, gather pictures of objects whose names begin with /p/. Have children take a picture and say its name, segmenting the initial sound. Model by holding up a picture of a pig as you say *p—ig.*

> p—ad   p—aw   p—en
> p—ie   p—in

LISTEN FOR FINAL /P/ Read the poem "Chicken Soup" several times, stressing words with the final /p/ sound. Then say the words *soup* and *cup.* Lead children to determine that both *soup* and *cup* end with /p/.

SIP SOUP FOR FINAL /P/ Say words aloud. Invite children to pretend they are drinking a cup of soup when they hear a word that ends with /p/.

> cap   sheep   tan
> map   pat   stop

Read Together

From Phonemic Awareness to Phonics

Objective: Identify /p/ *P, p*

IDENTIFY THE LETTERS Display the Big Book of Phonics Rhymes and Poems, pages 41 and 42. Point to the letters *P, p,* identify them, and say the /p/ sound.

REREAD THE POEMS Reread the poems. Point to each word, stressing those that begin or end with /p/.

FIND WORDS WITH *P, p* Have children use the classroom pointer to point out the letters *P* or *p* in the poems. Read the words and have children repeat them after you.

Pease Porridge Hot   Pp

Pease porridge hot,
 Pease porridge cold,
Pease porridge in the pot,
 Nine days old.
Some like it hot,
 Some like it cold,
Some like it in the pot,
 Nine days old.

Pp   **Chicken Soup**

Sip slurp chicken soup,
By the bowl or cup.
Sip slurp chicken soup,
Eat the noodles up.

Sip slurp chicken soup,
Chicken soup for dinner.
Sip slurp chicken soup,
Chicken soup is a winner!

Big Book of Phonics Rhymes and Poems, pages 41, 42

202B

OBJECTIVES

Children will:

- identify /p/*P, p*
- write and use letters *P,p*

. . . .

MATERIALS

- letter cards from the Word Building Book

TEACHING TIP

INSTRUCTIONAL

Children can make books of labeled pictures showing objects whose names begin or end in *p*. Mark each picture's corner with a square of masking tape on which children can write *p*. Use the bottom left corner if the word begins with *p*; use the bottom right corner if it ends with *p*.

ALTERNATE TEACHING STRATEGY

. . . .

LETTER /p/*p*

For a different approach to teaching this skill, see page T28.

▶ **Visual/Auditory/ Kinesthetic**

Review /p/ p

TEACH

Identify /p/ *P, p*   Tell children they will review the sound /p/ at the beginning and end of words and write the letters *P,p*. Write the letters, identify them, and make the /p/ sound. Write *p*___ on one side of the chalkboard and ___*p* on the other side. Explain that one model shows words that begin with /p/ and the other shows words that end with /p/. Ask children to point to the side of the chalkboard where each word belongs and say: *Put Pat's cap in your lap.* Write each word in the appropriate column, and read it aloud as you underline the *p*.

Form *P,p*   Make the following word cards and put them on the chalkboard ledge: *pan, pod, top, Pam, map, pad, mop.* Give children writing paper, and have them write *P* or *p* for every letter they see.

PRACTICE

Complete the Pupil Edition Page   Read the directions on page 202 to the children, and make sure they clearly understand what they are being asked to do. Identify each picture, and complete the first item together. Then work through the page with children or have them complete the page independently.

ASSESS/CLOSE

Identify and Use *P, p*   Rearrange the row of word cards displayed on the chalkboard ledge in the Teach activity. Have children write *P* or *p* to match the new arrangement.

Pp _p

Name_____

1. cup — p

2. p — pot

3. cap — p

4. p — paintbrush

5. sheep — p

Say the name of each picture. • Where do you hear the sound /p/p? • Write p in the correct position to show if it is the beginning sound (as in *pencil*) or the ending sound (as in *map*).

McGraw-Hill School Division

Pupil Edition, page 202

ADDITIONAL PHONICS RESOURCES

Practice Book, *page 202*
Phonics Workbook

McGraw-Hill School
TECHNOLOGY

Phonics **CD-ROM**
Activities for practice with Initial and Final Letters

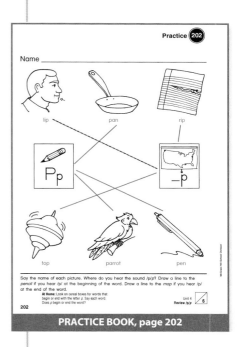

Practice 202

Name_____

lip   pan   rip

Pp   _p

top   parrot   pen

Say the name of each picture. Where do you hear the sound /p/p? Draw a line to the pencil if you hear /p/ at the beginning of the word. Draw a line to the map if you hear /p/ at the end of the word.

At Name: Look on cereal boxes for words that begin or end with the letter p. Say each word. Does p begin or end the word?

Unit 4
Review /p/p   6

202

PRACTICE BOOK, page 202

Meeting Individual Needs for Phonics

EASY	ON-LEVEL	CHALLENGE	LANGUAGE SUPPORT
Give each child magazine pages, a red crayon, and a blue crayon. Ask children to draw a circle around words that begin with *p* with a red crayon and words that end with *p* with a blue crayon. Discuss children's choices.	**For** this activity, you will need to make word cards for the following: *top, pan, pet, map, lip, pat, pot, cap.* Provide children with letter cards to match the letters in each word. Have children work together to match the individual letter cards with the letters on the word cards.	**Divide** the children into two groups, and ask children to listen carefully to your one-word instructions. If the word begins with the letter *p*, Group A mimes it; if it ends with *p*, Group B mimes it. Use such words as: *tap, point, clap, dip, pull, pat.*	**Help** ESL children remember the sound and symbol /p/P,p by chanting pairs of words that begin and end in *p*, such as: *pea soup, pine sap, pet pup, pink cap.*

Teacher Read Aloud

Listen

Hill of Fire

by Thomas P. Lewis

*T*he farmer in this story thinks nothing ever happens in his village community—until something big happens in his own field. In 1943 there really was a "hill of fire" in a small village in Mexico, and people had to leave their homes because of it. After the farmer moved to his new village, do you think he still complained that nothing ever happened? Why or why not?

Once there was a farmer who lived in Mexico. He lived in a little village in a house which had only one room. The farmer was not happy.

"Nothing ever happens," he said.

The people in the village thought the farmer was foolish. "We have everything we need," they said. "We have a school, and a market, and a church with an old bell that rings on Sunday. Our village is the best there is."

"But nothing ever happens," said the farmer.

Every morning, when the farmer woke up, the first thing he saw was the roof of his little house. Every morning for breakfast he ate two flat cakes of ground corn. His wife had made them the night before.

Continued on page T2

Oral Comprehension

LISTENING AND SPEAKING Ask children if they know what a volcano is. Explain that a volcano looks like a mountain with a big hole in the top. Share that when a volcano erupts, melted rock called lava shoots out of the hole. Then explain that you will read a story about a volcano that erupted in a farmer's backyard. Share that this is a true story. It happened in a small town in Mexico.

After you read the story, ask: *How was the farmer's life different after the fire? How was it the same?*

Activity Ask children to create a volcano using clay. Show them how to make the hole in the top. Using red clay, have them add lava coming out of the volcano.

▶ **Kinesthetic**

Real-Life Reading

old school · volcano · Farmer's new house · new sc[hool]

Farmer's old house

The farmer and his family moved away from the volcano.

26

Can you follow the road to their new house?

27

BIG BOOK OF REAL LIFE READING

Door · Funnel · Engine · Cars · Wheels

Big Book of Real-Life Reading, pages 26–27

Objective: Read a Map

READ THE PAGE If possible, display a local map, and discuss what it shows. Ask children to recall the story "Hill of Fire." Display the Big Book of Real-Life Reading and show children the table of contents. Explain that the contents page of a book gives information about where parts of the book are located. Help children find the "Hill of Fire" map on pages 26–27. Explain that the map shows the area where the man in the story lived. Read the labels on the page that show old house, new house, old school, new school, and volcano.

ANSWER THE QUESTION Ask a volunteer to trace the route to the farmer's new house. Discuss the many uses of maps; to find treasure, to get somewhere without getting lost, to figure out how far or close some place is.

CULTURAL PERSPECTIVES

POTTERY Explain that the story takes place in Mexico. In Mexico the art of making pottery is a skill that parents teach their children. Share that ceramic bowls are often painted bright colors after they dry.

Activity Provide clay. Show children how to make a bowl. Suggest that they draw decorations on their ceramics. When the clay dries, encourage children to paint their bowls.

▶ Spatial

OBJECTIVES

Children will:

- identify and read the high-frequency word *me*

MATERIALS

- word cards from the Word Building Book

TEACHING **TIP**

INSTRUCTIONAL Point out that the word *me* is never used at the beginning of a sentence. Give examples of sentences, such as *I have a hat. Give me the hat.*

Introduce High-Frequency Words: *me*

> **PREPARE**

Listen to Words

Explain to the children that they will be learning a new word: *me*. Say the following sentence: *Give me the ball.* Say the sentence again, and ask children to raise a finger when they hear the word *me*. Repeat with the sentence: *Pass me the cap.*

> **TEACH**

Model Reading the Word in Context

Give a word card to each child, and read the word. Reread the sentences, and have children raise their word cards when they hear the word.

Identify the Word

Write the sentences above on the chalkboard. Track print and read each sentence. Children hold up their word card when they hear the word *me*. Then ask volunteers to point to and underline the word *me* in the sentences.

> **PRACTICE**

Complete the Pupil Edition Page

Read the directions on page 203 to the children, and make sure they clearly understand what they are asked to do. Complete the first item together. Then work through the page with children, or have them complete the page independently.

> **ASSESS/CLOSE**

Review the Page

Review children's work, and note children who are experiencing difficulty or need additional practice.

Name_____

I.

Is my cat mad at <u>me</u>?

_____

2.

My cat is not mad at <u>me</u>.

_____

3.

My cat ran to <u>me</u>.

_____

4.

My cat sat on <u>me</u>!

_____

Read the sentence. • Draw a line under the word *me* in the sentence.

Unit 4   Introduce High-Frequency Words: *me*   **203**

Pupil Edition, page 203

ALTERNATE TEACHING STRATEGY

HIGH-FREQUENCY WORDS: *me*

For a different approach to teaching this skill, see page T27.

▶ **Visual/Auditory/Kinesthetic**

Practice 203

Name _____

I.

Is Min mad at <u>me</u>?

_____

2.

Is Nat mad at <u>me</u>?

_____

3.

Min and Nat are not mad at <u>me</u>!

_____

Read each sentence. Draw a line under the word me in each sentence.

3 | Unit 4
Introduce High-Frequency Words: *me*

At Home: Make up rhymes, such as "This is me climbing a tree." Have the child act out each rhyme.

203

PRACTICE BOOK, page 203

Meeting Individual Needs for Vocabulary

EASY	ON-LEVEL	CHALLENGE	LANGUAGE SUPPORT
Give each child the word card for *me*. Then give each child clay and have them roll out strips to place under the letters. Then have children run their fingers under the word while saying the word.	**Label** sheets of drawing paper: *This is __!* Children write and circle the word *me*. Then they draw pictures of themselves. Have children read the sentence. Display the pictures, and have children identify their friends.	**Write** *I* and *me* on the chalk-board. Then say sentences and have children complete them with one of the words: *Give __ the ball. ___ have a dog.* Children point to the correct word.	**Hold** a ball and sit across from a child. Say: *Roll the ball to me.* Hold up the word card: *me.* Then the child rolls the ball. Say: *I roll the ball.* Hold up the *I* word card. Then roll the ball to another child.

203

Develop Phonological Awareness

Listen

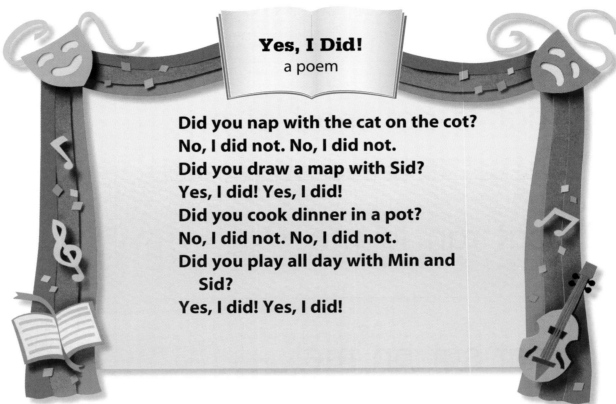

Yes, I Did!
a poem

Did you nap with the cat on the cot?
No, I did not. No, I did not.
Did you draw a map with Sid?
Yes, I did! Yes, I did!
Did you cook dinner in a pot?
No, I did not. No, I did not.
Did you play all day with Min and
    Sid?
Yes, I did! Yes, I did!

Objective: Focus on Context

READ THE POEM Read the poem "Yes, I Did!" Repeat the poem several times to familiarize children with the words.

RECALL CONTENT Ask children to tell you what the narrator in the poem did.

> The narrator drew a map with Sid.
> The narrator played all day with Min and Sid.

Ask children to tell what the narrator did not do.

> The narrator did not nap with the cat.
> The narrator did not cook dinner in a pot.

LISTEN AND RESPOND Tell children to listen carefully as you read the poem again. Have them nod when you say, *Yes, I did,* and shake their heads when you say, *No, I did not.*

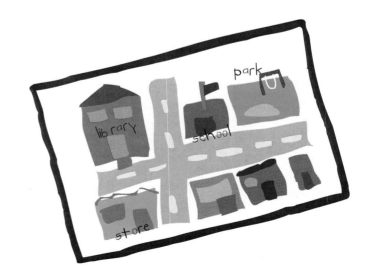

Objective: Blending With Short *a*, *i*, and *o*

LISTEN FOR THE SEGMENTED WORD Read the first line of "Yes, I Did!" As you read, say the word *nap* slowly, so children can hear each sound clearly. As you say /n/, place a piece of dry cereal in a paper cup. As you say /a/, place another piece of cereal in the cup. And as you say /p/, place a third piece of cereal in the cup. Then blend the sounds more quickly to say the word *nap*.

> **/n/-/a/-/p/**

BLEND WITH CEREAL Give each child a handful of cereal and a cup. Slowly, read the third line of the poem, emphasizing *map*. Guide children in placing one piece of cereal in the cup as you say /m/, another as you say /a/, and a third as you say /p/. Have children repeat the activity as they join you in saying /m/-/a/-/p/. Guide them in blending the sounds to say *map*. Continue with other short vowel words from the poem.

MORE BLENDING WITH CEREAL Choose one word from the poem, such as *did*, and have children practice blending the word on their own, using cereal and the cup.

Read Together

From Phonemic Awareness to Phonics

Objective: Identify Word Endings

LISTEN FOR RHYMING WORDS Read lines three and four of the poem, and ask children to identify rhyming words. Write the words on the chalkboard.

> **Sid   did**

IDENTIFY THE LETTERS Bend a pipe cleaner to make a "magic reading wand" with a loop on one end. Invite a volunteer to place the loop over the two letters the words have in common (*id*). Ask children to say each word.

NAME OTHER RHYMING WORDS Challenge children to name other words that end with the same sound as *Sid* and *did*. Write their ideas on the board. Invite other volunteers to use the reading wand to encircle letters the words have in common.

> **bid   hid   kid   lid**

CLIP THE WORDS Write the following words from the poem on separate index cards: *cot, not, did, Sid*. Place the cards on a table in random order. Read the words aloud, and ask children to find pairs of words with the same ending letters. Have volunteers use clothespins to clip rhyming sets of words together. Invite children to join you in chanting the word pairs.

OBJECTIVES

Children will:

- identify /a/*a*, /i/*i*, and /o/*o*
- blend and read short *a, i,* and *o* words
- write short *a, i,* and *o* words
- review /p/*p*, /c/*c*, and /m/*m*

MATERIALS

- letter cards from the Word Building Book

TEACHING TIP

INSTRUCTIONAL Write the following sentence on the chalkboard and have children read it aloud: *Pam and Tim sat on the cot.* Then ask volunteers to draw a line under and identify the words that have the /a/, /i/, and /o/ sounds.

ALTERNATE TEACHING STRATEGY

BLENDING SHORT *a, i, o*
For a different approach to teaching this skill, see Unit 1, page T32; Unit 2, page T32; Unit 3, page T30.
▶ **Visual/Auditory/ Kinesthetic**

Review Blending with short *a, i, o*

TEACH

Identify *a, i, o* as the Symbols for /a/, /i/, /o/
Tell children they will continue to read words with *a, i, o.*

- Display the *a* letter card and say /a/. Have children repeat the sound /a/.

BLENDING Model and Guide Practice
- Place the *p* letter card after the *a* card. Blend the sounds together and have children repeat after you.

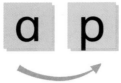 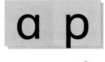

- Place an *m* card before the *a.* Blend the sounds to read *map.*

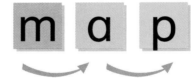 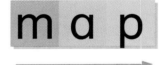

Use the Word in Context
- Ask children to use the word *map* in a sentence. Remind them of the different maps they have seen at school.

Repeat the Procedure
- Use the following words to continue modeling and for guided practice with short *a, i, o: pad, pot, cap, mop, pin, Pam, man.*

PRACTICE

Complete the Pupil Edition Page
Read aloud the directions on page 204. Identify each picture, and complete the first item together. Then work through the page with children, or have them complete the page independently.

ASSESS/CLOSE

Write Short *a, i, o* Words
Observe children as they complete page 204. Then have them write words with short *a, i,* or *o* that begin or end in *p, c, m, n, t.*

Name _____

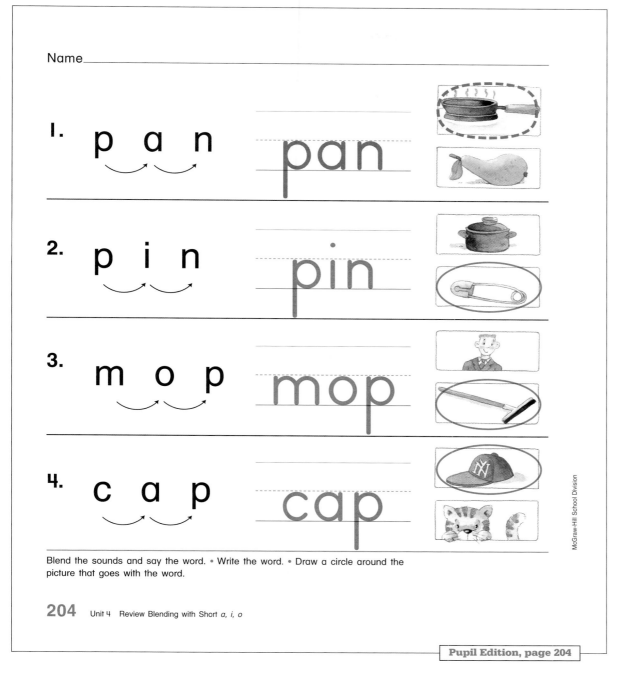

1. p a n   pan

2. p i n   pin

3. m o p   mop

4. c a p   cap

Blend the sounds and say the word. • Write the word. • Draw a circle around the
picture that goes with the word.

McGraw-Hill School Division

204 Unit 4 Review Blending with Short *a, i, o*

ADDITIONAL PHONICS RESOURCES

Practice Book, *page 204*
Phonics Workbook

McGraw-Hill School
TECHNOLOGY

Phonics CD-ROM
**Activities for practice with
Blending and Segmenting**

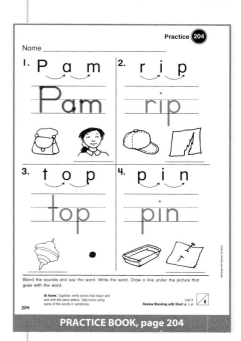

Practice 204

Name _____

1. P a m   2. r i p

   Pam   rip

3. t o p   4. p i n

   top   pin

Blend the sounds and say the word. Write the word. Draw a line under the picture that
goes with the word.

At Home: Together, write words that begin and
end with the same letters. Take turns using
some of the words in sentences.

204   Unit 4
                     Review Blending with Short *a, i, o*   8

PRACTICE BOOK, page 204

Meeting Individual Needs for Phonics

EASY	ON-LEVEL	CHALLENGE	LANGUAGE SUPPORT
Make word cards for the following words: *pan, pat, cap, pin, pot, pit, map, mop.* Point to each word, and ask children to blend the sounds together to read the words aloud. Have them sort the words that begin with /p/ in one group and the words that end with /p/ in another group.	**Write** the following words on the chalkboard: *pan, cap, dip, nap, sip, mop.* Have children blend and read the words; then ask them to write the word that completes a sentence you say, such as: *The sleepy cat took a (nap). She took a (sip) of juice. The (pan) was very hot.*	**Display** the following word cards on the chalkboard ledge in random order: *map, pod, dim, man, not, tap.* Ask children to arrange the words so that each word begins with the same letter with which the previous word ended (such as the order shown).	**Give** children additional practice in blending words that end with *p.* Make word cards for the following: *tip, sip, rip, mop, cap, nap.* Have children read each word and point to the final *p.*

204

Guided Instruction

BEFORE READING

PREVIEW AND PREDICT Take a brief **picture walk** through the book, focusing on the illustrations.

- Who is the story about? Where is the story taking place?

- What do you think will happen in the story?

- Do you think the story will be realistic, or will it be make-believe? Why?

SET PURPOSES Have the children think of questions to ask about the story, such as: What is the father doing to the tree?

TEACHING TIP

To put book together:
1. Tear out the story page.
2. Cut along dotted line.
3. Fold each section on fold line.
4. Assemble book.

INSTRUCTIONAL You may wish to bring in a bottle of maple syrup for children to taste. Ask them to describe the taste, and talk about the maple sugar process.

Tap the Sap

"I have the pot," said Pam.

3

"I can tap the sap to me," said Dad.

2

The sap ran.

4

Guided Instruction

DURING READING

☑ **Initial and Final *p***

☑ **Compare and Contrast**

☑ **Concepts of Print**

☑ **High-Frequency Words: *me***

(1) CONCEPTS OF PRINT Model how to run your finger from left to right under each word as you read the title page.

(2) HIGH-FREQUENCY WORDS Point out the word *me* on page 2. Have children use it in sentences that they create.

(3) CONCEPTS OF PRINT Ask children to count how many words are in the sentence on page 3. *(3)* Then talk about how each word is the same and how children might read the words.

(4) USE ILLUSTRATIONS Ask children to look at page 4 and ask them what is happening to the trees that have been tapped. *(Maple sap is coming out.)*

LANGUAGE SUPPORT

ESL Discuss the word *ran* on page 4. Explain that it applies to the movement of a liquid, such as maple sap.

Guided Instruction

DURING READING

⑤ PHONICS Ask children to find the two words on page 5 that end with *p*. *(sap, top)*

⑥ INITIAL AND FINAL *p* Ask children to look at page 6 and to point to the words that begin with *p*. (pan, Pam) Ask why *Pam* begins with a capital letter. (It is a name)

⑦ BLENDING WITH SHORT *i* Model: *Point to the word that begins with* s. *Each letter makes its own sound. Let's blend the sounds to read the word:* s i p sip.

⑧ COMPARE AND CONTRAST Ask children how the sap changed after it was boiled. *(It became syrup.)*

INFORMAL ASSESSMENT

COMPARE AND CONTRAST

HOW TO ASSESS Have children compare the two characters in the story, Pam and Dad. They might choose to focus on what they see in the pictures or on the words of the story. Have other children discuss what is the same or different.

FOLLOW UP Have children compare the interaction in this story with that of any other story they recall. Have them tell about another time in a story or real-life experience when a father and a daughter did an activity together.

"The sap is at the top," said Dad.

5

"Can I have a sip?" said Pam.

7

"I have the pan," said Pam.

6

"Fit the cap on the tin," said Dad.

8

Guided Instruction

AFTER READING

RETURN TO PREDICTIONS AND PURPOSES
Ask children if their predictions about the story were correct. Ask if their questions were answered, and revisit the story if necessary.

RETELL THE STORY As a class, have children retell the story. Pairs of children may want to act out the story, speaking the dialogue page by page.

LITERARY RESPONSE Have children respond to the story by asking:

• What was in Pam's bucket?

• What did Pam and Dad make with the sap?

Invite children to draw a picture of a tree near their home or school and to write about it. Encourage them to describe it and to write about what they like to do near the tree.

CENTER Activity

Cross Curricular: Language Arts

GIVING ART Make a tape of "The Giving Tree," by Shel Silverstein, and provide a copy of the book. Children can listen to the story and follow along. Invite children to design a poster that shows how trees can be used for food, fruit, wood, shelter, and so on.

▶ **Linguistic/Spatial**

OBJECTIVES

Children will:

- compare and contrast to understand a story

MATERIALS

- *Tap the Sap*

TEACHING TIP

INSTRUCTIONAL Ask children how the classroom looks at the beginning of the day. Then ask how it looks during center time. Compare and talk about how it is alike and how it is different.

Review Compare and Contrast

PREPARE

Recall the Story
Ask children to recall the story *Tap the Sap*. Ask who the characters are, and where the story takes place. Talk about how the girl's backyard is the same as and how it is different from children's backyards.

TEACH

Compare and Contrast Before and After
Reread the story together. After you read page 8, talk about how the sap changed. Then ask children about how other foods change after they are cooked, such as eggs, meat, and particular vegetables. Ask questions such as: *Is the (hamburger) the same color? Does it look the same? Does it smell the same?* List children's ideas in chart form on the chalkboard.

Rice

Before Cooking	After Cooking
• small grains	• larger in size
• very hard	• softer

PRACTICE

Complete the Pupil Edition Page
Read the directions on page 207 to the children, and make sure they clearly understand what they are asked to do. Identify each picture, and complete the first item together. Then work through the page with children or have them complete the page independently.

ASSESS/CLOSE

Review the Page
Review children's work, and note children who are experiencing difficulty.

Name_____

ALTERNATE TEACHING STRATEGY
....
COMPARE AND CONTRAST
For a different approach to teaching this skill, see page T30.

► **Visual/Auditory/ Kinesthetic**

1.

    ✔   ✔

2.

    ✔   ✔

3.

    ✔   ✗

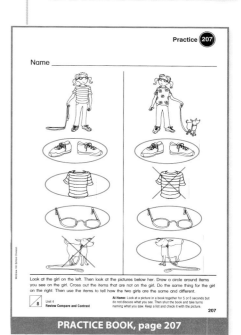

PRACTICE BOOK, page 207

Look at the two mice at the top of the page. • Then look at the pictures along the left side of the page. • Under each mouse, put a ✔ on the line if the mouse has that part. • Put an ✗ on the line if the mouse does not have that part.

Unit 4   Review Compare and Contrast   **207**

Pupil Edition, page 207

Meeting Individual Needs for Comprehension

EASY	ON-LEVEL	CHALLENGE	LANGUAGE SUPPORT
Show a picture of a waffle and a pancake. Explain that these foods are often eaten with maple syrup. Then have children talk about how these foods are alike and how they are different.	**Bring** in crackers with different tastes and textures, such as wheat, rye, and white. Have children compare and contrast the flavors, shapes, and colors.	**List** other toppings that go on pancakes: honey, different types of syrup, jam. Let children taste and compare the toppings. Have them dictate their ideas and make a comparison chart.	**Reinforce** the words *same* and *different* as children contrast and compare. Compare an apple and an orange and ask: *Are they the same color? Shape? Size? Do they taste the same? How are they different?*

Develop Phonological Awareness

Listen

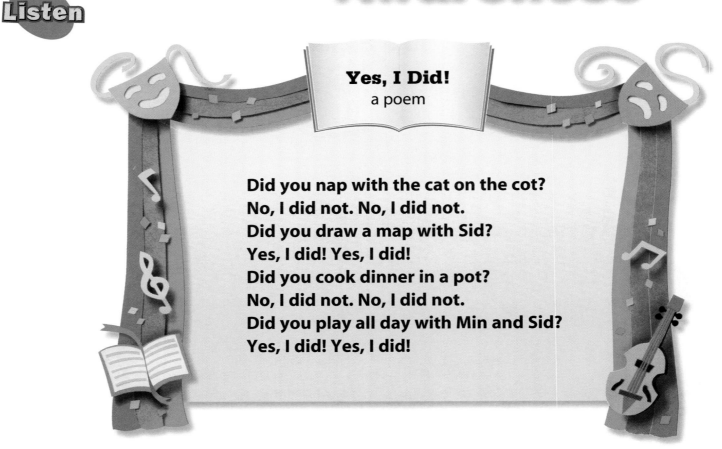

Yes, I Did!
a poem

Did you nap with the cat on the cot?
No, I did not. No, I did not.
Did you draw a map with Sid?
Yes, I did! Yes, I did!
Did you cook dinner in a pot?
No, I did not. No, I did not.
Did you play all day with Min and Sid?
Yes, I did! Yes, I did!

Objective: Focus on Context

REVISIT THE POEM Read the poem "Yes, I Did!" Ask children to tell you the four actions described in the poem.

> napping with the cat on the cot
> drawing a map with Sid
> cooking dinner in a pot
> playing all day with Min and Sid

PANTOMIME SENTENCE MEANING Tell children to listen carefully as you read the poem again. Invite volunteers to pantomime the four actions described as you read the poem.

Objective: Listen for Blending with Short *a*, *i*, and *o*

LISTEN FOR THE SEGMENTED WORD Read the first line of the poem. As you say *cat,* emphasize each sound individually by saying /c/-/a/-/t/.

> /c/-/a/-/t/

MODEL BLENDING Use plush cat toys to model blending. Say /c/, and place one cat at the end of a table to the children's left. Say /a/, and place another cat in the middle of the table. Say /t/, and place the last cat at the opposite end of the table. Starting from the children's left, say /c/-/a/-/t/ as you point to each cat. Invite children to join in as you gradually push the cats together and blend the sounds to say *cat.*

IDENTIFY A SOUND ACCORDING TO ITS PLACEMENT For a greater challenge, review each word by asking, *What sound do you hear at the beginning of the word? What sound do you hear in the middle of the word? What sound do you hear at the end?*

> **What sound do you hear at the beginning of the word *cat*?**

From Phonemic Awareness to Phonics

Read Together

Objective: Develop Letter/Sound Correspondence

LISTEN FOR SOUNDS Choose several three-letter CVC words from the poem, and write each on a sentence strip. Ask children to listen for the three sounds in each word as you read aloud.

> nap cat cot did
> not map Sid pot Min

ECHO GAME Read a sentence-strip word. Guide children in echoing the word, stretching out each sound as if it is echoing from a mountain top.

MAKE A WORD Divide the group into pairs. Tell children there are three letters/sounds in the word they just echoed. On index cards, write one letter per card from each word children have echoed. Ask pairs to place three index card letters in front of them. Display a sentence-strip word, and have children hold up the letters that match the word. Continue the activity with the rest of the sentence-strip words.

RECORD THE WORDS Have children glue the index cards to construction paper. Invite pairs to read a favorite word while the class echoes their reading.

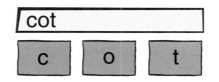

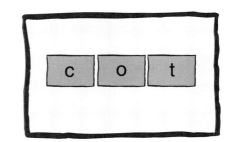

OBJECTIVES

Children will:

- identify /a/*a*, /i/*i*, and /o/*o*
- blend and read short *a*, *i*, and *o* words
- write short *a*, *i*, and *o* words
- review /p/*p*, /r/*r*, /f/*f*, /k/*c*, /t/*t*, /m/*m*, /s/*s*, /d/*d*, and /n/*n*

MATERIALS

- letter cards from the Word Building Book

TEACHING TIP

INSTRUCTIONAL

Demonstrate gestures children can use to pantomime the following words: *pat, mop, dip, sip, fan, tap, nap*. Show one word card at a time and ask volunteers to read the word aloud and act it out.

ALTERNATE TEACHING STRATEGY

BLENDING SHORT *a*, *i*, *o*

For a different approach to teaching this skill, see Unit 1, page T32; Unit 2, page T32; Unit 3, page T30.

▶ **Visual/Auditory/ Kinesthetic**

Review Blending with short *a, i, o*

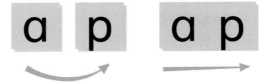

TEACH

Identify *a, i, o* as the Symbols for /a/, /i/, /o/

Tell children they will continue to read words with *a, i, o*.

- Display the *a* letter card and say /a/. Have children repeat the sound /a/.

BLENDING Model and Guide Practice

- Place the *p* card after the *a* card. Blend the sounds together and have children repeat after you.

- Place a *c* card before the *a*. Blend the sounds to read *cap*.

Use the Word in Context

- Ask children to use the word *cap* in a sentence. Ask whether any children own a cap.

Repeat the Procedure

- Use the following words to continue modeling and for guided practice with short *a, i, o: tip, mop, rip, pod, nap, sip, fan*.

PRACTICE

Complete the Pupil Edition Page

Read aloud the directions on page 208. Identify each picture, and complete the first item together. Then work through the page with children, or have them complete the page independently.

ASSESS/CLOSE

Build Short *a, i, o* Words

Observe children as they complete page 208. Have them use *p, r, f, c, t, m, s, d,* and *n* cards to build three-letter words with medial *a, i,* or *o*.

Name _____

1. 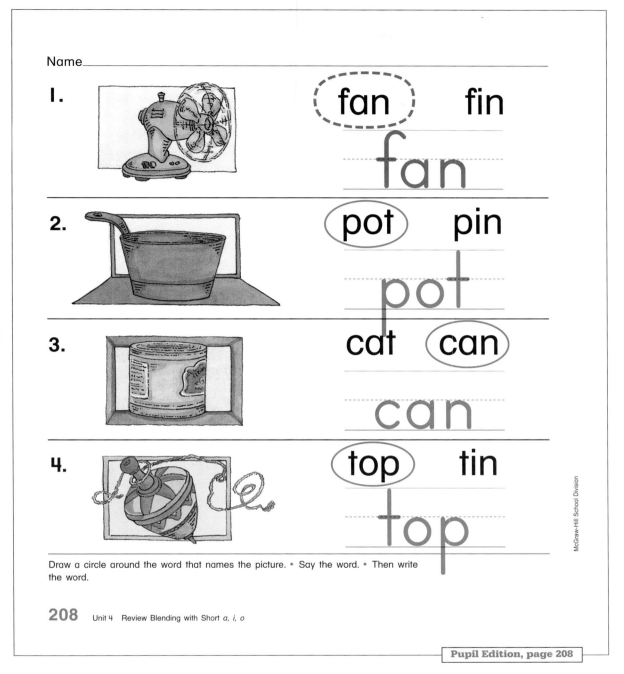 (fan)   fin

fan

2. (pot)   pin

pot

3. cat   (can)

can

4. (top)   tin

top

Draw a circle around the word that names the picture. • Say the word. • Then write the word.

McGraw-Hill School Division

Pupil Edition, page 208

ADDITIONAL PHONICS RESOURCES
Practice Book, *page 208*
Phonics Workbook

McGraw-Hill School
TECHNOLOGY

Phonics CD-ROM
Activities for practice with Blending and Segmenting

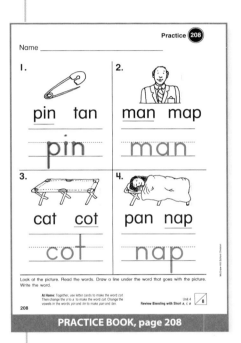

Practice **208**

Name _____

1. pin   tan

pin

2. man   map

man

3. cat   cot

cot

4. pan   nap

nap

Look at the picture. Read the words. Draw a line under the word that goes with the picture. Write the word.

At Home: Together, use letter cards to make the word *cot.* Then change the *o* to *a* to make the word *cat.* Change the vowels in the words *pin* and *tin* to make *pan* and *tan.*

Unit 4
8

208   Review Blending with Short *a, i, o*

PRACTICE BOOK, page 208

Meeting Individual Needs for Phonics

EASY	ON-LEVEL	CHALLENGE	LANGUAGE SUPPORT
Ask children to sort word cards to show words that begin or end with *p* and words that don't. Show the following word cards: *mop, mat, tip, tin, pad, dot.* Have children blend each word to read it aloud. Then ask them to use each word in a sentence.	**Give** each child one of the following word cards: *pan, nap, pot, top, tip, pit.* Ask children to find a partner whose word card has the first and last letter of their card in reverse order (as shown). Have children write the words and blend the sounds to say them aloud.	**Ask** children to write three-letter words that answer word clues such as the following: *to tear up (rip); opposite of bottom (top); you cook in it (pot, pan).* Display *a, i, o* and *p, r, f, c, t, m, s, d,* and *n* letter cards for children to choose from to write their words.	**Help** children blend and read the words *mop, pan, cap, map, pad.* Invite them to draw pictures of these objects and to label their pictures with the words.

Reread the Decodable Story

☑ **Initial and final p**

☑ **High-Frequency Words: me**

☑ **Compare and Contrast**

☑ **Concepts of Print**

Tap the Sap

Guided Reading

SET PURPOSES Tell children that when they read the story again, they can find out more about what happened. Explain that you also want them to look for and read words that begin or end with *p*. Remind them that they know the word *me,* and will see it again in this story.

REREAD THE BOOK As you guide children through the story, address specific problems they may have had during the first read. Use the following prompts to guide the lesson:

• **CONCEPTS OF PRINT** Remind children that the cover and title page help you to know what the story is going to be about. Ask what information they get from this title page.

• **COMPARE AND CONTRAST** Ask children to look at page 5. Ask them how the bucket has changed. (It is full of sap.)

RETURN TO PURPOSES Ask children if they found out what they needed to know from the story. See if they have any unanswered questions.

LITERARY RESPONSE Help children fold a sheet of paper into thirds. Have them draw and write about the steps of sugaring in the story: *Tap the tree. The sap runs. Sap boils into syrup.*

Ask children the following questions to prompt discussions about their drawings:

• *What is happening in each of your pictures?*

• *What do you think will happen after the sap is turned into syrup?*

TEACHING TIP

MANAGEMENT You may wish to reread the story with a small group of children who had difficulties during the first reading. Help children stay focused on the story by saying: *Let's turn the page and find out what happens next.*

INFORMAL ASSESSMENT

PHONICS: INITIAL AND FINAL p

HOW TO ASSESS Write the following words from the story: *Pam, pot, tap, cap, sip.* Have children find the words in the story, and identify the letter *p.*

FOLLOW UP If children have difficulty, let them hold the letter *p* as they look for words.

Read the Patterned Book

The Picnic

☑ **Initial and final /p/p**
☑ **Compare and Contrast**
☑ **High-Frequency Word:** *me*
☑ **Concepts of Print**

The Picnic

by Anne Miranda
illustrated by Carol Nicklaus

Guided Reading

PREVIEW AND PREDICT Read the title and the author's and the illustrator's name. Take a **picture walk** through pages 2–4, noting the setting of the story and the characters. Have children make predictions about what will happen in the story.

SET PURPOSES Have children decide what they want to find out from the story and to predict what might happen. Tell them that the story contains words with initial and final *p*.

READ THE BOOK Use the following prompts while the children are reading or after they have read independently. Remind them to run their fingers under each word as they read.

PAGES 2–3: Point to the last word in the sentence. *Let's read it together: me.*
High-Frequency Words

PAGES 4–5: *Model: I can use what I know about short a to read the name. Let's blend these sounds together: N-a-n. Let's do the same for the name on the next page, S-a-m.*
Phonics and Decoding

PAGES 6–7: *Let's think of all of the foods in the story. How are some of the foods the same? How are some of the foods different?* (They all begin with /p/. They are from different food groups.) *Compare and Contrast*

PAGE 8: *Who can point to the first word in this sentence?* (Have) *Who can point to the last word in this sentence?* (me)
Concepts of Print

RETURN TO PREDICTIONS AND PURPOSES Ask children if they found out what they needed to know from the story. See if their predictions were correct.

LITERARY RESPONSE The following questions will help focus children's responses:

• Could this story really happen? How do you know?

• What would you like to eat and do at a picnic? Draw a picture and write about it in your journal.

CENTER Activity

Cross Curricular: Science

FAVORITE FOODS
Make laminated picture cards showing different foods. Have children sort the cards according to basic food groups. You may wish to color code the cards on the back so that children can check their work independently.

OBJECTIVES

Children will:

- identify and read the high-frequency word *me*

MATERIALS

- word cards from the Word Play Book
- *Tap the Sap*

TEACHING TIP

MANAGEMENT Have children keep their own personal set of high-frequency word cards. You can make these cards from index cards or tagboard. Children can work in pairs to practice words.

Review *me, to, you*

PREPARE

Listen to Words

Explain to the children that they will review the word *me*.

Ask children to say words that rhyme: *be, fee, he, see, tee, we.*

TEACH

Model Reading the Word in Context

Have children reread the decodable book. Ask children to listen for the word *me*.

Identify the Word

Ask children to look at their word cards, and then ask them to look for the word in sentences. Have children point to the word *me* on each page as you read the story together. Have volunteers put a self-stick note below the word. (Have children move the self-stick note from page to page.)

Review High-Frequency Words

Hold up word cards for the following words: *the, a, my, that, I, and, said, we, are, is, have, to, you.* Children say the words.

PRACTICE

Complete the Pupil Edition Page

Read the directions on page 209 to the children, and make sure they clearly understand what they are asked to do. Complete the first item together. Then work through the page with children or have them complete the page independently.

ASSESS/CLOSE

Review the Page

Review children's work, and note children who are experiencing difficulty or need additional practice.

Name_____

1.

You said (to) me, "Pat the cat."

_____

2.

The cat ran to (you) and me.

_____

3.

The cat sat on (me)

_____

Read the sentences. Then do the following: **1.** Draw a circle around the word *to*.
2. Draw a circle around the word *you*. **3.** Draw a circle around the word *me*.

Unit 4   Review *me, to, you*   **209**

Pupil Edition, page 209

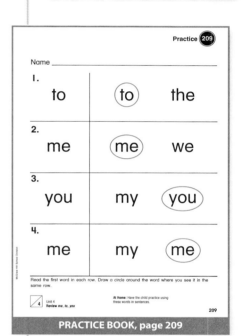

Practice 209

Name _____

1. to	(to)	the
2. me	(me)	we
3. you	my	(you)
4. me	my	(me)

Read the first word in each row. Draw a circle around the word where you see it in the same row.

Unit 4
Review *me, to, you*

At Home: Have the child practice using these words in sentences.

209

PRACTICE BOOK, page 209

Meeting Individual Needs for Vocabulary

EASY	ON-LEVEL	CHALLENGE	LANGUAGE SUPPORT
Write the letters *m* and *e* on index cards, and cut the cards apart to make puzzle pieces. Give children several cards. Have them find the matches, and read the word.	**Help** children to label a large sheet of drawing paper: ME. Have them draw pictures of themselves, showing what they like to do, family, friends, and so on.	**Have** children label a sheet of drawing paper: ME. Then have children draw a self-portrait, using a mirror as necessary. Display the portraits, and have other children guess the artists.	**Write** the word *me* on chart paper. Then have children follow directions using the word *me: Come with me. Bring a book to me. Please sit next to me.*

209

GRAMMAR/SPELLING CONNECTIONS

Model subject-verb agreement, complete sentences, and correct tense so that students may gain increasing control of grammar when speaking and writing.

Interactive Writing

Write a Class Book

Prewrite

LOOK AT THE STORY PATTERN Reread the story *The Apple Pie Tree*. Talk about the pattern of the story, focusing on how the story follows the changing of the seasons. Talk about how the apple tree changes. Then discuss the ending of the story. Make a list of other foods that are made with apples.

Draft

WRITE A CLASS BOOK Explain that children will work together to make a class book titled "Our Favorite Apple Foods." Have children choose their favorite apple food from the list.

- Give each child a sheet of drawing paper cut in the shape of an apple. Help children complete the phrase: *It's ___ for me.*

- Children illustrate their pages.

Publish

CREATE THE BOOK Bind the pages together. Read the book as a class.

It's apple pie for me.

Presentation Ideas

SOLVE A RIDDLE Reread the class book. Then give clues about a food in the book, and have children guess the food you are describing. Invite volunteers to give clues to others.

▶ **Listening/Speaking**

CREATE A COLLAGE Have children look in magazines to find pictures of foods mentioned in the class book. Make a collage, and have children point to appropriate foods when you reread the story.

▶ **Representing/Viewing**

COMMUNICATION TIPS

• **Speaking** When children are listening to or giving clues, remind them to focus on shape, color, size, and so on.

TECHNOLOGY TIP

Have children write the text for their pages of the book on the computer.

LANGUAGE SUPPORT

ESL Make picture cards showing different types of foods. Have children identify and describe the foods. Include foods from different cultures.

Meeting Individual Needs for Writing

EASY	ON-LEVEL	CHALLENGE
Make a Word List Ask children to think of other words that begin with the short *a* sound. Have them help you write a list.	**Categorize Foods** Brainstorm ways children could categorize the apple foods in the class book. Write the categories, and help children write the foods in the appropriate groups.	**Write a List** Have children write a shopping list of ingredients that would be needed to prepare the foods they wrote about in the class book. Children can make picture and word lists.

Nap in a Lap

Children will read and listen to a variety of stories about exploring nature and learning about the world.

Nap in a Lap

Listening
Library
Audiocassette

**Decodable Story,
pages 217–218 of the
Pupil Edition**

Let's Go!

by Suzanne Martinucci
illustrated by Thea Kliros

**Patterned Book,
page 221B**

The Clever Turtle

A Hispanic folktale
retold by Margaret H. Lippert

**Teacher Read Aloud,
page 215A**

Allie's Adventure
From A to Z

Written by Ellen Dreyer   Illustrated by Jui Ishida

Listening
Library
Audiocassette

**ABC Big Book,
pages 211A–211B**

NATURE SPY

written by SHELLEY ROTNER and KEN KREISLER
photographs by SHELLEY ROTNER

Listening
Library
Audiocassette

**Literature Big Book,
pages 213A–213B**

**Pupil Edition,
pages 210–221**

**Big Book of Real-Life Reading,
page 28**

**Big Book of Phonics Rhymes and
Poems, pages 31, 32**

 **Listening
Library
Audiocassette**

ADDITIONAL RESOURCES

**Practice Book,
pages 210–221**

- **Phonics Kit**
- **Language Support Book**
- **Alternate Teaching Strategies,**
  pages T27, T31, T33

McGraw-Hill School
TECHNOLOGY

Phonics CD-ROM Provides
extra phonics support.

inter NET CONNECTION Research & Inquiry Ideas.

Visit www.mhschool.com

Nap in a Lap

READING AND LANGUAGE ARTS

- **Phonological Awareness**
- **Phonics** *initial /l/*
- **Comprehension**
- **Vocabulary**
- **Beginning Reading Concepts**
- **Listening, Speaking, Viewing, Representing**

DAY 1

Allie's Adventure From A to Z
Written by Ellen Dreyer   Illustrated by Jui Ishida

Focus on Reading Skills

Develop Phonological Awareness, 210G–210H
"Lightning Bug" *Big Book of Phonics Rhymes and Poems,* 31

 **Introduce Initial /l/,** 210I–210
Practice Book, 210
Phonics/Phonemic Awareness
Practice Book

 Phonics CD-ROM

Read the Literature

Read *Allie's Adventure from A to Z* **Big Book,** 211A–211B
Shared Reading

Build Skills

☑ Over, Under, 211C–211
Practice Book, 211

DAY 2

NATURE SPY
written by SHELLEY ROTNER and KEN KRE
photographs by SHELLEY ROTNER

Focus on Reading Skills

Develop Phonological Awareness, 212A–212B
"The Lazy Little Lion" *Big Book of Phonics Rhymes and Poems,* 32

 **Review Initial /l/,** 212C–212
Practice Book, 212
Phonics/Phonemic Awareness
Practice Book

Phonics CD-ROM

Read the Literature

Read *Nature Spy* **Big Book,** 213A–213B
Shared Reading

Build Skills

☑ Main Idea, 213C–213
Practice Book, 213

- **Cross Curriculum**

   Language Arts, 211B

   Science, 213B

- **Writing**

   Writing Prompt: Write about your favorite vegetable.

   Journal Writing, 211B
  Letter Formation, 210I

   Writing Prompt: If you were a nature spy, where would you explore?

   Journal Writing, 213B
  Letter Formation, 212C

☑ = **Skill Assessed in Unit Test**

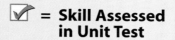

DAY 3

The Clever Turtle

Focus on Reading Skills

Develop Phonological Awareness, 214A–214B
"Lightning Bug" and "The Lazy Little Lion" *Big Book of Phonics Rhymes and Poems,* 31–32

 **Review /l/l,** 214C–214
Practice Book, 214
Phonics/Phonemic Awareness Practice Book

 CD-ROM

Read the Literature

Read "The Clever Turtle" Teacher Read Aloud, 215A–215B
Shared Reading
Read the Big Book of Real-Life Reading, 20–21
☑ Chart

Build Skills

☑ High-Frequency Word: *go* 215C–215
Practice Book, 215

 Cultural Perspectives, 215B

 Writing Prompt: What do you think the turtle did after it ran away? Draw a picture and write about it.

DAY 4

Nap in a Lap

Focus on Reading Skills

Develop Phonological Awareness, 216A–216B
"The Fire Is Lit"
Introduce Blending with Short *a, i, o,* 216C–216
Practice Book, 216
Phonics/Phonemic Awareness Practice Book

 **CD-ROM**

Read the Literature

Read "Nap in a Lap" Decodable Story, 217/218A–217/218D

☑ Initial and Final /p/*p;* Blending
☑ Main Idea
☑ High-Frequency Words: *go*
☑ Concepts of Print

Build Skills

☑ Main Idea, 219A–219
Practice Book, 219

 Math, 217/218D

 Writing Prompt: If you had your choice, where would you like to nap?

Letter Formation Practice Book, 217–218

DAY 5

Nap in a Lap

Let's Go!

by Suzanne Martinucci
Illustrated by Thea Kliros

Focus on Reading Skills

Develop Phonological Awareness, 220A–220B
"The Fire Is Lit"
Review Blending with Short *a, i, o,* 220C–220
Practice Book, 220
Phonics/Phonemic Awareness Practice Book

 **CD-ROM**

Read the Literature

Reread "Nap in a Lap" Decodable Story, 221A
Read "Let's Go" Patterned Book, 221B
Guided Reading
☑ Initial and Final /p/*p;* Blending
☑ Main Idea
☑ High-Frequency Words: *go*
☑ Concepts of Print

Build Skills

☑ High-Frequency Words: *go, to, me, you,* 221C–221
Practice Book, 221

 Social Studies, 221B

 Writing Prompt: Do you have a favorite type of weather? Write about it.

Interactive Writing, 222A–222B

210F

Develop Phonological Awareness

Listen

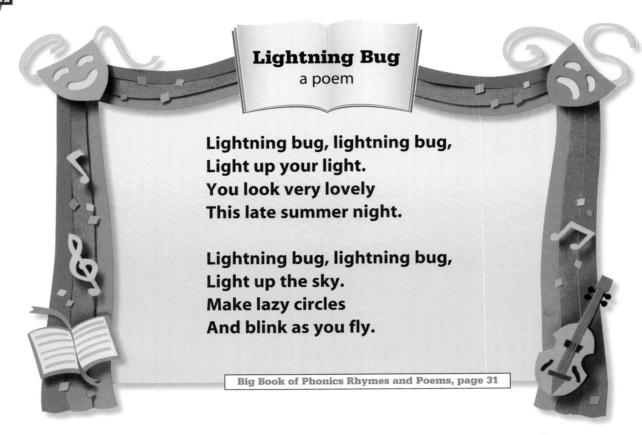

Lightning Bug
a poem

Lightning bug, lightning bug,
Light up your light.
You look very lovely
This late summer night.

Lightning bug, lightning bug,
Light up the sky.
Make lazy circles
And blink as you fly.

Big Book of Phonics Rhymes and Poems, page 31

Objective: Listen for Rhyming Words

LISTEN TO THE POEM

- Read the poem "Lightning Bug" aloud to children.

- Read the first stanza again; but have children listen for the rhyming words.

- Then ask children to think of other words that rhyme with light.

> light   night   right   fight

- Repeat the last stanza, and ask children which two words rhyme. Have children focus on the rhyming words: *sky* and *fly*.

- Then have children think of other words that rhyme with *sky*.

SUBSTITUTE WORDS

- Have children substitute rhyming words for the last word of each stanza. Discuss whether the word makes sense or not.

> This   late   summer   tight

- Continue with the last stanza.

- Again, focus on rhyming words *sky* and *fly*.

Objective: Listen for Initial /l/

SEGMENTING

- Say the word *light*. Segment the initial /l/ and have children repeat it with you.

> **l-ight**

- Then have children say the following words from the poem: *look, late, lightning*. Point out that the words begin with the /l/ sound.

- Then have children say the words without the /l/ sound.

LISTEN, LISTEN!

- Explain that children will play a listening game. Say the following rhyme:

  > Listen, listen, loud and clear.
  > What is the first sound that you hear?

- Say the word *listen,* and have children repeat it with you. Emphasize the initial /l/.

- Continue the game with the following words: *look, see, pen, loan, pad, lift.* Invite children to join in on the rhyme and then say the initial sound of the word.

Read Together

From Phonemic Awareness to Phonics

Objective: Identify Initial /l/L, l

IDENTIFY THE LETTER FOR THE SOUND Explain to children that the letter *l* stands for the sound /l/. Ask children to say the sound.

Display the Big Book of Phonics Poems and Rhymes, page 31. Point to the letters in the corner. Identify the letters as *l* and say the sound.

REREAD THE POEM Show children how to raise an index finger to show a lowercase *l*. Then read the poem again, pointing to each word. When you say a word that begins with /l/, children raise an index finger.

FIND L, l Slowly read each line of the poem. Ask volunteers to say each word that begins with *L* or *l* as you read. Count the words that begin with the letter *l* with the class.

FIND MATCHING WORDS Have children find two words in the poem that have the same letters. *(Lightning, light)* Then say the words *lightning* and *light*. Point to the words and show that *light* can be found in *lightning*.

Lightning Bug

Lightning bug, lightning bug,
Light up your light.
You look very lovely
This late summer night.

Lightning bug, lightning bug,
Light up the sky.
Make lazy circles,
And blink as you fly.

Big Book of Phonics Rhymes and Poems, page 31

OBJECTIVES

Children will:

- identify the letters *L,l*
- identify /l/*L,l*
- form the letters *L,l*

MATERIALS

- letter cards and word cards from the Word Building Book
- Big Book of Phonics Rhymes and Poems

TEACHING TIP

INSTRUCTIONAL Have children practice making the /l/ sound at the beginning of a word by singing a song with the syllable *la* instead of the words. Choose a song with a familiar tune, such as "Mary Had a Little Lamb."

ALTERNATE TEACHING STRATEGY

INITIAL /l/

For a different approach to teaching this skill, see page T31.

▶ **Visual/Auditory/ Kinesthetic**

Introduce Initial /l/ *l*

TEACH

Identify /l/ *L,l*   Tell children they will learn to write the sound /l/ with the letters *L,l*. Write the letters on the chalkboard, identify them, and have children say the sound. Then turn to page 31 in the Big Book of Phonics Rhymes and Poems and reread the poem, emphasizing the words that begin with *l*. Have children repeat some of the words.

Form *L,l*   Display the letters *L, l*, and trace them with your finger. With your back to the children, trace the letters *L* and *l* in the air. Ask children to do the same. Then have them fold a sheet of paper in fourths and write *L* and *l* in each of the four boxes.

PRACTICE

Complete the Pupil Edition Page   Read the directions on page 210 of the Pupil Edition, and make sure children clearly understand what they are being asked to do. Identify each picture, and complete the first item together. Then work through the page with children or have them complete the page independently.

ASSESS/CLOSE

Identify and Use *L,l*   Ask children to draw a circle around one pair of *l*'s on their sheet of paper each time they hear a word that being with /l/. Say "Linda has a lot of lettuce in her lunch." Write the sentence on the chalkboard. Ask children to turn their papers over and write *L* or *l* for every *l* they see at the beginning of a word.

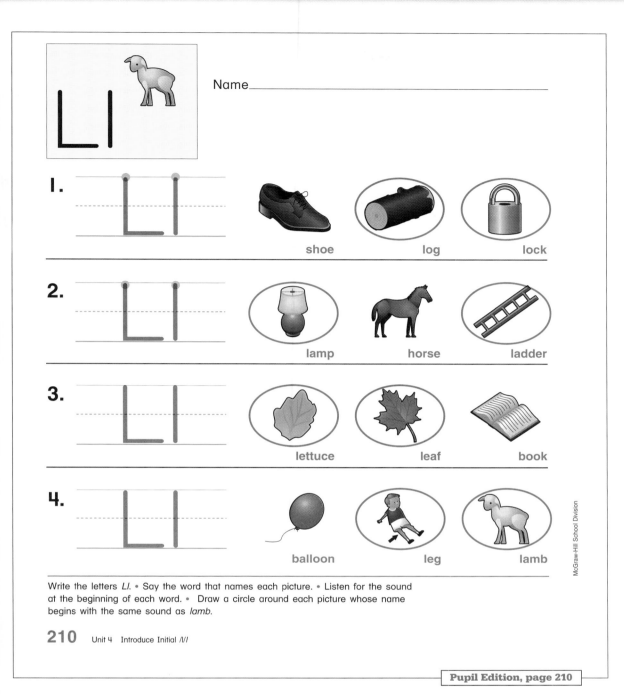

Name_____

1. L l

shoe   log   lock

2. L l

lamp   horse   ladder

3. L l

lettuce   leaf   book

4. L l

balloon   leg   lamb

Write the letters *Ll*. • Say the word that names each picture. • Listen for the sound at the beginning of each word. • Draw a circle around each picture whose name begins with the same sound as *lamb*.

McGraw-Hill School Division

210   Unit 4   Introduce Initial /l/

Pupil Edition, page 210

ADDITIONAL PHONICS RESOURCES

Practice Book, *page 210*
Phonics Workbook

McGraw-Hill School
TECHNOLOGY

Phonics CD-ROM
Activities for practice with Initial Letters

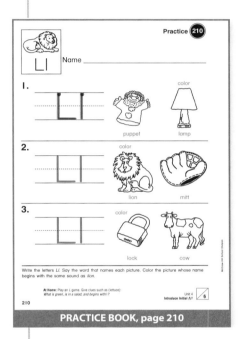

Practice **210**

L l   Name_____

1.   puppet   color   lamp

2.   color   lion   mitt

3.   color   lock   cow

Write the letters *Ll*. Say the word that names each picture. Color the picture whose name begins with the same sound as *lion*.

At Home: Play an *L* game. Give clues such as (lettuce): *What is green, is in a salad, and begins with l?*

210   Unit 4   Introduce Initial /l/   6

PRACTICE BOOK, page 210

Meeting Individual Needs for Phonics

EASY	ON-LEVEL	CHALLENGE	LANGUAGE SUPPORT
Hold up a lunch box, and ask children if they can guess what's inside. Tell them that only things whose names begin with the /l/ sound are in the lunch box. Ask *Is there a lemon in the lunch box? Is there a sandwich in the lunch box?* (licorice, lasagne, lemonade, lollipops)	**Have** children make new words by replacing the first sound in each word with /l/. Use words such as: *gate, book, night, cake, bike, song, duck, fast.* Have children write *l* on a strip of paper for each rhyme that is made.	**Have** children make up silly sentences by using as many words that begin with /l/ as they can. For example: *Liz likes lollipops a lot.*	**Help** children isolate the /l/ sound by saying a word without the beginning sound: "list," "ist." Continue with these words: *lunch, land, leaf, like, log, last.* Write each word part. Then add *l* and have children blend /l/ to say each whole word.

210

TESTED
OBJECTIVES

Children will:

- review letter identification and ABC order
- recognize words with initial *l*
- use story details

LANGUAGE SUPPORT

**ESL** Help children identify and gain understanding about other animals in the story. Use the pictures to have them identify the other animals. Ask questions such as: *Where does this animal live? How does it move?*

Read the Big Book

Before Reading

Develop Oral Language Sing "The Monkey Alphabet Song" with children. The song is on page 4 in the Big Book of Phonics Rhymes and Poems. Then give children letter cards, and sing the song again. Children hold up their letter cards when they hear that letter.

Remind children that they read a story about a kitten. Ask them to retell a favorite part of the story.

Set Purposes Ask children: *What does Allie see on her adventure?* (other animals) Discuss the different animals that Allie sees and note each so that children can refer to them when discussing the story.

When you reach page 14 of the story, stop before saying the word *lettuce*. Ask children to supply this word.

Allie sees a tiny **nose**.   She puts her paw **on** the nose.

Allie's Adventure from A to Z, pages 16–17

During Reading

Allie **jumps!**

Allie's Adventure from A to Z, page 12

Read Together

• Before you begin to read, point to the first word in the first sentence. Explain that this is where you will begin to read. Continue to track print as you read the story. *Tracking Print*

• As you read the story, omit words that begin with the highlighted letter. Have children say the word, using the picture and the letter. After children supply the key word, confirm their choice by saying, *That's correct. The word* Allie *begins with the letter* a. *Concepts of Print*

• After you read page 3, note that Allie saw an insect. Make a picture or word list of other animals that she sees as you continue reading. *Use Story Details*

• Make the /l/ sound, and have children say it with you. After you read pages 14–15, ask which word begins with that sound. *(lettuce) Phonics*

After Reading

Literary Response

JOURNAL WRITING Ask children to draw and write about another animal that Allie could see.

ORAL RESPONSE Ask questions, such as:
• *Where would Allie see this animal?*
• *What might Allie do?*

ABC Activity

Have children work in pairs. With his or her finger, one child writes a lowercase letter on another child's palm. The child guesses the letter. Children take turns.

INFORMAL ASSESSMENT

ABC ORDER AND LETTER IDENTIFICATION

HOW TO ASSESS Ask children to point to letters on an alphabet chart as you say them.

FOLLOW UP Cover certain letters on alphabet strips. Ask children to identify covered letter by looking at the letters around it.

Cross Curricular: Language Arts

ANIMAL ALPHABET Invite children to make an Animal Alphabet Book. Have them draw or cut out pictures of different animals. Have them write the corresponding initial letter. Help them to bind the books together.

▶ **Spatial/Logical**

OBJECTIVES

Children will:

- understand over and under

....

MATERIALS

- *Allie's Adventure from A to Z*

TEACHING TIP

INSTRUCTIONAL Make sure children have a point of reference to identify *over* and *under*. You may find it helpful to collect objects, such as a small towel, a rug space, and a small stuffed animal to use in the lesson.

Introduce Over, Under

PREPARE

Play a Game Play a game of "Teacher Says." Demonstrate by giving examples, such as: *Raise your hands over your head. Put your hand under your chin.*

TEACH

Recognize Over and Under Display the Big Book *Allie's Adventure from A to Z* and ask children to recall the story. Then turn to pages 14–15, and ask where the mouse is. (under the lettuce leaf)

Use Illustrations Take a picture walk through the book, and look for other examples that illustrate over and under. Then use a small towel and a small stuffed animal. Ask volunteers to follow your directions: *Put the bear under the towel. Is the towel over the bear?*

PRACTICE

Show Over and Under Read the directions on page 211 to the children, and make sure they clearly understand what they are asked to do. Identify each picture, and complete the first item. Then work through the page with the children, or have them complete the page independently.

ASSESS/CLOSE

Review the Page Check children's work on the Pupil Edition page. Note areas where children need extra help.

Name

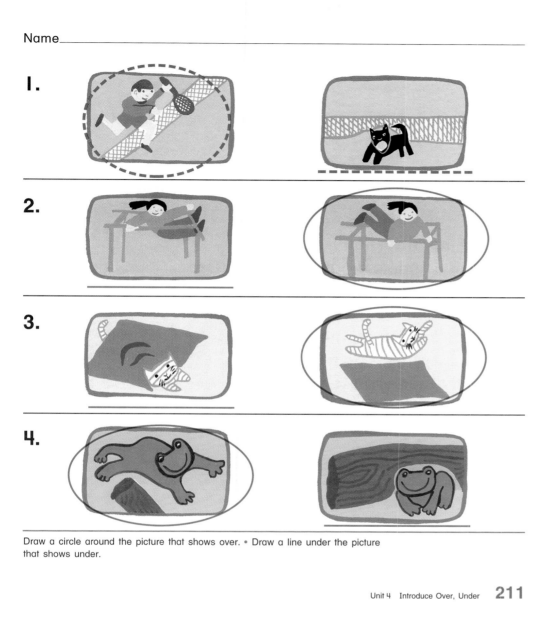

1.

2.

3.

4.

Draw a circle around the picture that shows over. • Draw a line under the picture that shows under.

Pupil Edition, page 211

ALTERNATE TEACHING
STRATEGY
....

OVER, UNDER
For a different approach to teaching this skill, see page T33.

▶ **Visual/Auditory/ Kinesthetic**

PRACTICE BOOK, page 211

Meeting Individual Needs for Beginning Reading Concepts

EASY	ON-LEVEL	CHALLENGE	LANGUAGE SUPPORT
Make each child a simple bear puppet from a craft stick. Draw a mountain on large paper, and then sing "The Bear Went Over the Mountain." Have children use their puppets to act out the song. Make up additional verses to focus on over and under.	**Draw** a simple bridge on large paper. Ask children to follow your directions to draw items that are over and under the bridge. Then ask children for their own ideas.	**Show** children how to make a simple weaving. Take a sheet of construction paper, and cut several horizontal lines, leaving at least an inch uncut at each side. Have children take thin construction paper strips and weave *over* and *under*. Encourage them to weave color patterns.	**Use** a stuffed animal and have children follow your directions: *Put the bear under the chair.* *Hold the bear over your head.* *Put the bear under the blanket.* Then have children give directions to you.

Develop Phonological Awareness

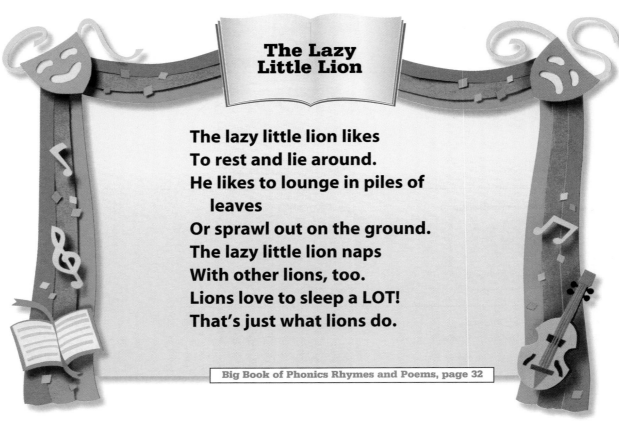

The Lazy Little Lion

The lazy little lion likes
To rest and lie around.
He likes to lounge in piles of
    leaves
Or sprawl out on the ground.
The lazy little lion naps
With other lions, too.
Lions love to sleep a LOT!
That's just what lions do.

Big Book of Phonics Rhymes and Poems, page 32

Objective: Strengthen Awareness of Words

LISTEN TO THE POEM

- Give each child 10 blocks or squares of paper. Explain that each block will show a word.

- Say the following sentence: *The lion sleeps.* Model how to repeat the sentence, and place three blocks with a space between each to show each word.

- Have children do the same. Encourage children to arrange the blocks from left to right to support directionality.

REPEAT THE SENTENCE

- Have children say the sentence with you, pointing to a block for each word. Then have the children count the blocks with you.

TRY A LONGER SENTENCE

- Read the poem "The Lazy Little Lion." Then repeat the above activity, using the last sentence.

Objective: Listen for Initial /l/

SEGMENTING

- Say the word *lazy.* Emphasize the /l/ sound and have children repeat it after you.

- Model how to say a word loudly if it begins with the /l/ sound.

- Read the following words. Have children say it loudly if it begins with /l/.

> lion   lazy   naps   rest
> lie   piles   leaves

DIFFERENTIATE BETWEEN INITIAL SOUNDS

- Say the following pairs of words. Children choose the word that begins with /l/ and repeat it loudly.

> let   get   gate   late
> no   low   bike   like

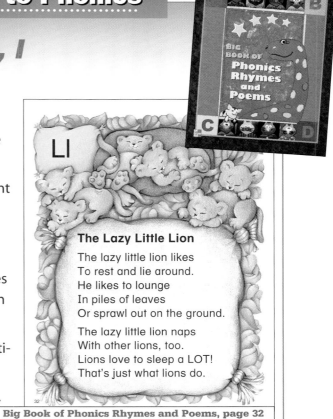

Read Together

From Phonemic Awareness to Phonics

Objective: Identify /l/L, l

IDENTIFY THE LETTER FOR THE SOUND

- Explain to children that the letters *L, l* sound like /l/. Have children repeat the sound.

- Display the Big Book of Phonics Rhymes and Poems, page 32. Identify the letters *L, l* in the corner of the page and say the letter names. Have children repeat the /l/ sound.

REREAD THE POEM

- Read the poem again, emphasizing the words that begin with /l/ as you point to each word.

FIND L,l

- Use a sheet of paper to isolate each line in the poem. Read the poem line by line.

- Ask volunteers to help you count the *l*'s in each line.

SUBSTITUTE OTHER ANIMALS

- Have children brainstorm names of other animals that begin with *l.* (lamb, lizard, llama)

- Then pick one animal and substitute its name for the word *lion.*

- Repeat the poem with children.

Ll

The Lazy Little Lion

The lazy little lion likes
To rest and lie around.
He likes to lounge
In piles of leaves
Or sprawl out on the ground.

The lazy little lion naps
With other lions, too.
Lions love to sleep a LOT!
That's just what lions do.

Big Book of Phonics Rhymes and Poems, page 32

212B

 OBJECTIVES

Children will:

- identify and use /l/ *L, l*
- write the letters *L,l*

MATERIALS

- letter cards and picture cards from the Word Building Book

TEACHING TIP

INSTRUCTIONAL To help children learn to distinguish between making the /l/ sound of initial *l* and the /r/ sound of intitial *r*, model the two sounds and describe how your mouth and tongue change position. Have children say *la la la* and then *rah rah rah*, and notice their mouths and tongues.

ALTERNATE TEACHING STRATEGY

INITIAL /l/

For a different approach to teaching this skill, see page T31.

▶ **Visual/Auditory/ Kinesthetic**

Review Initial /l/ *l*

TEACH

Identify and Use /l/ *L,l* Tell children they will review the sound /l/ and letters *L,l*. Write the letters on the chalkboard and have children repeat the /l/ sound. Say "Stop! Look! Listen!" and ask children to repeat the two words that begin with *l*. Then say the following sentence, asking children to hold up their hands in a Stop! gesture when they hear a word that begins with *l*: "Look at that lizard in Lee's jar."

Write *L,l* Display the letters *L,l* and have children trace them in the air with their fingers. Then ask them to write *L,l* on self-stick notes and use them to label pictures of things that begin with *l*, such as: *ladybug, lips, ladder, lamp, leaf, lion.*

PRACTICE

Complete the Pupil Edition Page Read the directions on page 212 of the Pupil Edition, make sure children clearly understand what they are being asked to do. Identify each picture, and complete the first item together. Then work through the page with children, or have them complete the page independently.

ASSESS/CLOSE

Identify and Use *L,l* Say the following list of words, and have children clap when they hear a word that begins with the letter *l*: *lap, mop, Kim, Lou, log, dog.*

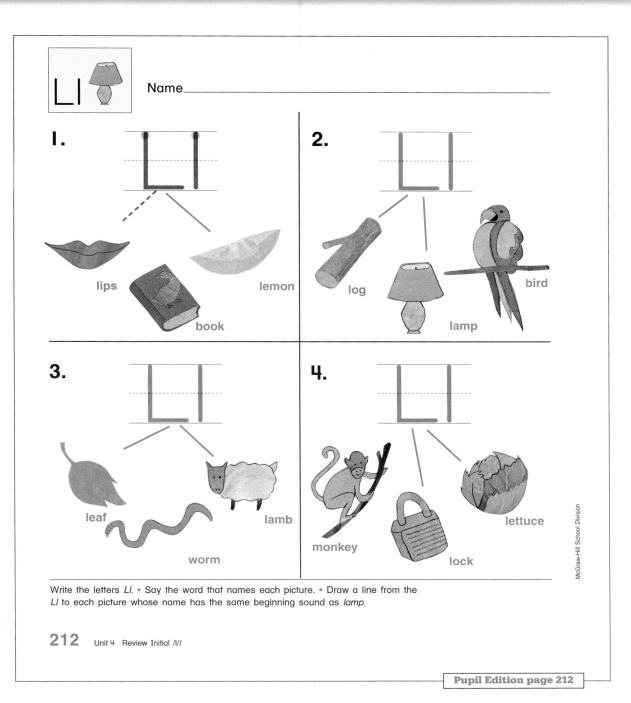

LI

Name

1.
LI
lips
book
lemon

2.
LI
log
lamp
bird

3.
LI
leaf
worm
lamb

4.
LI
monkey
lock
lettuce

McGraw-Hill School Division

Write the letters *Ll*. • Say the word that names each picture. • Draw a line from the *Ll* to each picture whose name has the same beginning sound as *lamp*.

212   Unit 4   Review Initial /l/

Pupil Edition page 212

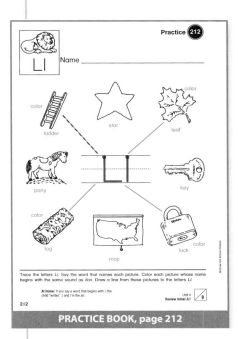

ADDITIONAL PHONICS RESOURCES

Practice Book, *page 212*
Phonics Workbook

McGraw-Hill School
TECHNOLOGY

Phonics **CD-ROM**
Activities for practice with Initial Letters

Practice **212**

LI   Name

color
color
color
ladder
star
leaf
pony
LI
key
color
log
map
lock
color

Trace the letters *Ll*. Say the word that names each picture. Color each picture whose name begins with the same sound as *lion*. Draw a line from these pictures to the letters *Ll*.

At Home: If you say a word that begins with *l*, the child "writes" *L* and *l* in the air.

212

Unit 4
Review Initial /l/   9

PRACTICE BOOK, page 212

Meeting Individual Needs for Phonics

EASY	ON-LEVEL	CHALLENGE	LANGUAGE SUPPORT
Write the letters *L, l* on the chalkboard and have children make the /l/ sound. Then point to parts of your body, and have children point to their body part when the word begins with /l/. Use the words *head, lips, neck, leg, hand.*	**Place** CVC word cards on the chalkboard ledge, choosing an equal number of words that begin with *l* and do not begin with *l*. Read the words aloud. Ask children to sort the words by placing the words that begin with *l* on the left, and the rest of the words on the right.	**Ask** children to search for letters *L* and *l* in newspapers and magazines. Have them cut out some of the letters and paste them on a sheet of paper. Ask children to use the letters to write a list of words that start with *L*.	**Sing** with children the song "Mary Had a Little Lamb." Ask them to join in with you on the repeated phrase *little lamb* as you emphasize the /l/ sound at the beginning of these words. Show pictures of *lambs* and other animals whose names begin with *l: lion, lizard, ladybug.*

212

- recognize words with initial /l/
- recognize the main idea of a story

SHELLEY ROTNER is a photographer and writer whose photographs have appeared in many magazines, including *National Geographic*. She also travels with UNICEF, documenting programs that deal with families and children.

KEN KREISLER is a writer who also has worked as a fisherman, a professor, and a yacht captain. He lives in Manhattan.

TEACHING TIP

INSTRUCTIONAL If possible, take children for a walk outside to collect objects from the natural world. If this is not practical, you may wish to collect the items yourself.

Read the Big Book

Before Reading

Build Background

EVALUATE PRIOR KNOWLEDGE Display a twig or a leaf and ask where it came from. Talk about other things from nature that children can find outside.

Make a Nature Tray Invite children to place on a tray something that they have found outside. Ask children to sit in a circle and place the tray in the middle of the circle. Have children take turns naming an item and describing one attribute about it, such as color, shape, or weight. Then ask children to take their item from the tray and look at it closely. Children can describe something different about the item from looking at it closely.

Preview and Predict

DISCUSS AUTHOR AND ILLUSTRATOR Display the Big Book cover, read the title, and read the author's name. Discuss what it means to spy. Share some background information about the authors and the photographer. Point out that two people worked together to write the story. Shelley Rotner also took the photographs.

TAKE A PICTURE WALK Ask children to describe what the girl on the cover is doing. Then take a picture walk through several pages of the book. Decide whether the story could really happen, or is a fantasy.

MAKE PREDICTIONS Ask children to make predictions about what will happen in the story.

My mother says I'm a curious kid. She calls me a nature spy.

10

Sometimes I look so closely, I can see the lines on a shiny green leaf.

11

Nature Spy, pages 10–11

During Reading

Read Together

- Before you begin to read, point to the first word in the first sentence. Explain that this is where you will begin to read. Continue to track print as you read the story. *Tracking Print*

- Review the /l/ sound. Then reread page 7 and ask children to say two words that begin with that sound. (like, look) *Phonics and Decoding*

- Invite children to look at the pictures of the leaves on page 11. Ask children to describe what they see. *Use Illustrations*

- After you have read the story, ask children to name the important idea that the writers wanted to share. (You can see new things if you look closely at nature.) *Understand Main Idea*

After Reading

Return to Predictions and Purposes

Return to the predictions that children made. Note if their questions were answered. Ask if any of the items on the classroom nature tray were seen in the book.

Literary Response

JOURNAL WRITING Invite children to draw a picture of something from the book or the nature tray. Have them write about it.

ORAL RESPONSE Then ask children to describe their item from nature. Ask questions such as:

- *What does the item look like?*

- *How does this item look different when you look at it close-up?*

UNDERSTAND THE MAIN IDEA

HOW TO ASSESS Pair children and ask them to tell their partner what this book is about. Walk around and listen to responses.

FOLLOW-UP Read other science books aloud. Have children share how the books are similar.

Cross Curricular: Science

NATURE CLOSE-UP Use the items from the classroom nature tray and set up a classifying project. Have children sort by color, weight, and size. Draw pictures or write sorting attributes on index cards. Use trays or paper plates for the different groups.

You may also wish to provide a magnifying glass. Invite children to look closely at the items and describe or draw what they see.

OBJECTIVES

Children will:

- use the main idea to understand a story

MATERIALS

- *Nature Spy*

TEACHING TIP

INSTRUCTIONAL Invite children to be "nature spies" at home. Have children explore their backyard, a park, or other nature setting. Have them draw a picture of what they see and report on their findings.

Review Main Idea

PREPARE

Take a Picture Walk

Ask children to recall the story *Nature Spy*. Take a picture walk through the book, having children describe some of their favorite parts of the story. Explain that children are describing *details* in the story.

TEACH

Understanding the Main Idea

Explain to children that the main idea of the story names the important idea that the writers wanted to share. After you take a picture walk, have children state the main idea of the story. Write down their ideas. Then restate the main idea clearly.

PRACTICE

Complete the Pupil Edition Page

Read the directions on page 213 to the children, and make sure they clearly understand what they are being asked to do. Identify each picture, and complete the first item together. Then work through the page with children, or have them complete the page independently.

ASSESS/CLOSE

Review the Page

Review children's work, and note children who are experiencing difficulty.

Name _____

1.  Dan can pat the cat.

Pam can pat the cat.

2.  The cap is on the cot.

Ron is on the cot.

3.  The pan and the pot are tan.

The can is on the pan.

Look at each picture. • Then read the sentences. • Draw a line under the sentence that tells what the picture is all about.

Pupil Edition, page 213

ALTERNATE TEACHING
STRATEGY
....
MAIN IDEA
For a different approach to teaching this skill, see page T26.
▶ **Visual/Auditory/ Kinesthetic**

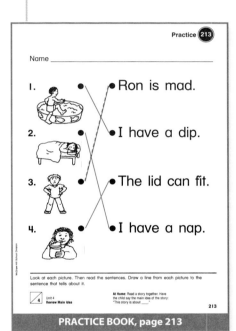

Practice 213

Name _____

1. • • Ron is mad.

2. • • I have a dip.

3. • • The lid can fit.

4. • • I have a nap.

Look at each picture. Then read the sentences. Draw a line from each picture to the sentence that tells about it.

Unit 4
Review Main Idea

At Home: Read a story together. Have the child say the main idea of the story: "This story is about ____."

213

PRACTICE BOOK, page 213

Meeting Individual Needs for Comprehension

EASY	ON-LEVEL	CHALLENGE	LANGUAGE SUPPORT
Help children focus on the main idea of *Nature Spy* by asking: *What is the story mainly about?* Then state the main idea. Have children draw a picture of what the story is about.	**Have** children reread stories from their Pupil Edition. Then have them draw a picture of the story and share the main idea of the story with the class.	**Provide** several main idea story starters, such as: *We got a new puppy. The Tigers won the basketball game.* Groups of children work together to illustrate a short class story. Children can dictate text to you.	**Read** short, simple stories to the children. Then help them state the main idea. If children focus on details, ask: *Does ____ tell us what the story is about, or tell us something about the story?*

Develop Phonological Awareness

Listen

The Lazy Little Lion
a poem

Pease Porridge Hot
a poem

The lazy little lion likes
To rest and lie around.
He likes to lounge
In piles of leaves
Or sprawl out on the
    ground.
The lazy little lion naps
With other lions, too.
Lions love to sleep a LOT!
That's just what lions do.

Pease porridge hot,
Pease porridge cold,
Pease porridge in the pot,
Nine days old.
Some like it hot,
Some like it cold,
Some like it in the pot,
Nine days old.

Big Book of Phonics Rhymes and Poems, pages 32, 41

Objective: Focus on Sentences

READ THE POEM Read the poem "The Lazy Little Lion." Invite children to name one thing the lazy little lion likes to do. Repeat children's response in a complete sentence. Explain that a sentence tells a complete thought or idea.

> The lazy little lion likes to sleep.

LISTEN FOR SENTENCES Read the poem, sentence by sentence. Have children listen carefully, clapping each time you come to the end of a sentence.

CREATING A SENTENCE Pantomime an activity that you like to do and then make up a sentence that tells about your activity. Invite children to take turns acting out what they like to do. Have others in the group say a sentence that tells what the child likes to do.

> He likes to swim.

Objective: Listen for /l/ and /p/

LISTEN FOR INITIAL /L/ Read the poem "The Lazy Little Lion," stressing words with the initial /l/ sound. Reread the poem and have children lift a leg if they hear /l/ at the beginning of a word.

NAME WORDS WITH INITIAL /L/ Have children listen as you sing the following to the tune of "Are You Sleeping."

> **Are you sleeping?**
> **Are you sleeping?**
> **Lazy lion, Lazy lion?**
> **Wake up! Let's name an /l/ word.**
> **Wake up! Let's name an /l/ word.**
> **/l/ /l/ /l/ /l/ /l/ /l/**

Invite children to join in the song and help the lion by naming words that begin with /l/.

LISTEN FOR INITIAL /P/ Read the poem "Pease Porridge Hot," stressing words with the initial /p/ sound. Have children repeat the words with you.

POP FOR /P/ Ask children to put their heads down. Then say words aloud, and have children pop their heads up when they hear a word that ends with /p/.

> mop   cap   bat   stop
> wig   dip   cup

Read Together

From Phonemic Awareness to Phonics

Objective: Identify /l/ L, l and /p/ P, p

IDENTIFY THE LETTERS Display the Big Book of Phonics Rhymes and Poems, pages 32 and 41. On each page, point to the letters, identify them, and say the sound they stand for.

REREAD THE POEMS Reread the poems, tracking the print and the words with initial /p/ or final /p/.

FIND WORDS WITH L, l, P, p Have children place self-stick notes under the words in the poems that have L, l, P, or p.

Ll

The Lazy Little Lion

The lazy little lion likes
To rest and lie around.
He likes to lounge
In piles of leaves
Or sprawl out on the ground.

The lazy little lion naps
With other lions, too.
Lions love to sleep a LOT!
That's just what lions do.

Pease Porridge Hot

Pease porridge hot,
Pease porridge cold,
Pease porridge in the pot,
Nine days old.
Some like it hot,
Some like it cold,
Some like it in the pot,
Nine days old.

Big Book of Phonics Rhymes and Poems, pages 32, 41

214B

OBJECTIVES

Children will:

- identify and discriminate between /l/ *L,l* and /p/ *P,p*
- write and use letters *L,l* and *P,p*

....

MATERIALS

- letter cards from the Word Building Book

TEACHING **TIP**

INSTRUCTIONAL Have children examine several tactile models of the two forms of *l* and *p*. Ask children to notice how the lowercase forms are similar to and different from the capital forms of the same letter.

ALTERNATE TEACHING **STRATEGY**

....

LETTERS /l/l AND /p/p

For a different approach to teaching this skill, see page T28, T31.

▶ **Visual/Auditory/ Kinesthetic**

Review /l/l, /p/p

TEACH

Identify and Discriminate Between /l/ *L,l* and /p/ *P,p*

Tell children they will review the sounds /l/ and /p/ at the beginning of words, and write letters *L, l, P,* and *p*. Write the letters, identify them, and have children say the sounds with you. Ask them to clap if they hear a word that begins with *p,* and say: *Pack pink lemonade in the picnic lunch.* Repeat for words that begin with *l.*

Write and Use *L,l* and *P,p*

Write the two forms of *l* and *p* on two sections of the chalkboard. Write the sentence you read, then repeat it as you track print with your hand. Have children point to the appropriate section of the chalkboard when they recognize an initial *l* or *p* word. Write the words as a list, then have children write *l* or *p* to match each first letter they recognize in the words of the sentence.

PRACTICE

Complete the Pupil Edition Page

Read the directions on page 214 to the children, and make sure they clearly understand what they are being asked to do. Identify each picture, and complete the first item together. Then work through the page with children, or have them complete the page independently.

ASSESS/CLOSE

Identify and Use *L,l* and *P, p*

Say the following, and have children hold up their *l* or *p* letter cards when they hear a word that begins with /l/ or /p/: *Pat has a little pet lamb.*

Name_____

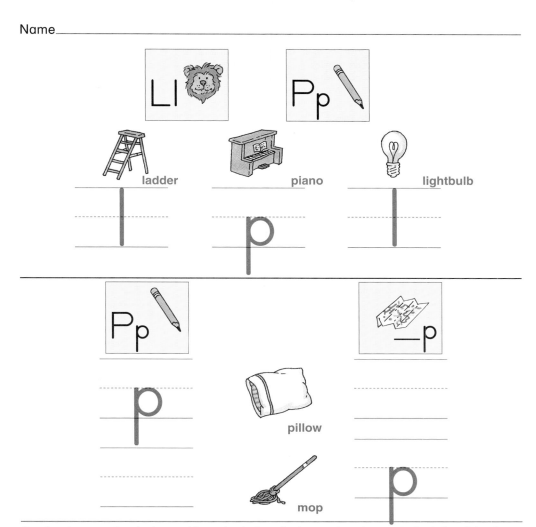

ladder   piano   lightbulb

pillow

mop

Top: Say the name of each picture. • Then write the letter for the sound you hear at the beginning of the picture name. • Bottom: Say the name of each picture. • If it begins with the sound /p/, write *p* to the left of the picture. • If it ends with the sound /p/, write *p* to the right of the picture.

McGraw-Hill School Division

214   Unit 4   Review /l/, /p/*p*

Pupil Edition, page 214

PRACTICE BOOK, page 214

Meeting Individual Needs for Phonics

EASY	ON-LEVEL	CHALLENGE	LANGUAGE SUPPORT
Give each child the letter cards for *P, p, L, l*. Write three of the letters on the chalkboard, and ask children to hold up the card that has the missing letter and form. Repeat with other arrangements. Ask children to think of a word for each letter.	**On** the chalkboard, write the sentence you read in Assess/ Close. Read it aloud. Give children letter cards for *P, p, L,* and *l*. Have them place the cards to show the same arrangement of *p*s and *l*s. Repeat with *Pat has a little pet lamb.*	**Children** can play "I've Got Something in My Backpack That Starts with *l*." Have children sit in a circle, and ask them to think of an object—any sort of object— whose name begins with /l/. Continue the game with objects whose names begin with *p*.	**Provide** more opportunities for ESL children to learn initial *p* and *l* words that are commonly used. Read aloud a few paragraphs of a picture book, and invite children to hold up *p* and *l* letter cards when they hear words that begin with the sounds /p/ and /l/.

Teacher Read Aloud

Listen

The Clever Turtle

A Hispanic folk tale
retold by Margaret H. Lippert

Wheet-weedle-whoo, wheet-weedle-whoo, wheet-wheet-wheet-whoo. Every day, Turtle sat by the Amazon River and played her flute. All the birds and animals loved to listen to her play.

One day, a man walking through the forest heard her beautiful music. Wheet-weedle-whoo, wheet-weedle-whoo, wheet-wheet-wheet-whoo.

He stopped to listen. When he saw that a turtle was playing the flute, he thought about dinner.

"Turtle soup would be a treat tonight," he thought. So he picked Turtle up and carried her home.

He put Turtle into a cage made of branches and closed the lid. "Don't let the turtle out of the cage," he said to his children. "Tonight we will have turtle soup." Then the father picked up his hoe and went to work in the garden. The children played in the yard.

Turtle did not want to be made into soup. She started to play her flute. Wheet-weedle-whoo, wheet-weedle-whoo, wheet-wheet-wheet-whoo. The children stopped their game and listened.

Continued on page T4

Oral Comprehension

LISTENING AND SPEAKING Ask children if they can recall any stories where characters tricked each other. Tell children that you will read a folk tale about a turtle who tricks a family. Explain that the story is a Hispanic folk tale. A folk tale is a story that people tell to their families and friends.

After you finish the story, ask: *How is a turtle like a rock? How is it different?* You may wish to make a list of children's responses to compare and contrast.

Activity Ask children to draw a picture of the man looking for the clever turtle. Ask them if they think the man ever found the turtle or if they think the turtle got away. Tell them to include their responses in their drawings.

▶ Spatial

Real-Life Reading

Can you find the clever turtle?

BIG BOOK OF
REAL LIFE READING

Big Book of Real-Life Reading, pages 28–29

Objective: Read a Map

READ THE PAGE Talk about how children can use pictures and maps to find things. Remind children of the folk tale they heard, "The Clever Turtle." Have children retell the story. Explain that children will see a picture and will give directions to find the turtle. Then discuss the picture. Identify the house, the forest, and the bank of the river.

ANSWER THE QUESTION Invite children to look for the turtle in the picture. Then read the question, and point to the picture of the man. Ask: *How can you give the man directions to find the turtle? Where should he walk? Should he turn left or right?* Ask volunteers to use their fingers to follow a path that children describe.

CULTURAL PERSPECTIVES

CAMOUFLAGE Explain that turtles live in most parts of the world. In many countries in Asia, Europe, and Latin America, turtle soup is considered a special meal. Turtles use their shells to hide from their enemies by blending into their environment.

Activity Provide circles of white paper, small pencils, and markers. Have children draw on their paper circles using several different colors. Push the small pencil through the center of the paper circle. Have children spin the circle on the pencil point. Elicit from children that the colors blur and blend together.

▶ **Kinesthetic**

215B

TESTED OBJECTIVES

Children will:

- identify and read the high-frequency word *go*

MATERIALS

- word cards from the Word Building Book

TEACHING TIP

INSTRUCTIONAL Show children the positions of the mouth when saying the word *go*. Invite children to say words that rhyme with *go*. Encourage them to say as many words as possible.

Introduce High-Frequency Words: *go*

PREPARE

Listen to Words

Explain to the children that they will be learning a new word: *go*. Say the following sentence: *Go to the mat*. Say the sentence again, and ask children to raise a finger when they hear the word *go*. Repeat with the sentence: *Let's go to the zoo*.

TEACH

Model Reading the Word in Context

Give a word card to each child, and read the word. Reread the sentences, and have children raise their hands when they hear the word.

Identify the Word

Write the sentences above on the chalkboard. Track print and read each sentence. Children hold up their word cards when they hear the word *go*. Then ask volunteers to point to and underline the word *go* in the sentences.

PRACTICE

Complete the Pupil Edition Page

Read the directions on page 215 to the children, and make sure they clearly understand what they are being asked to do. Complete the first item together. Then work through the page with children, or have them complete the page independently.

ASSESS/CLOSE

Review the Page

Review children's work, and note children who are experiencing difficulty or need additional practice.

Name_____

go

1.

"Go to Dad," said Mom to the cat.

2.

"Go to Pam," said Dad to the cat.

3.

"We can go to the cot," said Pam.

4.

"We can go and nap," said Pam.

Read the sentence. • Draw a line under the word *go* in the sentence.

Unit 4   Introduce High-Frequency Words: *go*   215

ALTERNATE TEACHING
STRATEGY
....

HIGH-FREQUENCY
WORD: *go*

**For a different approach to
teaching this skill, see page T27.**

▶ **Visual/Auditory/
Kinesthetic**

Practice 215

Name _____

1. "Can we go in?"
said Dan.

2. "We can go in."
said Mom.

3. "Can the cat go in?"
said Pam.

4. "The cat can go in,"
said Mom.

Read each sentence. Draw a line under the word *go* in each sentence.

4 Unit 4
Introduce High-Frequency Words: *go*   **At Home:** Use *go* in questions and
answers, such as *Can I go to the park?
You can go to the park.*   215

PRACTICE BOOK, page 215

Meeting Individual Needs for Vocabulary

EASY	ON-LEVEL	CHALLENGE	LANGUAGE SUPPORT
Give each child the word card for *go*. Then give children directions that use the word: *Please go to the front of the room. Go to the reading corner.* Children hold up the word card and follow your directions.	**Invite** children to retell the story "The Clever Turtle." Write the following sentence on drawing paper: *You let the turtle go.* Children circle the word *go* and draw a picture to illustrate that part of the story.	**Write** the following words on chart paper: *go, got, so, go, to, goes, do, go, gob.* Children circle the word *go* and count the number of words that they find.	**Draw** three vertical circles to represent a traffic light. Have volunteers color them red, yellow, and green. Children point to the green circle and say *go*.

215

Develop Phonological Awareness

Listen

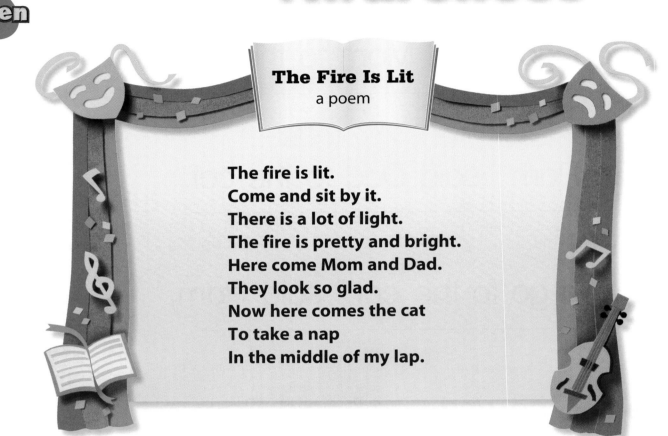

The Fire Is Lit
a poem

The fire is lit.
Come and sit by it.
There is a lot of light.
The fire is pretty and bright.
Here come Mom and Dad.
They look so glad.
Now here comes the cat
To take a nap
In the middle of my lap.

Objective: Focus on Context

READ THE POEM Read the poem "The Fire Is Lit." Ask children to name the images that come to mind when they hear the poem.

LISTEN FOR DESCRIBING WORDS Read the poem again. This time, ask children to listen for words that describe the fire. After reading, ask children what they know about the fire.

> a lot of light
> pretty and bright

OMIT A WORD Tell children you will read the first line of the poem and leave out a word. Then say: *The fire is___*. Ask children to suggest a word, not the one already in the poem, to fill the blank. Continue with other lines.

> Come and _____ by it.
> There is a lot of _____.
> The fire is _____ and bright.

Objective: Listen for Blending with Short *a, i, o*

LISTEN FOR THE SEGMENTED WORD Ask children to listen carefully as you read the first line of the poem. Tell them you will say one word louder than the others. Say the word *lit* in a loud voice: /l/-/i/-/t/.

BLEND WITH A WORD CHANT Teach children a chant about the word *lit.* As you say the following chant, invite children to fill in the blank:

It begins with /l/.
It ends with /it/.
Put them all together
And they say _____.

Repeat the chant with *lot* and *lap.*

> /l/-/it/ /l/-/ap/ /l/-/ot/

MORE BLENDING WITH THE WORD CHANT Use the chant to help children blend other short *a, i,* and *o* words that begin with *l,* such as: *lad, lab, lip, lid, lob,* and *log.*

lap!

Read Together

From Phonemic Awareness to Phonics

Objective: Associate Sounds with Letters

BRAINSTORM SHORT a AND i WORDS THAT BEGIN WITH /l/ Write *lot* and *lap* on the chalkboard. Help children brainstorm a variety of three-letter short *o* and *a* words that begin with /l/. Write the words in two columns on the chalkboard.

> lot lap
> lob lad
> log lab

REPEAT DISTINCT SOUNDS Read each listed word. Explain that each word has three letters. Invite children to repeat after you as you reread the list and stretch out each word to say the distinct sounds. Then name all the letters in each word.

PASTA WORDS Give each child pieces of dry spaghetti, a piece of construction paper, and glue. Invite children to use the pasta pieces to form the letters of a word on the list. Have children glue the pasta pieces to construction paper,

then trace over the letters and say the sound each letter stands for. Children can trade papers to "sound out" classmates' words.

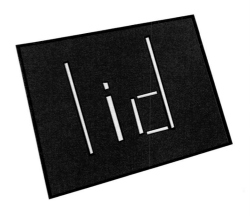

OBJECTIVES

Children will:

- identify /a/*a*, /i/*i*, and /o/*o*
- blend and read short *a, i,* and *o* words
- write short *a, i,* and *o* words
- review /l/*l*

MATERIALS

- **letter cards from the Word Building Book**

TEACHING TIP

INSTRUCTIONAL Write the words *sit, sad, sip,* and *sap* on the chalkboard. Have children use their letter cards to make the same words. Then ask children to remove the initial *s* from the words and substitute the letter *l*. Have children read the new words.

ALTERNATE TEACHING STRATEGY

BLENDING SHORT *a, i, o*

For a different approach to teaching this skill, see Unit 1, page T32; Unit 2, page T32; Unit 3, page T30.

▶ **Visual/Auditory/ Kinesthetic**

216C *Nap in a Lap*

Review Blending with short *a, i, o*

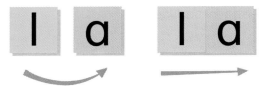

TEACH

Identify *a, i, o* as the Symbols for /a/, /i/, /o/

Tell children they will continue to read words with *a, i, o.*

- Display the *a* letter card and say /a/. Have children repeat the sound /a/.

BLENDING Model and Guide Practice

- Place the *l* letter card before the *a* card. Blend the sounds together and have children repeat after you.

- Place a *p* card after *a*. Blend the sounds to read *lap.*

Use the Word in Context

- Ask: *What part of your body disappears when you stand up?* (your lap). Invite children to make their laps disappear and reappear.

Repeat the Procedure

- Use the following words to continue modeling and for guided practice with short *a, i, o: lit, lid, lad, lip, lot, Lin.*

PRACTICE

Complete the Pupil Edition Page

Read aloud the directions on page 216. Identify each picture, and complete the first item together. Then work through the page with children, or have them complete the page independently.

ASSESS/CLOSE

Write Short *a, i, o* Words

Observe children as they complete page 216. Then have each child write one word that begins with *l;* uses a medial short *a, i,* or *o;* and ends with *p, t, d,* or *n.*

Name_____

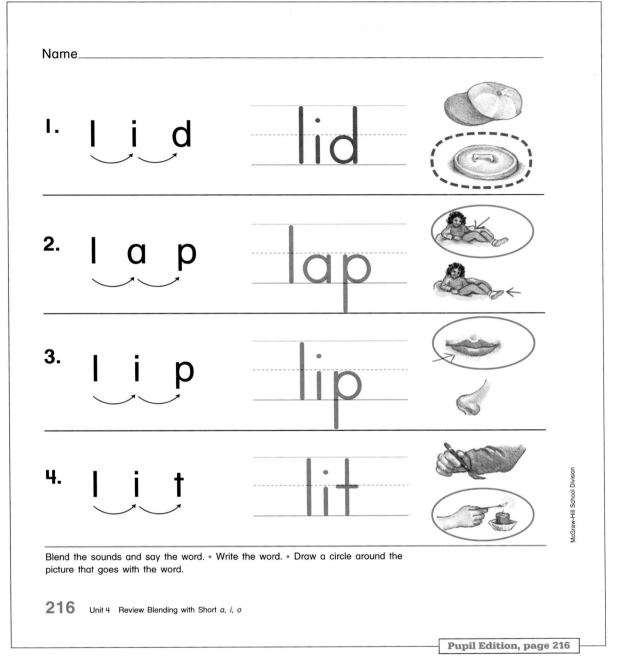

1. l i d   lid

2. l a p   lap

3. l i p   lip

4. l i t   lit

Blend the sounds and say the word. • Write the word. • Draw a circle around the picture that goes with the word.

216   Unit 4   Review Blending with Short *a, i, o*

McGraw-Hill School Division

Pupil Edition, page 216

ADDITIONAL PHONICS RESOURCES

Practice Book, *page 216*
Phonics Workbook

McGraw-Hill School
TECHNOLOGY

Phonics CD-ROM
Activities for practice with
Blending and Segmenting

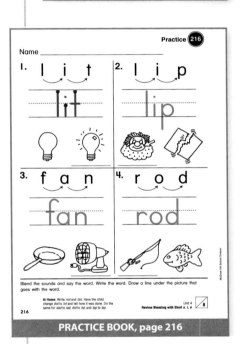

PRACTICE BOOK, page 216

Meeting Individual Needs for Phonics

EASY	ON-LEVEL	CHALLENGE	LANGUAGE SUPPORT
Ask children to name and then sort the following pictures into two groups showing things whose names begin with /l/ or /p/: *lip, pan (pot), lid, lad, pad, pin*. Blend the sounds of each word together to read it aloud with children.	**Write** the following list of words on the chalkboard: *lit, lid, lap, lad, lip, Lin*. Ask riddles that children can answer using one of the words, such as: *it's a name* (Lin); *it's next to your teeth* (lip); *another word for boy* (lad). Ask children to write each word.	**Write** *l__t* on one side of the chalkboard and *a, i, o* on the other side. Ask children to use the corresponding letter cards to complete a word, then ask them to use the word in a sentence. Continue with these incomplete words: *l_t, l_d, L_n*.	**Begin** a chart listing CVC names children can read and write, and revisit each time children add a consonant or vowel to their repertoire.

216

Guided Instruction

BEFORE READING

PREVIEW AND PREDICT Take a brief **picture walk** through the book, focusing on the illustrations.

- Who is the story about? Where does the story take place?

- What do you think will happen in the story?

- Do you think the story will be realistic, or will it be make-believe? Why?

SET PURPOSES Have children brainstorm ideas as to what might happen in the story. Have them guess which character will be the main character in the story.

TEACHING TIP

To put book together:
1. Tear out the story page.
2. Cut along dotted line.
3. Fold each section on fold line.
4. Assemble book.

INSTRUCTIONAL Use this story to talk about "fair shares." Show two crackers and ask how three children could share fairly. Elicit creative responses.

Nap in a Lap

"Nat, go to the mat and nap," said Mom.

3

"Ron, go to the mat and nap," said Mom.

2

"Can I nap?" said Lin.

4

Guided Instruction

DURING READING

☑ **Initial /**
☑ **Main Idea**
☑ **Concepts of Print**
☑ **High-Frequency Words:** *go*

(1) CONCEPTS OF PRINT Help children with the return sweep on pages 2 and 3. Model how to run your finger from left to right under each word as you read.

(2) HIGH-FREQUENCY WORDS Point to the word *go* on page 2. Help children read it and track print.

(3) USE ILLUSTRATIONS Look at the picture on page 3. Ask children why they think Mom is pointing to the mat.

(4) CONCEPTS OF PRINT Have children identify the question mark on page 4. Explain that this type of punctuation is used when a question is being asked. Ask children who is asking the question. (Lin)

LANGUAGE SUPPORT

ESL Explain that *nap* means "to take a nap." A *nap* is a short sleep, usually in the middle of the day. Relate this to the children's own experiences in taking naps.

Guided Instruction

DURING READING

5 **INITIAL *I*** Ask children what word on page 5 begins with *I*. *(Lin)* Ask why the letter is capital. *(It is a name.)*

6 **CONCEPTS OF PRINT** After you read the sentence on page 6 together, ask if the sentence tells or asks. Have children frame the question mark.

7 **MAKE PREDICTIONS** After children have read page 7, ask them what they think will happen next. Encourage creative responses.

8 **MAIN IDEA** After children read the story, ask what the most important idea of the story is about. *(children who are looking for a place to nap)*

MAIN IDEA

HOW TO ASSESS Have children summarize the action of the story. Have pairs of children work together if some children have difficulty remembering the story. You may wish to ask children to use the pictures in their book to aid their recall.

FOLLOW UP Have children draw pictures on cards to show the most important parts of the story. Have children mix up the cards and then have other children put them in the correct order.

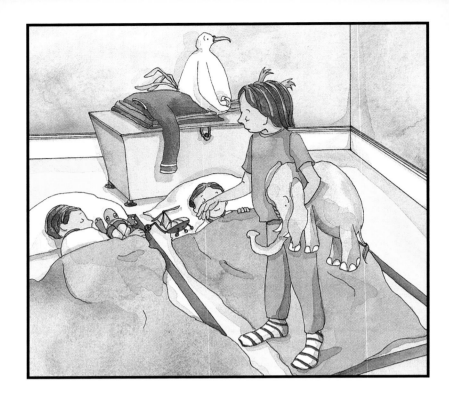

Lin ran to the mat.

5

Lin ran to Mom.

7

"Can I have a mat?"
said Lin.

6

"You can nap in my lap,"
said Mom.

8

Guided Instruction

AFTER READING

RETURN TO PREDICTIONS AND PURPOSES
Ask children if their predictions about the story were correct. Ask if their questions were answered, and revisit the story if necessary.

RETELL THE STORY As a class, have children retell the story. Have children refer to the story to check sequence of story events, if necessary.

LITERARY RESPONSE Ask children to draw and write a different ending for the story. Then invite small groups to act out the story for others. Use mats from the classroom, if they are available.

OBJECTIVES

Children will:

- recognize the main idea to understand a story

MATERIALS

- *Nap in a Lap*

TEACHING TIP

INSTRUCTIONAL Help children notice the rhyming words in the title. Ask the class to think of other places where children can take naps. Encourage both rhyming and non-rhyming responses.

Review Main Idea

PREPARE

Recall the Story
Ask children to recall the story *Nap in a Lap.* Ask children who the characters are, and what Lin wants to do.

TEACH

Identify Main Idea
Reread the story together. Then ask children to tell in a few words how the story begins, what happens, and how the story ends. Explain that the main idea of a story briefly tells what the story is about.

PRACTICE

Complete the Pupil Edition Page
Read the directions on page 219 to the children, and make sure they clearly understand what they are asked to do. Identify each picture, and complete the first item together. Then work through the page with children or have them complete the page independently.

ASSESS/CLOSE

Review the Page
Review children's work, and note children who are experiencing difficulty.

Name_____

1.  Nan can sit on the cot.

   Tim and the cat have a nap.

2.  Pam can fit the lid on the pot.

   "I have a mop," said Pam.

3.  "Sit on my lap," said Mom.

   "Pat the cat," said Dad.

Look at each picture. • Then read the sentences. • Draw a line under the sentence
that tells what the picture is all about.

Pupil Edition, page 219

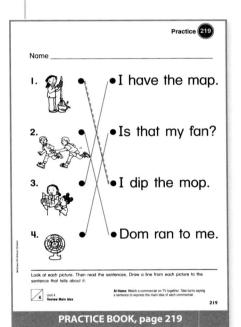

Practice 219

Name_____

1. •   •I have the map.

2. •   •Is that my fan?

3. •   •I dip the mop.

4. •   •Dom ran to me.

Look at each picture. Then read the sentences. Draw a line from each picture to the
sentence that tells about it.

At Home: Watch a commercial on TV together. Take turns saying
a sentence to express the main idea of each commercial.

Unit 4
Review Main Idea   219

PRACTICE BOOK, page 219

Meeting Individual Needs for Comprehension

EASY	ON-LEVEL	CHALLENGE	LANGUAGE SUPPORT
Reread the story together. Direct the children to what the story is mainly about by asking: *What did Lin want to do? How did the story end?*	**Help** children to recount the main idea of the story, asking how the story began and how Lin solved the problem. Then have children write a new ending to the story by asking: *What if there were three mats?*	**Brainstorm** other words that mean about the same as the word *nap,* such as *rest* or *sleep.* Reread the story, substituting one of the words for *nap.* Then ask if the main idea of the story changed.	**Ask** children where they like to nap, and role play getting ready for a nap. Have children act out the story, and then say what the main idea is.

ALTERNATE TEACHING
STRATEGY
·······································
MAIN IDEA
For a different approach to
teaching this skill, see
page T26.
▶ Visual/Auditory/
Kinesthetic

Develop Phonological Awareness

Listen

The Fire Is Lit
a poem

The fire is lit.
Come and sit by it.
There is a lot of light.
The fire is pretty and bright.
Here come Mom and Dad.
They look so glad.
Now here comes the cat
To take a nap
In the middle of my lap.

Objective: Focus on Syllables

REVISIT THE POEM Read "The Fire Is Lit." Ask children, "What will the cat do? How do Mom and Dad look?"

> **The cat will nap.**
> **Mom and Dad look glad.**

MODEL HOW TO CLAP IT OUT Model for children how to clap out the rhythm of the poem by clapping out loud and chanting the first two lines several times.

CLAP IT OUT Read the rest of the poem as children clap out rhythm with you. Before reading lines four and nine, tell children there is a word in the line that needs two claps. After reading those lines, ask children to tell you which words need two claps. (pretty, middle)

Objective: Listen for Blending Short *a, i, o*

SEGMENT A WORD Read the first line of "The Fire Is Lit." Stop reading when you get to the word *lit*. Say the word slowly to pronounce each distinct sound. Have children repeat the sounds /l/-/i/-/t/. With children, blend the word several times, speaking faster and faster each time to say *lit*.

> /l/-/i/-/t/

PLAY "STOP" Tell children you will read each line of the poem. Have them shout "Stop!" whenever they hear one of the following words: *lit, lot, lap*. After you say each of these words, stop to segment with children. Gradually, say the sounds faster and faster until you and the children have blended the sounds to say the word.

PLAY "STOP" WITH OTHER WORDS Complete the activity a second time. This time, ask children to stop you at the words *sit, glad, cat*, and *nap*.

Read Together

From Phonemic Awareness to Phonics

Objective: Associate Sounds with Letters

LISTEN FOR SOUNDS Read the first line of the poem, and ask children to identify the word with /l/ at the beginning. *(lit)* Write the word on the chalkboard. Read the third line of the poem, and ask children to identify the word with /o/ in the middle. *(lot)* Read the last line of the poem, and ask children to identify the word with /p/ at the end. *(lap)*

> lit   lot   lap

SEGMENT WORDS Explain that each of these words has three separate sounds. Help children say each word slowly, so each sound is distinct.

ASSOCIATE SOUNDS WITH LETTERS Explain that each sound in the words has a letter to match it. For the word *lit*, write ___ *it* on the chalkboard. For the word *lot*, write *l* ___ *ot* on the chalkboard. And for the word *lap*, write ___ *ap* on the board. Tape cardboard cutouts of of three *l*'snext to the partially-written words.

Ask children to choose from the letters to make the first word *lit*. When children choose the *l*, tape it on the blank and say: /l/-/i/-/t/, *lit*. Continue until *lot* and *lap* are complete.

OBJECTIVES

Children will:

- identify /a/*a*, /i/*i*, and /o/*o*
- blend and read short *a, i,* and *o* words
- write short *a, i,* and *o* words
- review /l/*l*, /p/*p*, /r/*r*, /f/*f*, /k/*c*, /t/*t*, /m/*m*, /s/*s*, /d/*d*, and /n/*n*

....

MATERIALS

- letter cards from the Word Building Book

```
┌─────────────────────────────┐
│  TEACHING TIP                │
│                              │
│  INSTRUCTIONAL Review        │
│  the difference in the initial│
│  sounds of letters l and r, by│
│  having children repeat the fol-│
│  lowing words: lid, lap, lot, rid,│
│  rap, rot. Write the words in │
│  two rows on the chalkboard  │
│  and point to each word as chil-│
│  dren repeat after you.      │
└─────────────────────────────┘
```

ALTERNATE TEACHING STRATEGY
....

BLENDING SHORT *a, i, o*

For a different approach to teaching this skill, see Unit 1, page T32; Unit 2, page T32; Unit 3, page T30.
▶ **Visual/Auditory/ Kinesthetic**

220C *Nap in a Lap*

Review Blending with short *a, i, o*

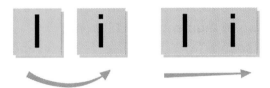

TEACH

Identify *a, i, o* as the Symbols for /a/, /i/, /o/

BLENDING Model and Guide Practice

Tell children they will continue to read words with *a, i, o.*

- Display the *i* letter card and say /i/. Have children repeat the sound /i/.
- Place the *l* card before the *i* card. Blend the sounds together and have children repeat after you.

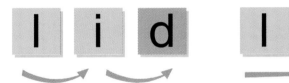

- Place a *d* card after the *i.* Blend the sounds to read *lid.*

```
  l     i d      l i d
```

Use the Word in Context

- Ask children to use the word *lid* in a sentence. You may want children to point out several lids in the classroom—on jars, cans, and so on.

Repeat the Procedure

- Use the following words to continue modeling and for guided practice with short *a, i, o: lad, lap, man, fit, dip, rod, pat.*

PRACTICE

Complete the Pupil Edition Page

Read aloud the directions on page 220. Identify each picture, and complete the first item together. Then work through the page with children, or have them complete the page independently.

ASSESS/CLOSE

Write Short *a, i,* and *o* Words

Observe children as they complete page 220. Write *l, p, t, r, s, d, n* on the chalkboard. Ask children to use the letters to write words with an *a, i,* or *o* in the middle.

Name_____

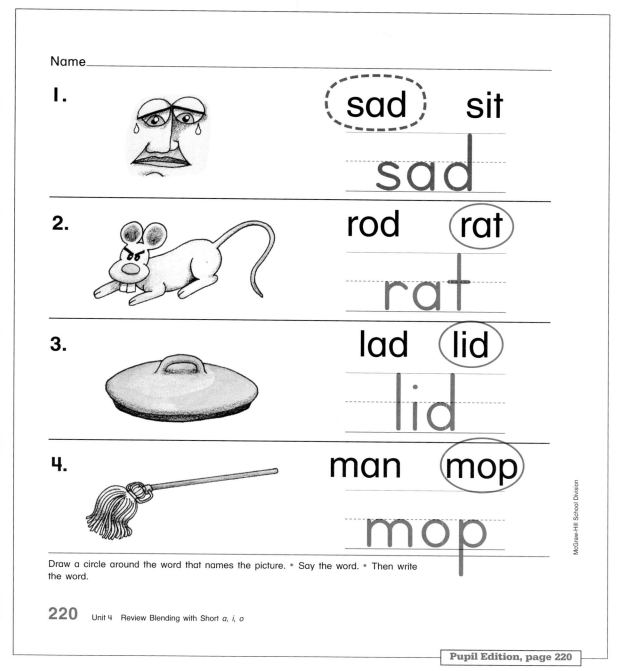

1. (sad) sit

    sad

2. rod (rat)

    rat

3. lad (lid)

    lid

4. man (mop)

    mop

Draw a circle around the word that names the picture. • Say the word. • Then write the word.

McGraw-Hill School Division

220 Unit 4 Review Blending with Short *a, i, o*

ADDITIONAL PHONICS RESOURCES

Practice Book, *page 220*
Phonics Workbook

McGraw-Hill School
TECHNOLOGY

Phonics CD-ROM
Activities for practice with Blending and Segmenting

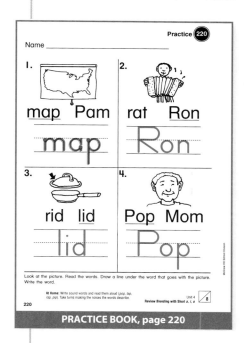

Practice **220**

Name_____

1. map Pam

   map

2. rat Ron

   Ron

3. rid lid

   lid

4. Pop Mom

   Pop

Look at the picture. Read the words. Draw a line under the word that goes with the picture. Write the word.

At Home: Write sound words and read them aloud *(pop, tap, rap, pip)*. Take turns making the noises the words describe.

220   Review Blending with Short *A, I, O*   Unit 4 / 8

PRACTICE BOOK, page 220

Meeting Individual Needs for Phonics

EASY	ON-LEVEL	CHALLENGE	LANGUAGE SUPPORT
Write *a, i, o* on three different areas of the chalkboard; then write: *lap, fit, sit, mat, tip, rip.* Ask children to point to the letter that shows the short *a, i,* or *o* sound in the middle. Then have one child read a word while another child draws a circle around it.	**On** the chalkboard write: *dip, fit, lap, sad, lid, lot.* Ask children to write the word that completes each sentence, such as: *Cats like to nap a* (lot). *Babies like to sit on a person's* (lap). *Unscrew the* (lid) *of the jar.* Have children read each word they wrote.	**Ask** children to work in groups of three and look for all the ways they can sort the following words into three groups: *pat, lap, lid, tip, tot, pod.* (initial *l, p, t;* final *p, t, d;* medial *a, o, i*)	**Help** children practice the /l/ sound at the beginning of words. Write and then blend sounds to read: *lap, lot, lip, Lin, lit.* Invite children to repeat each word with you. To reinforce meaning, ask children to use each word in a sentence.

220

Reread the Decodable Story

Nap in a Lap

- ☑ **Initial /l/ _L, l_**
- ☑ **Main Idea**
- ☑ **High-Frequency Word:** _go_
- ☑ **Concepts of Print**

Nap in a Lap

Guided Reading

SET PURPOSES Have children discuss what their purpose is for rereading the story. Children may have more questions about the story.

REREAD THE BOOK As you reread the story, keep in mind any problems children experienced during the first reading. Use the following questions to guide reading.

- **MAIN IDEA** Ask why Lin is looking sad. _(She doesn't have a place to nap.)_ Focus children's attention on pages 5 and 6 of the story if they have difficulty with this conclusion.

- **INITIAL /l/ _L, l_** Ask children to find the word on page 8 that begins with _l_. _(lap)_ Blend the sounds to read the word: _l a p lap_. Then ask what word in the sentence rhymes with _lap_. _(nap)_

- **CONCEPTS OF PRINT** Explain that if someone is speaking directly to another person, the speaker may address them and say their name first. Point out examples on pages 2 and 3. _(Ron, Nat)_

RETURN TO PURPOSES Ask children if they found out what they needed to know from the story. See if they have any unanswered questions.

LITERARY RESPONSE Ask children to write about and draw places where they like to take a nap. Have volunteers share their experiences.

INFORMAL ASSESSMENT

HIGH-FREQUENCY WORD: _go_
HOW TO ASSESS Have children identify the word _go_ throughout the story. Then ask them to make up their own sentences using the word _go_.

FOLLOW-UP For children who are having difficulty, help them to place green dots under the word _go_ so that the word can be easily identified.

Read the  Patterned Book

Let's Go!

☑ **Initial /l/**
☑ **Main Idea**
☑ **High-Frequency Word:** *go*
☑ **Concepts of Print**

by Suzanne Martinucci
illustrated by Thea Kliros

Guided Reading

PREVIEW AND PREDICT Read the title and the author's and the illustrator's name. Take a **picture walk** through pages 2–4, noting the setting of the story and the characters. Ask if they think the story will be realistic or a fantasy. Have children make predictions about what will happen in the story.

SET PURPOSES Have children decide what they want to find out from the story and predict where the children might go. Tell them that the story contains words with initial *l*.

READ THE BOOK Use the following prompts while the children are reading or after they have read independently. Remind them to run their fingers under each word as they read.

PAGES 2–3: Point to the word that begins with *g*. Let's read it together: go. *High-Frequency Words*

PAGES 4–5: Point to the word *Let's. The word Let's begins with the letter l. Who knows what sound the letter l makes?* (/l/) *Let's read the word together: Lets. Phonics and Decoding*

PAGES 6–7: *Point to page 6. Who can find a capital L on this page?* (Let's) *Who can find a lowercase l on this page?* (look, lilies) *Concepts of Print*

PAGE 8: *What is this story about?* (children who are visiting a park) *Main Idea*

RETURN TO PREDICTIONS AND PURPOSES Ask children if they found out what they needed to know from the story. See if their predictions were correct.

LITERARY RESPONSE The following questions will help focus children's responses:

• What was your favorite place in the story? Why?

• Draw and write about a park that you would like to visit.

LANGUAGE SUPPORT

 Read the story again, and have children role-play the activities that the children did. Then have pairs of children reread the story together.

CENTER Activity

Cross Curricular: Social Studies

SAFETY SIGNS Talk about safety signs that children have seen in parks and other public places. If possible, display some signs. Then have children draw posters to illustrate safety in a park. Give examples such as: Swim with an adult. Keep dogs on leashes.

OBJECTIVES

Children will:

- identify and read the high-frequency word *go*

....

MATERIALS

- word cards from the Word Building Book
- *Nap in a Lap*

+--+
| TEACHING **TIP** |
| |
| **MANAGEMENT** You may |
| wish to make a word wall with |
| high-frequency words. Children |
| will have ready access to the |
| words for their own writing. |
+--+

Review *go, to, me, you*

PREPARE

Listen to Words Explain to the children that they will review the word *go*. Ask children to say words that rhyme: *blow, slow, mow, toe, bow, no,* and so on.

TEACH

Model Reading the Word in Context Have children reread the decodable book. Ask children to listen for the word *go*.

Identify the Word Ask children to look at their word cards, and then ask them to look for the word in sentences. Have children point to the word go on each page as you read the story together. Have volunteers put a self-stick note below the word. (Have children move the self-stick note from page to page.)

Review High-Frequency Words Give each child one word card of a high-frequency word (*go, to, me, you, the, a, my, that, I, and, said, we, are, is, have*). As you say each word, a child holds up the appropriate card.

PRACTICE

Complete the Pupil Edition Page Read the directions on page 215 to the children, and make sure they clearly understand what they are being asked to do. Complete the first item together. Then work through the page with children or have them complete the page independently.

ASSESS/CLOSE

Review the Page Review children's work, and note children who are experiencing difficulty or need additional practice.

Name_____

1.

"Go to the top," said Ron.

_____

2.

"You can go," said Dad.

_____

3.

"Go," Mom said to me.

Read the sentences. Then do the following: **1.** Draw a circle around the words *go* and *to*. **2.** Draw a circle around the word *you*. **3.** Draw a circle around the word *me*.

Unit 4   Review *go, to, me, you*   **221**

Pupil Edition, page 221

ALTERNATE TEACHING
STRATEGY
·······························
HIGH-FREQUENCY
WORDS
For a different approach to teaching this skill, see page T27.
▶ **Visual/Audiory/**
   Kinesthetic

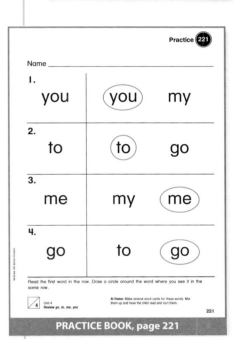

PRACTICE BOOK, page 221

Meeting Individual Needs for Vocabulary

EASY	ON-LEVEL	CHALLENGE	LANGUAGE SUPPORT
Write these sentences on chart paper and read them aloud: *Let's go to the park. Let's go home. Let's go outside.* Children circle the word *go* in each sentence. Then have children dictate their sentences to you, using the word *go*.	**Write** the following words on the chalkboard: *go, so, go, to, do, go, go, no, so, go, do.* Children circle the word *go* and read it. Then they use the word in a sentence.	**Use** empty milk cartons to make word cubes. Write the following words on each side: *go, the, me, that, go, you.* Children roll the cube, read it, and use the word in a sentence. They score a point, and take turns.	**Invite** children to help you make a picture list of places children can go. Then read the list together.

Interactive Writing

Write a Book of Riddles

**GRAMMAR/SPELLING
CONNECTIONS**
Model subject-verb
agreement, complete
sentences, and correct
tense so that students
may gain increasing con-
trol of grammar when
speaking and writing.

Prewrite

LOOK AT THE STORY PATTERN Reread
the story *Nature Spy*. Talk about the pattern
of the story: the pictures show an animal or
object from nature, and then the photographs show a closer look. Have children
help you make a list of items from nature
that interest them. Include some items that
you have available, such as a rock, leaf, or
pine cone.

Draft

MAKE A CLASS BOOK Explain that children are going to work together to make a
class book of riddles.

• Explain that you are going to write some
  clues that describe one of the items from
  the list. Choose an item that you have
  available and write simple clues:

  It is green.

  It has pointy edges.

  It is flat.

• Read the clues together as you track print,
  and ask volunteers to guess. *(The answer is
  leaf.)* Show the item, and talk about how
  the clues match.

• Have each child write three clues to
  describe an item from nature. Help as
  needed. Then have children draw the item
  on the back of their papers.

Publish

CREATE THE BOOK Bind the pages
together to make a book. Volunteers may
create a book cover.

It has petals.
It can be many colors.
It smells good.

a daisy

Presentation Ideas

GUESS THE RIDDLES Have children take turns reading their riddles and having other children guess. Help as needed.

▶ Listening/Speaking

READ WITH A PARTNER Have partners read the book together. One child can read the clues, and the partner guesses. The child who is reading can also offer other clues.

▶ Listening/Speaking

COMMUNICATION TIPS

- **Speaking** When children read, remind them to read clearly and in a voice that everyone can hear. You may wish to have children read their riddles with you before reading to the class.

TECHNOLOGY TIP

Help children use the computer to write their riddles.

LANGUAGE SUPPORT

ESL Have children find items from nature and describe them to you.

Meeting Individual Needs for Writing

EASY	ON-LEVEL	CHALLENGE
Use Pictures Use picture cards with objects from nature, and have partners give each other clues. After they guess, help the child write the answer to the riddle.	**Descriptive Words** Hold up an object from nature, and have children write as many words as possible to describe it. Count the words in the list. Repeat with another object.	**Classroom Riddles** Invite children to write riddles about classroom objects. Children write three clues, and partners guess. Help them focus on color, size, and shape.

Mud Fun

The variety of literature in this lesson will offer children opportunities to read and listen to stories about interactions and relationships in nature.

Mud Fun

Listening Library Audiocassette

Decodable Story, pages 229–230 of the Pupil Edition

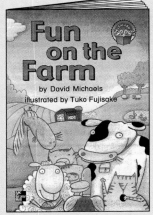

Patterned Book, page 0233B

How Many Spots Does a Leopard Have?
(An African folk tale retold by Julius Lester)

Teacher Read Aloud, page 227A

ABC Big Book, pages 223A–223B

Listening Library Audiocassette

Literature Big Book, pages 225A–225B

**Pupil Edition,
pages 222–233**

**Big Book of Real-Life Reading,
page 30**

**Big Book of Phonics Rhymes and
Poems, pages 52, 53**

 **Listening
Library
Audiocassette**

ADDITIONAL RESOURCES

**Practice Book,
pages 222–233**

- **Phonics Kit**
- **Language Support Book**
- **Alternate Teaching Strategies,**
  pages T27, T30, T32

McGraw-Hill School
TECHNOLOGY

Phonics **CD-ROM** Provides
extra phonics support.

interNET **Research & Inquiry Ideas.**
CONNECTION
Visit www.mhschool.com

Mud Fun

READING AND LANGUAGE ARTS

- **Phonological Awareness**
- **Phonics** *initial and medial /u/u*
- **Comprehension**
- **Vocabulary**
- **Beginning Reading Concepts**
- **Listening, Speaking, Viewing, Representing**

DAY 1

Allie's Adventure
From A to Z
Written by Ellen Dreyer   Illustrated by Jui Ishida

 **Phonics**

Focus on Reading Skills
Develop Phonological Awareness, 222G–222H
"Umbrellas" *Big Book of Phonics Rhymes and Poems,* 52
Introduce Initial /u/u, 222I–222
Practice Book, 222
Phonics/Phonemic Awareness Practice Book

Phonics CD-ROM

Read **Read the Literature**
Read *Allie's Adventure from A to Z* **Big Book,** 223A–223B
Shared Reading

Build Skills
☑ Up, Down, 223C–223
Practice Book, 223

DAY 2

NATURE SP
written by SHELLEY ROTNER and KEN KI
photographs by SHELLEY ROTNER

 **Phonics**

Focus on Reading Skills
Develop Phonological Awareness, 224A–224B
"Snug as a Bug" *Big Book of Phonics Rhymes and Poems,* 53
Introduce Medial /u/u, 224C–224
Practice Book, 224
Phonics/Phonemic Awareness Practice Book

Phonics CD-ROM

Read **Read the Literature**
Read *Nature Spy* **Big Book,** 225A–225B
Shared Reading

Build Skills
☑ Compare and Contrast, 225C–225
Practice Book, 225

- **Cross Curriculum**

 Activity Language Arts, 223B

 Activity Cultural Perspectives, 225B

- **Writing**

 Writing Prompt: Write your own adventure story of being on a farm.

 Journal Writing, 223B
Letter Formation, 222I

 Writing Prompt: Pick something in nature to write about.

 Journal Writing, 225B
Letter Formation, 224C

DAY 3

How Many Spots Does a Leopard Have?

Focus on Reading Skills

Develop Phonological Awareness, 226A–226B
"Umbrellas" and "Snug as a Bug" *Big Book of Phonics Rhymes and Poems,* 52–53

 **Review /u/u,** 226C–226
Practice Book, 226
Phonics/Phonemic Awareness Practice Book

 CD-ROM

Read the Literature

Read "How Many Spots Does a Leopard Have?" Teacher Read Aloud, 227A–227B
Shared Reading
Read the Big Book of Real-Life Reading, 30–31
☑ Map

Build Skills

☑ High-Frequency Word: *do*
227C–227
Practice Book, 227

 Activity Cultural Perspectives, 227B

 Writing Prompt: Do you have a favorite way to count? Write about how you do it.

DAY 4

Mud Fun

Focus on Reading Skills

Develop Phonological Awareness, 228A–228B
"A Pup Named Tom"
 **Introduce Blending with Short *u*,** 228C–228
Practice Book, 228
Phonics/Phonemic Awareness Practice Book

 **CD-ROM**

Read the Literature

 Read "Mud Fun" Decodable Story, 229/230A–229/230D

☑ Initial and Medial /u/u; Blending
☑ Compare and Contrast
☑ High-Frequency Words: *do*
☑ Concepts of Print

Build Skills

☑ Compare and Contrast, 231A–231
Practice Book, 231

 Activity Math, 229/230D

 Writing Prompt: What would you make if you were playing with mud? Write about it.

Letter Formation Practice Book, 229–230

DAY 5

Mud Fun

Focus on Reading Skills

Develop Phonological Awareness, 232A–232B
"A Pup Named Tom"
 **Review Blending with Short *u, o*,** 232C–232
Practice Book, 232
Phonics/Phonemic Awareness Practice Book

CD-ROM

Read the Literature

Reread "Mud Fun" Decodable Story, 233A
Read "Fun on the Farm" Patterned Book, 233B
Guided Reading
☑ Initial and Medial /u/u; Blending
☑ Compare and Contrast
☑ High-Frequency Word: *do*
☑ Concepts of Print

Build Skills

☑ High-Frequency Words: *do, go, I, and me,* 233C–233
Practice Book, 233

 **Activity** Math, 233B

Writing Prompt: If you could visit a farm, what animal would you most like to see? Write about it.

Interactive Writing, 234A–234B

Develop Phonological Awareness

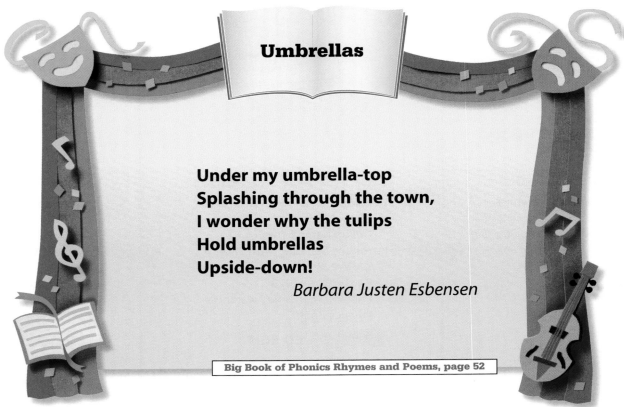

Umbrellas

Under my umbrella-top
Splashing through the town,
I wonder why the tulips
Hold umbrellas
Upside-down!

Barbara Justen Esbensen

Big Book of Phonics Rhymes and Poems, page 52

Objective: Listen for Changes in a Poem

LISTEN TO THE POEM

- Read the Poem "Umbrellas." Draw a simple tulip shape on the chalkboard, and discuss how the shape of the tulip looks like an umbrella.

- Reread the first two lines, changing the word *splashing* to *running*. Ask children which word was changed in the poem.

- Reread the first two lines again, changing *town* to *street*.

CREATE NEW WORDS

- Say the first two lines again. Then invite volunteers to think of a word to change. Others decide which word was changed.

Objective: Listen for Short /u/

SEGMENTING

- Say the word *umbrella*. Emphasize the short /u/ sound, and have children repeat it after you. Have them segment the sound.

- Then say the word *up*, and ask if the word has the same beginning sound as *umbrella*.

STAND UP FOR *U*

- Say words from the poem. Ask a volunteer to repeat the word and to determine if the word begins with short /u/. If it does, invite the child to come and stand under an open umbrella.

> under   tulips   umbrella
> hold   upside-down

From Phonemic Awareness to Phonics

Objective: Identify /u/*U, u*

IDENTIFY THE LETTER FOR THE SOUND

- Explain to children that the letters *U, u* stand for the sound /u/. Say the sound and have children say it with you.

- Display the Big Book of Phonics Rhymes and Poems, page 52. Point to the letters in the corner. Identify them, and have children say the short /u/ sound.

REREAD THE POEM

- Reread the poem. Have children say the word when they hear a word that begins with *u*.

CAN YOU FIND A *U*?

- Invite children to find the upper-case and lowercase letters in the poem. Have children frame the letter *u* with their index fingers.

Uu Umbrellas

Under my umbrella-top,
Splashing through the town,
I wonder why the tulips
Hold umbrellas
Up-side-down!

Barbara Juster Esbensen

Big Book of Phonics Rhymes and Poems, page 52

OBJECTIVES

Children will:

- identify the letters *U,u*
- identify /u/ *U,u*
- form the letters *U,u*

....

MATERIALS

- letter cards and word cards from the Word Play Book

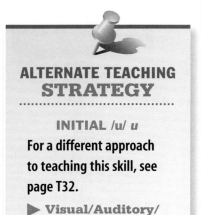

ALTERNATE TEACHING STRATEGY
....

INITIAL /u/ *u*

For a different approach to teaching this skill, see page T32.

▶ **Visual/Auditory/ Kinesthetic**

Introduce Initial /u/u

TEACH

Identify /u/ *U, u* Tell children they will learn to write the sound /u/ with the letters *U, u*. Write the letters on the chalkboard, identify them, and say the short *u* sound. Have children repeat the sound after you. Then play "Thumbs Up." Ask children to turn their thumbs up and to say "thumbs up" when they hear a word that begins with /u/. Say, for example, *up, at, under, end, ugly, us, ink.*

Form *U,u* Display letters *U,u* and, with your back to the children, trace the letters in the air with your finger. Invite children to do the same. Have children write four sets of the letters *U,u* on letter strips. Then display letter cards *N,n,* and compare the lowercase forms of *n* and *u*.

PRACTICE

Complete the Pupil Edition Page Read the directions on page 222 of the Pupil Edition, and make sure children clearly understand what they are being asked to do. Identify each picture and complete the first item together. Then work through the page with children, or have them complete the page independently.

ASSESS/CLOSE

Identify and Use *U, u* Show pictures, and ask children to identify the objects and circle a *u* on their letter strips for every object whose name begins with *u*, for example: *umbrella, nest, under, egg, up (arrow), apple.*

Name

I.

 hat

 up

 under

2.

 umpire

 cat

 umbrella

3.

 upside down

 nest

 up

4.

 newspaper

 under

 umpire

Write the letters *Uu*. • Say the word that names each picture. • Listen for the sound at the beginning of each word. • Draw a circle around each picture whose name begins with the same sound as *umbrella*.

McGraw-Hill School Division

222   Unit 4 Introduce Initial /u/u

Pupil Edition, page 222

ADDITIONAL PHONICS RESOURCES

Practice Book, *page 222*
Phonics Workbook

McGraw-Hill School
TECHNOLOGY

Phonics **CD-ROM**
Activities for practice with Initial Letters

PRACTICE BOOK, page 222

Meeting Individual Needs for Phonics

EASY	ON-LEVEL	CHALLENGE	LANGUAGE SUPPORT
Give children objects, and ask them to place them under other objects. Say, for example: *Put the pencil under the chair.* Emphasize the /u/ sound, and have children write the letter *u*.	**Ask** children to act out action words that begin with /u/: *untie, unbend, unwind, unlock.* Help them think of more action words beginning with *un-* by asking: *What do you do when you open a present?* (unwrap) *when you take off a jacket?* (unbutton or unzip)	**Have** children play "Go Upstairs." Draw a staircase on the chalkboard, and invite children to suggest initial *u* word. Each time they say a word, write in on one step or move to the next step. Children write a *u* on their letter strips for every step up.	**Give** ESL children pantomime directions, and check to see if they are having trouble with word meanings. For example: *Put the umbrella up. Look under the desk. Untie your shoes. Unwrap your sandwich. Unlock the door. Unzip your raincoat.*

222

OBJECTIVES

Children will:

- review letter identification
- recognize words with initial *u*
- make inferences

LANGUAGE SUPPORT

ESL Help children understand words that describe feelings. Have children role-play situations, such as: *What is something that makes you happy? How do you look when you are happy?* Have children smile and practice saying the word *happy*. Repeat this activity using other emotions and facial expressions.

Read the Big Book

Before Reading

Develop Oral Language Read "The Alphabet Name Game" on page 5 in the Big Book of Phonics Rhymes and Poems with children. Then have them use their first names and perform the actions to the song.

Remind children that they have read a story about a kitten named Allie. Ask them to tell how the story begins.

Set Purposes Explain to children that as they reread the story, they will think about how Allie might be feeling.

Ask questions, such as *How do you think you would feel if you were on an adventure? Name some of the different emotions you think Allie may be feeling.*

Then ask children to notice the order of the letters on the alphabet chart and the order of the highlighted words throughout the story. Ask: *What's the same?* (The words follow the ABC order.)

Allie curls up in a **sunny** spot. She is very **tired**.

Allie's Adventure from A to Z, pages 22–23

During Reading

Read Together • Before you begin to read, point to the first word in the sentence. Explain that this is where you will begin to read. Continue to track print as you read the story. *Tracking Print*

• After you read pages 2–3, ask which two letters will come next. Then turn the page and confirm. Continue as you read the story. *Phonics*

• After you read pages 6–7, ask children how Allie might be feeling and why. Continue to ask when Allie might be tired, excited, and happy. *Make Inferences*

• Make the short *u* sound and have children say it with you. After you read pages 24–25, ask which word begins with that sound. *(up) Phonics*

Zack missed Allie.

Allie's Adventure from A to Z, page 32

After Reading

Literary Response **JOURNAL WRITING** Have children draw and write about how Allie might have felt when she saw the insect.

ORAL QUESTIONS Ask questions such as:
• *How do you think Allie feels? Why?*

ABC Activity Say the letters of the alphabet slowly, stopping and omitting some letters. Children write the letters that you do not say.

CENTER Activity

Cross Curricular: Language Arts

PICTURE THIS Make simple drawings of the places Allie visited. Have children arrange the pictures to show the sequence of the story. Then have children say the letter that begins each identifying word, such as *f* for *field*.

▶ **Spatial/Logical**

OBJECTIVES

Children will:
- describe up and down

....

MATERIALS
- *Nature Spy*

TEACHING TIP

INSTRUCTIONAL Look for opportunities to use the words *up* and *down* during the day. For example, talk about going up the stairs and down the stairs. You may also want to use cut-out arrows or hand signals to show *up* and *down*.

Introduce Up, Down

PREPARE

Follow Directions
Ask children to look up, and invite them to describe what they see. Then have them look down and do the same. Talk about what they would see if they were outside.

TEACH

Identify Up and Down
Display the Big Book *Nature Spy* and recall the story. Then take a picture walk through the book, discussing illustrations that show up and down: the girl walking down the steps, the girl looking up at the tree.

PRACTICE

Find Up and Down
Read the directions on page 223 to the children, and make sure they clearly understand what they are asked to do. Identify each picture, and complete the first item. Then work through the page with children, or have them complete the page independently.

ASSESS/CLOSE

Review the Page
Check children's work on the Pupil Edition page. Note areas where children need extra help.

Name _____

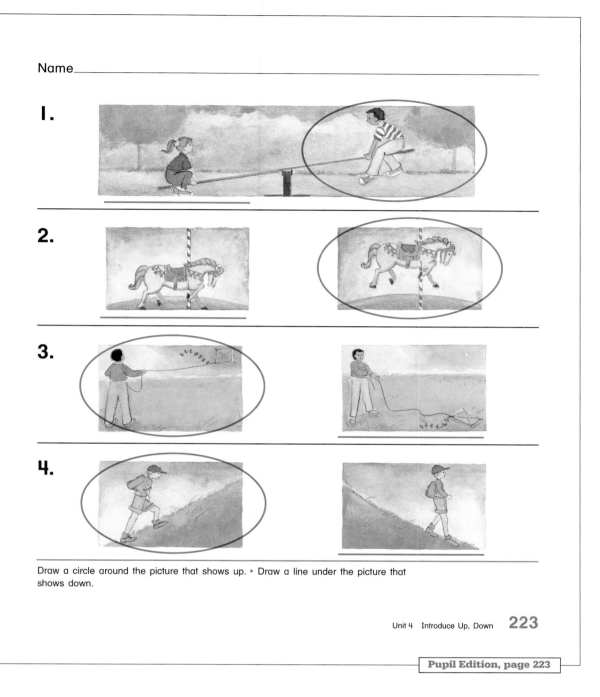

1.

2.

3.

4.

Draw a circle around the picture that shows up. • Draw a line under the picture that shows down.

Unit 4 Introduce Up, Down **223**

Pupil Edition, page 223

ALTERNATE TEACHING STRATEGY

UP, DOWN

For a different approach to teaching this skill, see page T33.

▶ **Visual/Auditory/ Kinesthetic**

PRACTICE BOOK, page 223

Meeting Individual Needs for Beginning Reading Concepts

EASY	ON-LEVEL	CHALLENGE	LANGUAGE SUPPORT
Draw a set of stairs on the chalkboard. Have children use their fingers to walk up the stairs. Ask them to use a sentence to explain what they are doing: *I am walking up the steps.* Then continue, moving down the stairs.	**Show** pictures of animals. Ask children if they would be more likely to see each animal up in the sky or down in the ground. Animals may include different types of birds and insects.	**Invite** children to pretend to be birds flying in the sky. Ask them to look down and to draw a picture of what they might see. You may wish to show some aerial-view photographs before children begin.	**Recite** the nursery rhyme "Hickory, Dickory, Dock." Children move their hands up and down to show the story. Hickory, dickory, dock. The mouse ran up the clock. The clock struck one and down he fell. Hickory, dickory, dock.

Develop Phonological Awareness

Listen

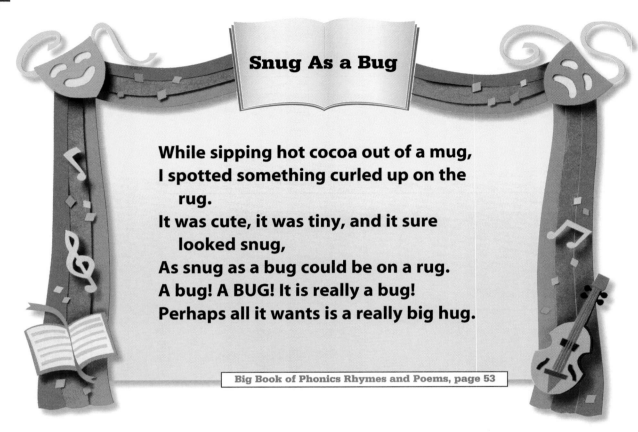

Snug As a Bug

While sipping hot cocoa out of a mug,
I spotted something curled up on the
    rug.
It was cute, it was tiny, and it sure
    looked snug,
As snug as a bug could be on a rug.
A bug! A BUG! It is really a bug!
Perhaps all it wants is a really big hug.

Big Book of Phonics Rhymes and Poems, page 53

Objective: Identify Long and Short Words

LISTEN TO THE POEM

- Read the poem "Snug as a Bug." Then say the words *sipping* and *hot*. Clap as you clap for each syllable.

- Repeat, having children say the words and clap with you. Determine that they clapped twice when they said *sipping* and once when they said *hot*. Ask which word is longer.

WHICH WORD IS LONGER?

- Say the following pairs of words. Repeat, and have children clap for each syllable as you say them.

- Children then determine which word is longer.

> rug   something   sipping mug
>   it   really   perhaps   hug

Objective: Listen for Medial u

SEGMENTING

- Say the word *up*. Emphasize the short *u* sound, and have children say the sound with you. Then say the word *pup* and have children repeat it. Point out that both words have the /u/ sound.

THUMBS UP!

- Demonstrate how to give the "thumbs up" signal. Point out the /u/ sound in both of these words. Then say the following words. Children say "thumbs up" and give the signal if the word has the /u/ sound.

bug	cat	drum
pat	cut	hid
lunch	road	crunch

Read Together

From Phonemic Awareness to Phonics

Objective: Identify /u/ u

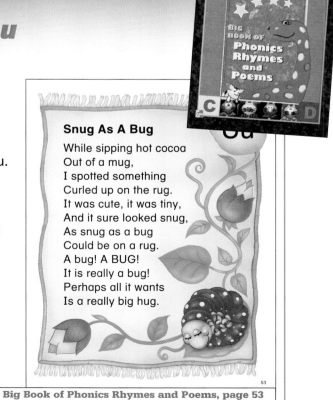

IDENTIFY THE LETTER FOR THE SOUND

- Explain to children that the letter *u* stands for the sound /u/. Invite children to say the sound with you.

- Display the Big Book of Phonics Rhymes and Poems, page 53. Point to the letters in the upper left corner and identify them. Have children say the sound with you.

REREAD THE POEM

- Reread the poem. Frame each word that has a medial *u*, and emphasize the /u/ sound. Have children say the words with you.

FIND WORDS WITH /u/

- Make word cards to match words in the poem with medial *u*. Invite volunteers to find the words in the poem. Read them together.

Snug As A Bug

While sipping hot cocoa
Out of a mug,
I spotted something
Curled up on the rug.
It was cute, it was tiny,
And it sure looked snug,
As snug as a bug
Could be on a rug.
A bug! A BUG!
It is really a bug!
Perhaps all it wants
Is a really big hug.

53

Big Book of Phonics Rhymes and Poems, page 53

OBJECTIVES

Children will:

- identify the letter *u*
- identify /u/ *u*
- form the letter *u*

....

MATERIALS

- letter cards and picture cards from the Word Building Book

TEACHING **TIP**

INSTRUCTIONAL Ask children a number of questions that begin *Would you rather . . .* and then use words with medial /u/, such as: *play in mud or play in the sun? eat a nut or eat a bun? drink from a cup or drink from a mug? hug a pup or hug a cub?* Repeat the medial /u/ words, and ask children what sound they hear in the middle of each word.

ALTERNATE TEACHING
STRATEGY
....

MEDIAL /u/*u*

For a different approach to teaching this skill, see page T32.

▶ **Visual/Auditory/ Kinesthetic**

Introduce Medial /u/ *u*

TEACH

Identify /u/ *u*   Tell children they will learn to write the sound /u/ in the middle of the word with the letter *u*. Write the letter on the chalkboard, identify it, and say the sound with the children. Say, *Let's have fun with mud*, and ask children to identify the sound that's the same in *fun* and *mud*. Then ask, *Would a pup have fun in the mud? Can a bug have fun in the mud?*

Form *u*   Display the letter *u*, and have children trace the letter with you in the air with their fingers. Then write the following words on the chalkboard and read them aloud: *sun, cap, cup, nut, not, mud*. Ask children to write the letter *u* on a letter strip each time they hear a word that has the sound /u/ in the middle.

PRACTICE

Complete the Pupil Edition Page   Read the directions on page 224 to children, and make sure they clearly understand what they are being asked to do. Identify each picture and complete the first item together. Then work through the page with children, or have them complete the page independently.

ASSESS/CLOSE

Identify and Use *u*   Show picture cards for words that have the sound /u/ in the middle, and have children identify the pictures. Give them incomplete word cards for each picture, and ask them to fill in the missing *u*. Help children match word cards to picture cards, and observe as they write the letters.

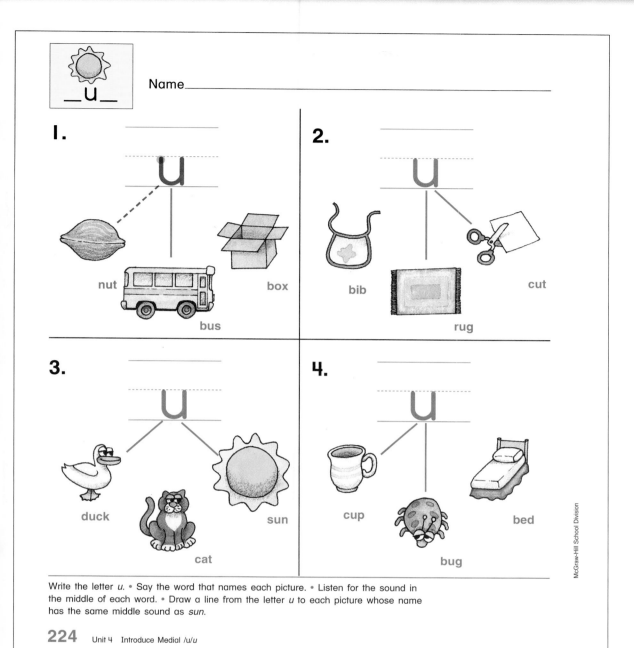

Name _____

1.
u
nut
box
bus

2.
u
bib
cut
rug

3.
u
duck
cat
sun

4.
u
cup
bug
bed

Write the letter *u*. • Say the word that names each picture. • Listen for the sound in the middle of each word. • Draw a line from the letter *u* to each picture whose name has the same middle sound as *sun*.

224 Unit 4 Introduce Medial /u/*u*

McGraw-Hill School Division

Pupil Edition, page 224

ADDITIONAL PHONICS RESOURCES

Practice Book, *page 224*
Phonics Workbook

McGraw-Hill School
TECHNOLOGY

Phonics **CD-ROM**
Activities for practice with Medial Letters

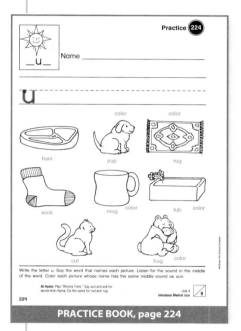

PRACTICE BOOK, page 224

Meeting Individual Needs for Phonics

EASY	ON-LEVEL	CHALLENGE	LANGUAGE SUPPORT
Say the word *fun* and ask children what sound they hear in the middle of the word. Then give children a sheet of drawing paper, and ask them to draw a picture of something that is fun to do. Children can label their pictures with the word *fun*.	**Have** children complete each sentence by saying a word that has /u/*u* in the middle: I ___ (cut) a piece of paper with my scissors. The sky is blue and the ___ (sun) is shining. I drank a ___ (cup) of hot chocolate. I had ___ (fun) at the park. We sat on the ___ (rug) and watched TV.	**Have** children work together with you on a medial /u/ sound Add-On story. Tell children that the story will be about a *pup* named *Gus*. Call on children to contribute sentences as you write them on chart paper. Each sentence must contain a word with /u/*u* in the middle.	**Help** ESL children practice medial /u/ words by using them in sentences that you and the children can act out together, such as: *Let's cut a piece of butter. Let's wash the mud off the rug. Let's shoo away that bug. Let's give the pup a hug.*

224

LANGUAGE SUPPORT

ESL Use illustrations in the book to review words that describe color, position, and size. Ask questions such as: *What color are the lily pads? Are corn kernels big or small?*

TEACHING TIP

MANAGEMENT You may wish to have children reread *Nature Spy* independently or with a partner. Pair children who may be having difficulty with more fluent readers.

Read the Big Book

Before Reading

Develop Oral Language

Share the following finger play with the children:

Beehive
Here is the beehive, where are the bees?
(Hold out a clenched fist.)
Hidden away where nobody sees!
(Look at your fist; shake your head.)
Here they come creeping out of the hive,
(Open fist gradually.)
One, two, three, four, five,
ZOOM, ZOOM, ZOOM, see they're alive!
(Flutter fingers in rhythm.)

After children perform the finger play, display a copy of "Nature Spy." Ask children to recall some of the things that the girl sees in the story.

Set Purposes

Model: We know that this story is mainly about a girl who looks closely at nature. When we read the story today, let's find out more about the animals in the story. What animals in the book do you remember?

or the golden eye of a frog.

16

During Reading

Read Together

- Before you begin to read, point to the first word in the first sentence. Explain that this is where you will begin to read. Continue to track print as you read the story. *Tracking Print*

- Reread pages 8–9. Point to the comma on page 8, and note the period on page 9. Explain that this sentence does not end on one page, but carries over the two pages. *Concepts of Print*

- Ask children to look at the three photographs of the frog. Talk about how the frog looks the same and different in the photographs. Have children describe the eye of the frog in each photograph. *Compare and Contrast*

- Make the short *u* sound, and have children repeat it. Reread the last sentence in the book. Ask children which word has the /u/ sound. (up) *Phonics and Decoding*

I notice the feathers of a bird.
14

Nature Spy, page 14

After Reading

Retell the Story

Have children name some of the animals in the story. Ask them to describe what the animals look like.

Literary Response

JOURNAL WRITING Ask children to choose an animal from the story and to draw a picture of it. Have them complete a sentence that describes the animal, such as: *The frog is <u>green</u>. The spider is <u>small</u>.*

ORAL RESPONSE Engage children in a discussion by asking questions such as:

- *Have you ever seen this animal? Where?*

- *Where does this animal usually live?*

- *Would this animal make a good pet?*

CULTURAL PERSPECTIVES

NATURE Talk about how going for a walk every day helps us to notice nature and the changes in the seasons. Point out that in different places in the world, children experience nature in different ways. In Belize, where it is warm all the time, a child might swim every day. In siberia, where there are few cars and great dis-

tances between things, a child might ride a horse every day. In Beijing, China, where most people travel by bike, a child might ride through city streets on a bike with her mom every day.

▶ **Verbal**

Activity Take children on a walk. Tell them to act like nature spies. At the end of the walk, ask children what they noticed. Make a list as a class. Gather nature specimens, if possible.

OBJECTIVES

Children will:

- compare and contrast information from a story

MATERIALS

- *Nature Spy*

TEACHING TIP

INSTRUCTIONAL Show children how to use a magnifying glass properly, moving the glass away to enlarge the item that is being examined.

Review Compare and Contrast

PREPARE

Make a List Ask children to recall the Big Book story *Nature Spy*. Ask where the story takes place and what the girl likes to do. Discuss some of the things in the story that the girl looks at. Make a picture or word list.

TEACH

Compare and Contrast Reread *Nature Spy,* and discuss ways in which things look alike and different when they are seen both up close and far away. Ask children to describe the frog shown on pages 16 and 17 in detail. Then compare and contrast other things from the picture or word list.

PRACTICE

Compare Plants on the Pupil Edition Page Read the directions on page 225 to the children, and make sure they clearly understand what they are asked to do. Identify each picture, and complete the first item together. Then work through the page with children or have them complete the page independently.

ASSESS/CLOSE

Review the Page Review children's work on the Pupil Edition page, and note any children who are experiencing difficulty.

Name_____

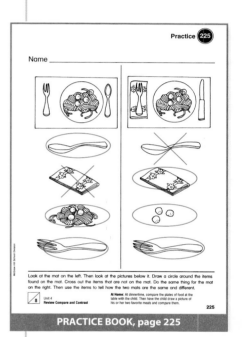

1.

2.

3.

Look at the two plants at the top of the page. • Then look at the pictures along the left side of the page. • Under each plant, put a ✔ on the line if the plant has that part. • Put an ✘ on the line if the plant does not have that part.

Pupil Edition, page 225

ALTERNATE TEACHING
STRATEGY
....
COMPARE AND
CONTRAST
For a different approach to teaching this skill, see page T30.
▶ **Visual/Auditory/ Kinesthetic**

Practice **225**

Name _____

Look at the mat on the left. Then look at the pictures below it. Draw a circle around the items found on the mat. Cross out the items that are not on the mat. Do the same thing for the mat on the right. Then use the items to tell how the two mats are the same and different.

Unit 4
Review Compare and Contrast

At Home: At dinnertime, compare the plates of food at the table with the child. Then have the child draw a picture of his or her two favorite meals and compare them.

225

PRACTICE BOOK, page 225

Meeting Individual Needs for Comprehension

EASY	ON-LEVEL	CHALLENGE	LANGUAGE SUPPORT
Invite each child to choose an animal from *Nature Spy*. Talk about how the animals look alike and how they look different. Make a list of observations.	Choose two types of berries, such as strawberries and raspberries. Provide samples to small groups of children and have them compare and contrast by describing size, color, texture, smell, and taste. Record the observations.	Ask children to choose an animal or item from *Nature Spy*. Help them create a Venn diagram to compare and contrast the animal's appearance from close up and from far away. Begin by discussing how the animal or item is the same in each photograph.	Go on a rock hunt, and have children collect some different rocks. Compare and contrast the rocks, talking about how they are alike and how they are different. Children may also wish to sort the rocks.

225

Develop Phonological Awareness

Listen

Snug As a Bug
a poem

Umbrellas
a poem

While sipping hot cocoa
Out of a mug,
I spotted something
Curled up on the rug.
It was cute, it was tiny
And it sure looked snug,
As snug as a bug
Could be on a rug.
A bug! A BUG!
It is really a bug!
Perhaps all it wants
Is a really big hug.

Under my umbrella-top,
Splashing through the town,
I wonder why the tulips
Hold umbrellas
Up-side-down!

Barbara Justen Esbensen

Big Book of Phonics Rhymes and Poems, pages 53, 52

Objective: Focus on Rhyming Words

READ THE POEM Read the poem "Snug As a Bug." In repeated readings, pause before the rhyming words and invite children to provide them: *mug, rug, snug, bug, hug.*

EXTEND THE RHYME Say three rhyming words and call on volunteers to name other words that rhyme with the three words. Begin with *jet, set, bet* and then continue with other sets of rhyming words.

> club, hub, grub small, tall, call
> plan, fan, van knock, lock, dock

ADD A RHYMING WORD Have children sit in a circle. Ask children to listen carefully as you say: *I see a cat.* Encourage volunteers to repeat your sentence and add a word that rhymes with *cat.* Repeat with other objects.

cat   can
hat   man
mat   Dan

Objective: Listen for /u/

LISTEN FOR INITIAL /U/ Read the poem "Umbrellas," emphasizing words with initial /u/. Say the words *under* and *umbrellas*. Help children see that both words begin with *u*.

LOOK UNDER FOR INITIAL /u/ Say words one at a time, and have children put one hand under the other each time they hear a word that begins with *u*.

> uncle over umpire
> ugly inch untie

LISTEN FOR MEDIAL /U/ Read the poem "Snug As a Bug," stressing words with the medial /u/ sound. Have children repeat the words *rug* and *bug* several times, listening for the medial /u/ sound.

GIVE A HUG FOR MEDIAL /U/ Invite children to hug themselves each time they hear you say a word that has *u* in the middle.

> cub ten hat mud hum
> box duck sit cup run

Read Together

From Phonemic Awareness to Phonics

Objective: Identify /u/ *U, u*

IDENTIFY THE LETTERS
Display the Big Book of Phonics Rhymes and Poems, pages 52 and 53. Point to the letters as you identify them. Tell children that the letters *U* and *u* stand for the /u/ sound.

REREAD THE POEMS Reread the poems. Point to each word, emphasizing those with /u/.

FIND WORDS WITH *U, u* Have children find words with *U* or *u* in the poems. Provide them with self-stick dots to place under the words.

Uu Umbrellas

Under my umbrella-top,
Splashing through the town,
I wonder why the tulips
Hold umbrellas
Up-side-down!
Barbara Juster Esbensen

Snug As A Bug

While sipping hot cocoa
Out of a mug,
I spotted something
Curled up on the rug.
It was cute, it was tiny,
And it sure looked snug,
As snug as a bug
Could be on a rug.
A bug! A BUG!
It is really a bug!
Perhaps all it wants
Is a really big hug.

Big Book of Phonics Rhymes and Poems, pages 52, 53

226B

OBJECTIVES

Children will:

- identify /u/*U, u*
- discriminate between initial and medial *u*
- write and use letters *U, u*

....

MATERIALS

- picture cards from the Word Building Book

TEACHING TIP

INSTRUCTIONAL Invite children to make up a story using words that begin with the sound /u/ or have the sound /u/ in the middle. Start them off with *Once upon a time . . .* ; then keep suggesting words and help children weave them into a tale. Use words such as: *bug, ugly, mud, until, fun, hug, sun, under.*

ALTERNATE TEACHING STRATEGY

....

LETTER /u/*u*

For a different approach to teaching this skill, see page T32.

▶ **Visual/Auditory/ Kinesthetic**

Review /u/u

TEACH

Identify and Discriminate Between Initial and Medial /u/ U, u

Tell children they will review the sound /u/ at the beginning and middle of words and write the letters *U, u*. Write the letters, identify them, and make the /u/ sound. Write *u*___ on one part of the chalkboard and ___*u*__ on another part. Say the following sentence, and ask children to point to the part of the chalkboard that shows the position of *u* in a word: *The sun came up. Gus took his pup for a run.*

Write and Use U, u

First have children fold a sheet of paper to make two columns and copy the headings you wrote on the chalkboard: *u*___ and ___*u*__. Write the above sentences on the chalkboard, and repeat them as you track print with your hand. When children recognize a word that has initial or medial short *u*, have them clap. Stop and ask volunteers to draw a circle around the word and underline the *u* while the rest of the children write *u* under the appropriate heading on their papers.

PRACTICE

Complete the Pupil Edition Page

Read the directions on page 226 to the children, and make sure they clearly understand what they are being asked to do. Identify each picture, and complete the first item together. Then work through the page with children or have them complete the page independently.

ASSESS/CLOSE

Identify and Use U, u

Have children fold a sheet of paper and make two columns as before, headed *u*___ and ___*u*__. Show pictures of objects, such as: *mud, umbrella, up (arrow), cup, nut.* Ask children to write *u* in the appropriate column.

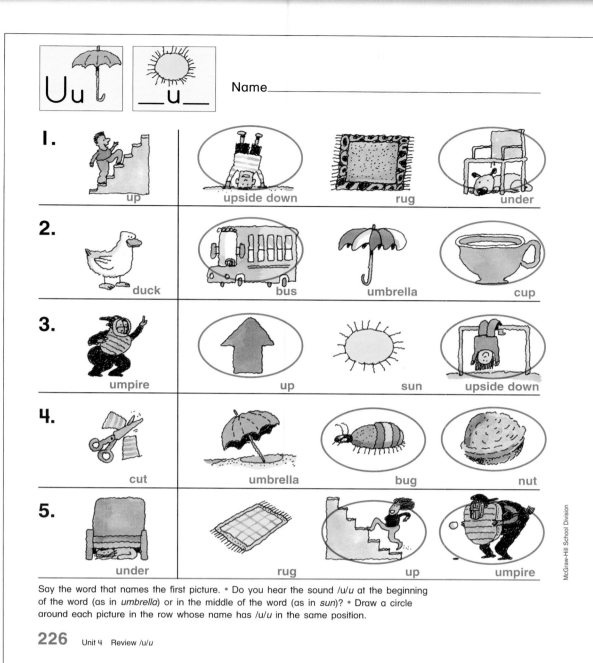

Name_____

1.	up	upside down	rug	under
2.	duck	bus	umbrella	cup
3.	umpire	up	sun	upside down
4.	cut	umbrella	bug	nut
5.	under	rug	up	umpire

Say the word that names the first picture. • Do you hear the sound /u/u at the beginning of the word (as in *umbrella*) or in the middle of the word (as in *sun*)? • Draw a circle around each picture in the row whose name has /u/u in the same position.

226   Unit 4   Review /u/u

McGraw-Hill School Division

Pupil Edition, page 226

ADDITIONAL PHONICS RESOURCES

Practice Book, *page 226*
Phonics Workbook

McGraw-Hill School
TECHNOLOGY

Phonics CD-ROM
Activities for practice with Initial and Medial Letters

PRACTICE BOOK, page 226

Meeting Individual Needs for Phonics

EASY	ON-LEVEL	CHALLENGE	LANGUAGE SUPPORT
Show word cards for words that have *u* at the beginning and in the middle of the word, such as: *up, run, us, pup, under, cut*. Ask children to sort the cards into two groups to show initial and medial *u*. Read the words, and have children make up sentences using each word.	**Have** children work in groups to make an initial *u* mobile and a medial *u* mobile. Each child can draw a picture of one object that begins with the sound /u/ and one that has the sound /u/ in the middle. When children have completed their drawings, help them create their mobiles.	**Give** children clues that can be answered with words that have the sound /u/ at the beginning or in the middle, such as: *To move very fast.* (run) *Kites go this way.* (up) *The opposite of over.* (under) *A baby dog.* (pup)	**Give** ESL children additional opportunities to recognize medial *u* words and to write the letter *u*. Read the following words aloud and ask children to write the letter *u* each time they hear a word with /u/ in the middle: *cap, cup, cot, sun, cut, fin, fun, pup, mad, mud.*

Teacher
Read Aloud

Listen

How Many Spots Does a Leopard Have?

an African folk tale
retold by Julius Lester

One morning Leopard was doing what he enjoyed doing most. He was looking at his reflection in the lake. How handsome he was! How magnificent was his coat! And, ah! The spots on his coat! Was there anything in creation more superb?

Leopard's rapture was broken when the water in the lake began moving. Suddenly Crocodile's ugly head appeared above the surface.

Leopard jumped back. Not that he was afraid. Crocodile would not bother him. But then again, one could never be too sure about Crocodile.

"Good morning, Leopard," Crocodile said. "Looking at yourself again, I see. You are the most vain creature in all of creation."

Leopard was not embarrassed. "If you were as handsome as I am, if you had such beautiful spots, you, too, would be vain."

"Spots! Who needs spots? You're probably so in love with your spots that you spend all your time counting them."

Now there was an idea that had not occurred to Leopard. "What a wonderful idea!" he exclaimed.

Continued on page T5

Oral Comprehension

LISTENING AND SPEAKING Explain that the word *vain* means being too proud. Ask children if they can remember a story character who was vain. Explain that they will hear an African folk tale about a vain leopard. Remind them that a folk tale is a story with animals who act and talk like humans. A folk tale usually teaches a lesson.

After you read, talk about the lesson that the animals learned. Then ask: *How are the animals alike and different?* If possible, provide pictures of animals. Ask: *Which animals in the story have four legs? Which animals can fly?*

Activity Help children to make a class chart that shows how the animals are alike and how they are different. Create headings such as *two legs, four legs, fur, feathers, flies, runs.* Children draw and cut out pictures in each category to compare and contrast the animals.

▶ **Logical/ Spatial**

Real-Life Reading

Help the leopard cub find its way to its mother!

Big Book of Real-Life Reading, pages 30–31

Objective: Read a Map

READ THE PAGE Display the Big Book of Real-Life Reading and show children the title page. Explain that the title page of a book tells information about that book. You may wish to discuss such items as the copyright date. Ask children if they remember where the folk tale "How Many Spots Does a Leopard Have?" takes place. Then explain that children will use a map that is set in Africa. Read the question, and have volunteers point out these elements on the map: tall grass, the pond, trees, the animals.

ANSWER THE QUESTION Invite volunteers to trace the path for the cub to follow. Ask: *What animal will the cub pass first? Where will she go next?* Provide crayons and paper. Have children create their own map with a path by which the cub finds its mother.

CULTURAL PERSPECTIVES

COUNTING Share that people all over the world use many different objects to count. Many people in Europe and the United States use a calculator. In China and the Middle East, some people use an abacus to count. Still others count in their heads!

Activity Provide beans, an abacus, a calculator, paper, and pens. Provide simple addition equations and encourage children to use counting tools to find the answers.

▶ Logical/Mathematical

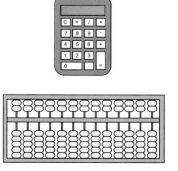

OBJECTIVES

Children will:

- identify and read the high-frequency word *do*

MATERIALS

- word cards from the Word Building Book

TEACHING TIP

INSTRUCTIONAL Play a concentration game to review high-frequency words. Make pairs of words, and place them face down in a grid. Have children turn over cards two at a time and try to make pairs.

Introduce High-Frequency Words: *do*

PREPARE

Listen to Words
Tell children that they will be learning a new word, *do*. Say the following sentence: *Do you have spots?* Read the sentence again, and ask children to raise their hands when they hear the word *do*. Repeat with the sentence: *Do not come in.*

TEACH

Model Reading the Word in Context
Give a word card to each child, and read the word. Reread the sentences, and have children raise their hands when they hear the word.

Identify the Words
Write the sentences above on the chalkboard. Track print and read each sentence. Have children hold up their word cards when they hear the word *do*. Then ask volunteers to point to and underline the word *do* in the sentences.

Write the Word
Review how to write the letters *d* and o. Then have children practice writing the word *do*.

PRACTICE

Complete the Pupil Edition Page
Read the directions on page 227 to children, and make sure they clearly understand what they are being asked to do. Complete the first item together. Then work through the page with children or have them complete the page independently.

ASSESS/CLOSE

Review the Page
Review children's work, and guide children who are experiencing difficulty or need additional practice.

Name_____

1.

Do you have a cat?

2.

I do not have a cat.

3.

Do you have a pup?

4.

I do have a tan pup!

Read the sentence. • Draw a line under the word *do* in the sentence.

Unit 4 Introduce High-Frequency Words: *do* **227**

Pupil Edition, page 227

Practice **227**

Name_____

1. Do you run in
the sun?

2.
I do run in the sun.

3.
Do you have fun?

4.
I do have fun!

Read each sentence. Draw a line under the word *do* in each sentence.

Unit 4
Introduce High-Frequency Words: *do*

At Home: Have the child draw a picture of something he
or she does and write *I do* on the picture.

227

PRACTICE BOOK, page 227

Meeting Individual Needs for Vocabulary

EASY	ON-LEVEL	CHALLENGE	LANGUAGE SUPPORT
Have children write the word *do* on the chalkboard. Then have them use the word to form a sentence.	**Have** children look through magazines and newspapers for the word *do*. They can cut out the words and make a collage showing an activity that people do.	**Write** the following words on chart paper: *do, to, does, do, go, dot, do, did, do, so, do, do, go.* Have children circle the word *do* and count how many times they find it.	**Make** tactile letter cards for *d* and *o*. Children can trace the letters with their fingers as they say the word. Then have them arrange the letters to form the word.

Develop Phonological Awareness

Listen

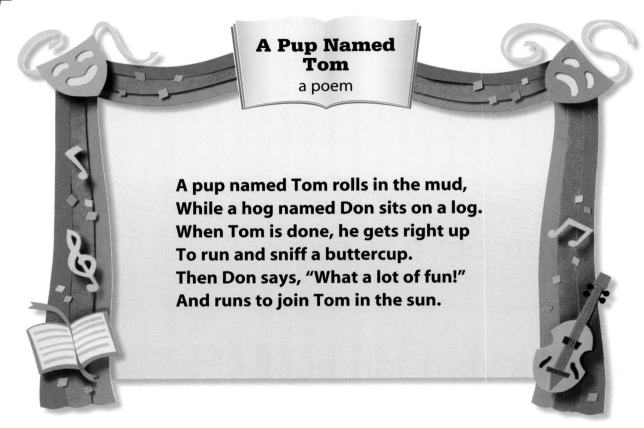

A Pup Named Tom
a poem

A pup named Tom rolls in the mud,
While a hog named Don sits on a log.
When Tom is done, he gets right up
To run and sniff a buttercup.
Then Don says, "What a lot of fun!"
And runs to join Tom in the sun.

Objective: Focus on Context

READ THE POEM Read the poem "A Pup Named Tom." Read it several times until children are familiar with the words and content.

LISTEN FOR THINGS THAT COULD REALLY HAPPEN Read the poem again. This time, ask children to listen for things that could happen in real life to a pup and a hog. Have children name things that could really happen.

> A pup could roll in the mud.
> A hog could sit on a log.
> A pup could sniff a buttercup.
> A hog could join a pup.

LISTEN FOR THINGS THAT COULD NOT HAPPEN Read the poem again. This time, have children listen for one thing that could not happen in real life. Guide children in recognizing that a hog cannot talk.

> A hog could not say,
> "What a lot of fun!"

Objective: Listen for Blending Short *u* with
p, r, f, c, t, m, s, d, and *n*

LISTEN FOR WHISPERED WORDS Read the first line of "A Pup Named Tom." Ask children to listen carefully for two words that you will whisper. As you read, whisper the words *pup* and *mud*. When children identify the words, whisper each one slowly to emphasize individual sounds: /p/- /u/-/p/, /m/-/u/-/d/. Have children repeat the "whisper sounds" several times, faster and faster each time, until the words are blended.

> /p/-/u/-/p/   /m/-/u/-/d/

WHISPER SOUNDS Read the rest of the poem and repeat the "whisper sounds" activity with the following words: *up, run, fun, sun.*

WHISPER WITH A PARTNER Divide the class into pairs. Ask each child to think of a favorite "whispered word" and lead a partner in whispering each sound of the word slowly, then blending it faster and faster to say the word.

Read Together

From Phonemic Awareness to Phonics

Objective: Identify Word Endings

LISTEN FOR RHYMING WORDS Read the last two lines of "A Pup Named Tom," emphasizing the rhyming words at the ends of the lines. Write the words on an overhead projector transparency.

> fun sun

IDENTIFY THE LETTERS Invite a volunteer to place rubber bands around the letters that are the same in each word. *(un)* Identify the letters, and ask children to say the sounds these letters stand for.

"RUBBER BAND" OTHER WORDS Ask children to name other words that rhyme with *fun* and *sun*. Add the rhyming words that end in *-un* to the overhead. Use new rubber bands to encircle *un* in these words. Invite children to repeat each word after you say it.

> bun nun pun run

OBJECTIVES

Children will:

- identify /u/*u*
- blend and read short *u* words
- write short *u* words
- review /p/*p*, /r/*r*, /f/*f*, /k/*c*, /t/*t*, /m/*m*, /s/*s*, /d/*d*, and /n/*n*.

······································

MATERIALS

- letter cards and word cards from the Word Building Book

TEACHING TIP

INSTRUCTIONAL Write this sentence, then read it aloud as you point to each word: *The pup sat in the sun.* Invite volunteers to underline the words that have the /u/*u* sound in the middle. Blend and read these words aloud with children.

ALTERNATE TEACHING STRATEGY

·······························

BLENDING SHORT *u*
For a different approach to teaching this skill, see page T32.

▶ **Visual/Auditory/ Kinesthetic**

Introduce Blending with short *u*

TEACH

Identify *u* as the Symbol for /u/
Tell children that today they will be reading and writing words with the letter *u* that stands for the sound /u/.

- Display the *u* letter card and say /u/. Have children repeat the sound /u/ after you as you point to the *u* card.

BLENDING Model and Guide Practice
- Place an *n* letter card to the right of the *u* card. Blend the sounds together and have children repeat after you: *un.*

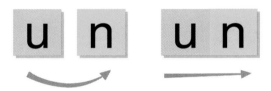

- Place an *f* letter card before the *un* cards. Blend the sounds in the word to read *fun*. Have children repeat after you.

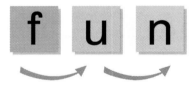

Use the Word in Context
- Invite children to use the word *fun* in a sentence. Encourage them to talk about the kinds of things they like to do.

Repeat the Procedure
- Use the following words to continue modeling and for guided practice with short *u*: *cup, mud, nut, run, cup, sun, pup.*

PRACTICE

Complete the Pupil Edition Page
Read aloud the directions on page 228 to the children, and make sure they clearly understand what they are being asked to do. Identify each picture, and complete the first item together. Then work through the page with children, or have them complete the page independently.

ASSESS/CLOSE

Build Short *u* Words
Observe children as they complete page 228. Then have them use letter cards *p, r, f, c, t, m, s, d, n* to build three-letter words with short *u* in the middle.

Name_____

1. s u n   sun

2. c u p   cup

3. n u t   nut

4. p u p   pup

Blend the sounds and say the word. • Write the word. • Draw a circle around the picture that goes with the word.

McGraw-Hill School Division

228   Unit 4   Introduce Blending with Short *u*

Pupil Edition, page 228

ADDITIONAL PHONICS RESOURCES

Practice Book, *page 228*
Phonics Workbook

McGraw-Hill School
TECHNOLOGY

Phonics CD-ROM
Activities for practice with
Blending and Segmenting

PRACTICE BOOK, page 228

Meeting Individual Needs for Phonics

EASY	ON-LEVEL	CHALLENGE	LANGUAGE SUPPORT
Review letters *p, r, f, c, t, m, d, n* by having children join you as you blend and read these words written on the chalkboard: *sun, mud, pup, cut, fun.* Ask children to name the first and last letter of each word, and to underline the letter as they name it.	**Give** children the following word cards in random order: *sun, run, rut, nut, cut, cup.* Ask them to arrange the cards so *sun* is the first word and each word after that shows only one letter different from the previous word. Have children blend sounds to read the words.	**Give** children letter cards: *p, r, f, c, t, m, s, d, n.* Ask them to find a partner with whom they can build a word by placing *u* between their letters. Be sure there are enough *n, p,* and *t* cards, which are frequently used as the final letters.	**Ask** children to put their hands up when they hear a word that has *u* in the middle. Say: *cup, cap, pup, pod, not, nut.* Write the words on the chalkboard and have children blend sounds with you to read each word aloud.

Guided Instruction

BEFORE READING

PREVIEW AND PREDICT Take a brief **picture walk** through the book, focusing on the illustrations.

- Who is the story about? Where is the story taking place?

- What do you think will happen in the story?

- Do you think the story will be realistic, or will it be make-believe? Why?

SET PURPOSES Guide children in a brief discussion of what they want to find out as they read the story. Have volunteers tell what activities they see taking place. (washing dishes; playing in mud) Ask them to think about how these two activities might be related. (some of the containers used in two ways)

TEACHING **TIP**

To put book together:
1. Tear out the story page.
2. Cut along dotted line.
3. Fold each section on fold line.
4. Assemble book.

INSTRUCTIONAL Talk about different types of clothing that are appropriate for playing outside. Help children compile a list or have them draw pictures of clothes suitable to wear in the rain, in the mud, in the snow, and in the sun.

Mud Fun

"I do have a pot," said Nan.

3

"Do you have a pot?"
said Pam.

2

"Do you have a cup?"
said Pam.

4

Guided Instruction

DURING READING

☑ **Blending with Short *u***

☑ **Compare and Contrast**

☑ **Concepts of Print**

☑ **High-Frequency Words: *do***

① **CONCEPTS OF PRINT** Ask children to count the number of words on the title page. (2) Ask how many letters are in each word. (3)

② **HIGH-FREQUENCY WORDS** Have children point to the word *do* on page 2. As children read the sentence, point out how the word *do* adds emphasis to the meaning.

③ **COMPARE AND CONTRAST** Have children compare the picture on page 3 with that of the title page. Ask how they are alike and how they are different.

④ **USE ILLUSTRATIONS** Point out the labeled bottle shown on page 4. Explain that the word *danger* always means that something may be harmful.

LANGUAGE SUPPORT

ESL Discuss different names for kitchen objects that children may be familiar with. For example, *pot* (pages 2–3) may also be called *pan*.

229/230B

Guided Instruction

DURING READING

5 **BLENDING WITH SHORT _u_** Point to the word on page 5 that begins with _c_. Blend the sounds of these letters together to read the word: _c u p cup._

6 **CONCEPTS OF PRINT** Ask children to look at page 6 and tell how many words are in the sentence. (7) Ask how many words have three letters. (4)

7 **USE ILLUSTRATIONS** Ask children to look at page 7 and to determine what Pam did with the pot and the cup. (played in the mud and made a castle)

8 **PHONICS** Ask which two words on page 8 have a _u_ and the /u/ sound. (mud, fun)

INFORMAL ASSESSMENT

COMPARE AND CONTRAST
HOW TO ASSESS Ask children to point to two pictures that show something that is the same and two that show a difference. (two sisters are different heights; clothes and kitchen items start clean and get muddy)

FOLLOW UP Extend comparison to include the text of the story, asking children to compare the pair of sentences on pages 2 and 3 as well as those on pages 4 and 5. (question and its corresponding answer) Ask children to compare the punctuation on each pair of pages.

"I do have a cup,"
said Nan.

5

"I do have mud on me,"
said Pam.

7

"You have mud on you!"
said Nan.

6

"Mud is fun!" said Pam.

8

Guided Instruction

AFTER READING

RETURN TO PREDICTIONS AND PURPOSES
Ask children if their predictions about the story were correct. Ask if their questions were answered, and revisit the story if necessary. Have volunteers talk about the two activities shown in the story.

RETELL THE STORY Have pairs of children work together to retell the story. One child could role-play the part of Pam and another could pay Nan, reading the appropriate pages if they need help retelling the story. (*Pam*—pages 2, 4, 7, 8; *Nan*—pages 3, 5, 6)

LITERARY RESPONSE Ask children to draw and write about how they would like to play in the mud. Have them describe any changes in their appearance and show any toys or household objects they might use in their play.

Activity

Cross Curricular: Math

POUR IT ON Provide measuring cups, a small pot, and a large bowl with rice or sand for pouring. Have children choose a measuring cup and estimate how many (half-cups) the pot will hold. Ask them to record their guesses and then check.

▶ Logical/Mathematical

OBJECTIVES

Children will:

- compare and contrast to understand a story

MATERIALS

- *Mud Fun*

TEACHING TIP

INSTRUCTIONAL Make sure children understand the meaning of some simple comparative words, such as: *alike, different,* and *similar.*

Review Compare and Contrast

PREPARE

Recall the Story
Ask children to recall the story *Mud Fun*. Ask them who the characters are, and how the story begins.

TEACH

Compare and Contrast Story Characters
Read pages 2–3, and ask how Pam and Nan are alike and how they are different. Children may respond that both are girls, they are dressed the same, Nan is older. Continue through the story, comparing and contrasting the sisters. You may wish to make a word or picture chart to record the results.

PRACTICE

Complete the Pupil Edition Page
Read the directions on page 231 to the children, and make sure they clearly understand what they are asked to do. Identify each picture, and complete the first item together. Then work through the page with children or have them complete the page independently.

ASSESS/CLOSE

Review the Page
Review children's work, and note children who are experiencing difficulty.

Name _____

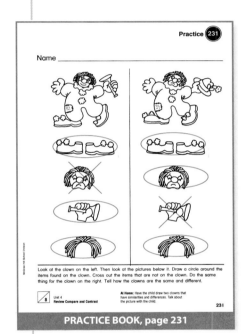

ALTERNATE TEACHING
STRATEGY

COMPARE AND CONTRAST
For a different approach to teaching this skill, see page T30.

▶ Visual/Auditory/ Kinesthetic

1.   ✔   ✔

2.   ✔   ✘

3.   ✘   ✔

Look at the two snails at the top of the page. • Then look at the pictures along the left side of the page. • Under each snail, put a ✔ on the line if the snail has that part. • Put an ✘ on the line if the snail does not have that part.

Unit 4   Review Compare and Contrast   **231**

Pupil Edition, page 231

PRACTICE BOOK, page 231

Meeting Individual Needs for Comprehension

EASY	ON-LEVEL	CHALLENGE	LANGUAGE SUPPORT
Show children two blocks. Ask how they are the same, and how they are different. Continue with other classroom objects, such as two trucks, two stuffed animals, or a marker and a pencil.	**Talk** about ways children make castles: mud, sand, clay, boxes, blocks, and so on. Have children compare and contrast the different materials. Then take a vote to see which is the most popular.	**Give** partners clay, and invite each of them to make a castle. Then they make a picture or word list and find two ways that the castles are the same, and two ways that they are different.	**Display** some kitchen utensils, such as pots, lids, measuring cups, bowls, and so on. Talk about what each is used for, and how they are alike and how they are different.

Develop Phonological Awareness

Listen

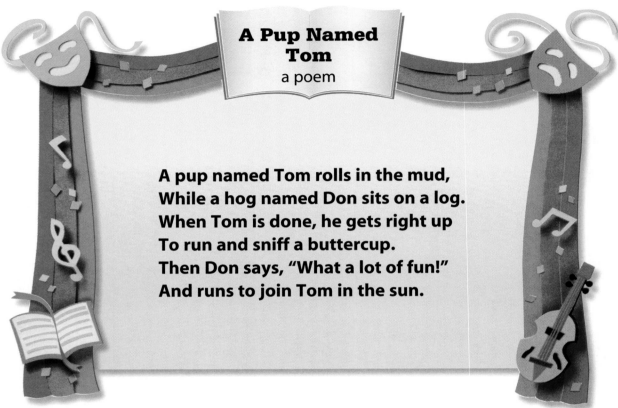

A Pup Named Tom
a poem

A pup named Tom rolls in the mud,
While a hog named Don sits on a log.
When Tom is done, he gets right up
To run and sniff a buttercup.
Then Don says, "What a lot of fun!"
And runs to join Tom in the sun.

Objective: Focus on Context

REVISIT THE POEM Read the poem "A Pup Named Tom." Ask children to tell you the name of the dog and the name of the hog in the poem.

LISTEN FOR THINGS THAT TOM DOES Read the poem again. This time, ask children to listen for things Tom does. Have children name the activities.

> Tom rolls in the mud.
> Tom gets up.
> Tom runs and sniffs a buttercup.
> Tom is in the sun.

LISTEN FOR THINGS THAT DON DOES Read the poem again. Have children listen for things Don does. Invite children to tell you about Don's activities.

> Don sits on a log.
> Don says "What a lot of fun!"
> Don runs to join Tom and sniffs the buttercup.

Objective: Listen for Blending Short *u* and *o* with *l, p, r, f, c, t, m, s, d,* and *n*

LISTEN FOR THE SEGMENTED WORD Read the first line of "A Pup Named Tom." When you get to the word *Tom,* sing each distinct sound in the word to segment it, /t/-/o/-/m/. Ask children to tell you which word you sang.

/t/-/o/-/m/

MODEL THE "NAME GAME" Invite children to play the "Name Game." Repeat the following chant, using the name *Tom:*

I know a name.
It's always the same.
The sounds are /t/ /o/ /m/.
If you know it,
Tell me to show it!

Have children say the name *Tom.* Repeat the chanting game with the name *Don.*

PLAY THE "NAME GAME" WITH A PARTNER Invite pairs to play the "Name Game" with more rhyming names they have thought of, such as: *Ron, Lon, Jon, Von, Dom,* and *Mom.*

/r/ /o/ /n/

Read Together

From Phonemic Awareness to Phonics

Objective: Associate Sounds with Letters

IDENTIFY LETTERS Encourage children to listen as you read the first line in the poem. Ask them to tell you which word is a name. *(Tom)* Then ask which word shows what you have when you add water to dirt. *(mud)* Read the first line. When children identify the words *Tom* and *mud,* write them on the chalkboard.

MAKE LETTER CARDS Point to the letters in each word, name them, and tell children the sound each letter represents. Make a set of five index cards for each child.

Each set should include *T, o, m, u, d.*

PLAY "SIMON SAYS" Play a letter/sound version of "Simon Says," by giving directions such as the following:

Simon says, "Touch the first letter in the word *mud.*"
Simon says, "Place the *d* on your head."
Simon says, "Place the letter that says /t/ on your foot."
Simon says, "Turn over the letter that says /o/."

PLAY "SIMON SAYS" WITH A PARTNER Divide the group into pairs. Have children take turns playing "Simon Says" with their partners, giving directions for identifying both letters and sounds.

OBJECTIVES

Children will:

- identify /u/u, /o/o
- blend and read short *u* and *o* words
- write short *u* and *o* words
- review /l/l, /p/p, /r/r, /f/f, /k/c, /t/t, /m/m, /s/s, /d/d, and /n/n

....

MATERIALS

- letter cards from the Word Building Book

TEACHING TIP

INSTRUCTIONAL Give each child two of the following letter cards: *l, p, r, f, c, t, m, s, d, n.* Ask them to work with a partner to build CVC words with short *o* and *u.*

ALTERNATE TEACHING STRATEGY

....

BLENDING SHORT *u, o*
For a different approach to teaching this skill, see Unit 3, page T32; Unit 4, page T32.

▶ **Visual/Auditory/ Kinesthetic**

Review Blending with short *u, o*

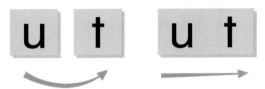

TEACH

Identify *u* as the Symbols for /u/
Tell children they will continue to read and write words with the letter *u* that stands for the sound /u/.

- Display the *u* letter card and say /u/. Have children repeat the sound /u/ after you as you point to the *u* card.

BLENDING Model and Guide Practice
- Place *l, p, r, f, c, t, m, s, d* and *n* letter cards apart from the *u* card. Place a *t* card after the *u* card. Blend the sounds together and have children repeat after you: *ut.*

u t   u t

- Place an *n* card before *ut* to show *nut.* Blend the sounds to read *nut.* Have children repeat them.

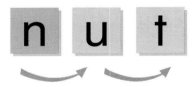

n u t

Use the Words in Context
- Hold up several objects and ask *Is this a nut?* Ask children to answer in a complete sentence that includes the word *nut.* Hold up a real nut and ask children to answer again.

Repeat the Procedure
- Use the following words to continue modeling and for guided practice with short *u* and *o*: *sun, mop, pot, cut, mud, nod, pup.*

PRACTICE

Complete the Pupil Edition Page
Read aloud the directions on page 232. Identify each picture, and complete the first item together. Work through the page with children, or have them complete the page independently.

ASSESS/CLOSE

Build Short *u* and Short *o* Words
Observe children as they complete page 232. Then have them use letter cards to build two short *u* and two short *o* words that begin with the letters *p, c, m,* or *n* and end with the letters *p, t, m,* or *n.*

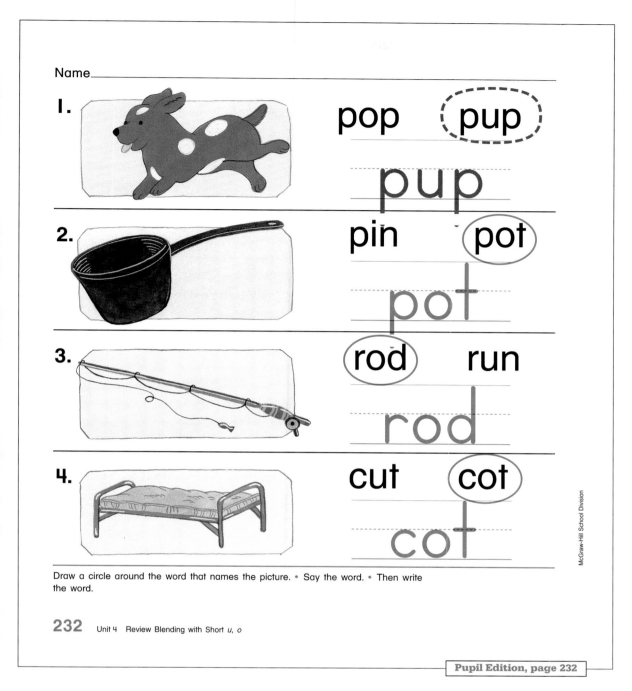

Name

1. pop (pup)

pup

2. pin (pot)

pot

3. (rod) run

rod

4. cut (cot)

cot

Draw a circle around the word that names the picture. • Say the word. • Then write the word.

McGraw-Hill School Division

Pupil Edition, page 232

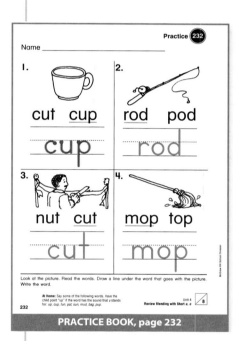

ADDITIONAL PHONICS RESOURCES

Practice Book, *page 232*
Phonics Workbook

McGraw-Hill School
TECHNOLOGY

Phonics CD-ROM
Activities for practice with Blending and Segmenting

Practice 232

Name

1. cut cup

cup

2. rod pod

rod

3. nut cut

cut

4. mop top

mop

Look at the picture. Read the words. Draw a line under the word that goes with the picture. Write the word.

At Home: Say some of the following words. Have the child point "up" if the word has the sound that *u* stands for: up, cup, fun, pat, sun, mud, bag, pup.

232   Review Blending with Short *u, o*   Unit 4   8

PRACTICE BOOK, page 232

Meeting Individual Needs for Phonics

EASY	ON-LEVEL	CHALLENGE	LANGUAGE SUPPORT
Write *rut* and *rot* on the chalkboard and ask children to say the sound of the letter you underline (first *u*, then *o*). Repeat with other short *u* and *o* words, such as: *mud, rod, mop, pup, cut, dot.* Blend sounds to read each word aloud with children.	**Form** a circle with children and pass a bag containing slips of paper on which you have written words such as *cot, fun, top, cup, mud, rod.* Each child takes a slip of paper, reads the word aloud, and then makes up a sentence using the word.	**Have** children write the short *u* and *o* words they built in **Assess/Close.** Then ask them to work in groups and make up a story that uses each child's word at least once. Record the stories and invite children to perform them.	**Have** children blend the following words with you to reinforce recognition of short *u* and *o*: *cut, cot, nut, not, pup, pop.* Be sure children understand the meaning of each word; then have them say the words as you point to them.

Reread the Decodable Story

Mud Fun

☑ **Blend with Short _u_**
☑ **Compare and Contrast**
☑ **High-Frequency Word:** _do_
☑ **Concepts of Print**

Mud Fun

Guided Reading

SET PURPOSES Have children discuss what their purpose is for rereading the story. Children may wish to have a better understanding of the story.

REREAD THE BOOK As you reread the story, keep in mind any problems children experienced during the first reading. Use the following questions to guide reading.

- **CONCEPTS OF PRINT** Ask children to point to the quotation marks, and remind them that they show that someone is speaking. For example, ask who is speaking on page 2. (Pam)

- **COMPARE AND CONTRAST** Ask children to describe how Pam looks and how Nan looks. Focus on how they look alike and how they look different.

- **HIGH-FREQUENCY WORDS** Review with children how the word _do_ is sometimes used to begin a question, as on pages 2 and 4.

- **BLEND WITH SHORT _u_** Write the words _mud, cup, fun_ on the chalkboard. Ask children to blend the sounds and read the words. Have them complete the words and recognize the short _u_ sound in each word. Elicit other words with short _u_. (_sun, up, run, cut, nut_ and so on)

RETURN TO PURPOSES Ask children if they found out what they needed to know from the story. See if they have any unanswered questions.

LITERARY RESPONSE Ask children to write about or draw a picture of something else that Pam could make in the mud.

Read the Patterned Book

Fun on the Farm

☑️ **Short /u/**
☑️ **Compare and Contrast**
☑️ **High-Frequency Word:** *do*
☑️ **Concepts of Print**

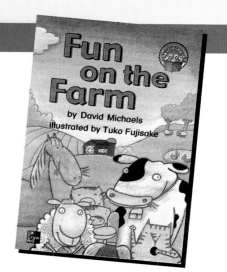

Guided Reading

PREVIEW AND PREDICT Read the title and the author's and the illustrator's name. Take a **picture walk** through pages 2–4, noting the setting of the story and the characters. Have children make predictions about what will happen in the story.

SET PURPOSES Have children decide what they want to find out from the story and predict what might happen at the farm. Tell them that the story contains words with short *u*.

READ THE BOOK Use the following prompts while the children are reading or after they have read independently. Remind them to run their fingers under each word as they read.

PAGES 2–3: Point to the last word in the sentence. *Let's read it together: do.*
High-Frequency Words

PAGES 4–5: *How are the pigs and sheep the same? How are they different?* (Answers will vary.) *Compare and Contrast*

PAGES 6–7: *Model: I can use what I know about short* u *to read the word that begins with s. Let's blend these sounds together: s-u-n.*
Phonics and Decoding

PAGE 8: *Listen as I read the sentences. Who can find the letter u in the middle of a word on this page?* (hugs) *Concepts of Print*

RETURN TO PREDICTIONS AND PURPOSES Ask children if they found out what they needed to know from the story. Ask if they have any questions that were not answered.

LITERARY RESPONSE The following questions will help focus children's responses:

- What other animal in the story is similar to a cow? How are they the same? How are they different?

- What would you like to see and do at a farm? Draw a picture and write in your journal.

LANGUAGE SUPPORT

ESL Sing the familiar song "Old McDonald" with children, using animals from the story. Then read the story again, and encourage children to use the illustrations to help read words with you.

Cross Curricular: Math

CATS OF A DIFFERENT COLOR Cut out circular cat faces in red, green, blue, and yellow. Have the cat faces be two sizes. Invite children to sort by size and color. Then have children copy and extend color and size patterns. Encourage children to make their own patterns, and have others continue them.

OBJECTIVES

Children will:

- identify and read the high-frequency word *do*

....

MATERIALS

- word cards from the Word Play Book
- *Mud Fun*

TEACHING TIP

INSTRUCTIONAL Make a class list of questions beginning with the word *do*. They can be questions to ask family members or friends about the things they like to do.

Review *do, go, I, and, me*

PREPARE

Listen to Words
Explain to the children that they will review the word *do*.

Ask children to raise their hands when they hear the word *do* in a sentence: *Do you like soup? What do you do after school? Where do you play?*

TEACH

Model Reading the Word in Context
Have children reread the decodable book. Ask children to listen for the word *do*.

Identify the Word
Ask children to look at their word cards, and then ask them to look for the word in sentences. Have children point to the word *do* on each page as you read the story together. Have volunteers put a self-stick note below the word. (Have children move the self-stick note from page to page.)

Write the Word
Review how to write the letters *d* and *o*. Then children practice writing the word.

Review High-Frequency Words
Hold up word cards for the following words: *the, a, my, that, and, you, said, we, are, is, have, to, go, I, and, me.* Have children say the words.

PRACTICE

Complete the Pupil Edition Page
Read the directions on page 233 to the children, and make sure they clearly understand what they are being asked to do. Complete the first item together. Then work through the page with children or have them complete the page independently.

ASSESS/CLOSE

Review the Page
Review children's work, and note children who are experiencing difficulty or need additional practice.

Name_____

I.

Pam said to (me), "Do you have a mat?"

_____

2.

(I) said, "(I) do not have a mat."

_____

3.

Pam said, "(Go) and sit on my mat."

_____

Read the sentences. Then do the following: **I.** Draw a circle around the word *me*. Draw a line under the word *do*. **2.** Draw a circle around the word *I* each time you see it. Draw a line under the word *do*. **3.** Draw a circle around the word *go*. Draw a line under the word *and*.

Unit 4 Review *do, go, I, and, me* **233**

Pupil Edition, page 233

ALTERNATE TEACHING STRATEGY

HIGH-FREQUENCY WORDS

For a different approach to teaching this skill, see page T27.

▶ **Visual/Auditory/ Kinesthetic**

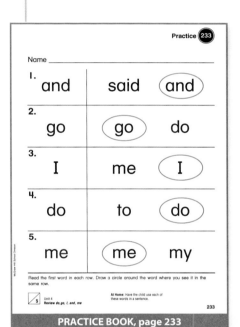

Practice **233**

Name_____

I. and	said	(and)
2. go	(go)	do
3. I	me	(I)
4. do	to	(do)
5. me	(me)	my

Read the first word in each row. Draw a circle around the word where you see it in the same row.

At Home: Have the child use each of these words in a sentence.

5 Unit 4 Review *do, go, I, and, me*

233

PRACTICE BOOK, page 233

Meeting Individual Needs for Vocabulary

EASY	ON-LEVEL	CHALLENGE	LANGUAGE SUPPORT
Write the word *do* on chart paper and read it together. Then ask questions about activities in the day that use the word: *What do we do after circle time? What do we do before snack? What do we do before we go home?*	**Write** the following words on the chalkboard: *do, to, so, do, go, do, no, do, do, so, to, do.* Have children erase words, except for the word *do*. Then children use the word *do* in sentences.	**Write** the following rhyme on the chalkboard: What would you do At the zoo? Have children repeat the rhyme, emphasizing the word *do*. Then they role-play their answer.	**Ask** children to draw pictures of things that they like to do. Label each picture with the word *do*.

233

Interactive Writing

Write a New Version

GRAMMAR/SPELLING CONNECTIONS

Model subject-verb agreement, complete sentences, and correct tense so that students may gain increasing control of grammar when speaking and writing.

Prewrite

LOOK AT THE STORY PATTERN Revisit *Nature Spy,* talking about how the story follows a pattern. The photographs show an object from nature, and then the close-up photos show different details. Invite children to help you write a word/picture list of classroom objects that children could describe.

Draft

WRITE A NEW STORY Explain to children that they will write a book titled "Classroom Spy." They will follow the pattern of *Nature Spy.*

- Have children work in pairs. Children think of an object and complete the sentence: *Do you see the ____ on the ____?*

- Children then draw two pictures to illustrate: a picture of the object and a close-up picture of part of the object.

Publish

CREATE THE BOOK Compile the pages of the book. Invite volunteers to help make a book cover. Reread the book together.

Do you see the scales on the fish?

Presentation Ideas

READ THE BOOK Invite volunteers to read their parts of the story aloud. Children can point to or use the classroom object to talk about their choices.

▶ Speaking/Listening

MAKE A TAPE Have children read their parts of the story and make a cassette tape. Keep the tape and the story in your reading corner so children can share the book.

▶ Speaking/Listening

COMMUNICATION TIPS

- **Listening** When children listen to others read, remind them to be supportive.

- **Speaking** Demonstrate proper placement of the tape recorder microphone. Children may wish to practice reading before they do their taping.

TECHNOLOGY TIP

Look for Web sites that show pictures of items in nature.

LANGUAGE SUPPORT

ESL Play a game of "I Spy" using classroom objects. Give clues and have children guess the object.

Meeting Individual Needs for Writing

EASY	ON-LEVEL	CHALLENGE
Draw Pictures Invite children to draw pictures of classroom objects and label them.	**Add to the Story** Have children use the same object and create another page for the book. Demonstrate how to look for other details and complete the same sentence: *Do you see the ___ on the ___?*	**Play a Guessing Game** Draw simple pictures of five classroom objects and label each. Children take turns giving clues about one of the items. Others write their guess and then check. Children take turns.

Fun in the Sun

Children will read and listen to a variety of stories about exploring nature and making new discoveries.

Fun in the Sun

**Decodable Story,
pages 241–242 of the
Pupil Edition**

 **Listening
Library
Audiocassette**

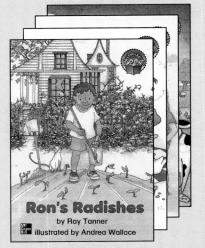

Ron's Radishes
by Ray Tanner
illustrated by Andrea Wallace

**Patterned Book,
page 245B**

**Every Time I Climb
a Tree**
by David McCord

**Teacher Read Aloud,
page 239A**

Allie's Adventure
From A to Z

Written by Ellen Dreyer   Illustrated by Jui Ishida

**ABC Big Book,
pages 235A–235B**

 **Listening
Library
Audiocassette**

**The
Apple Pie
Tree**

BY Zoe Hall

ILLUSTRATED BY
Shari Halpern

**Literature Big Book,
pages 237A–237B**

 **Listening
Library
Audiocassette**

**Pupil Edition,
pages 234–245**

**Big Book of Real-Life Reading,
page 24**

**Big Book of Phonics Rhymes and
Poems, pages 32, 42, 45**

Listening
Library
Audiocassette

ADDITIONAL RESOURCES

**Practice Book,
pages 234–245**

- **Phonics Kit**
- **Language Support Book**
- **Alternate Teaching Strategies,**
  pages T24–T33

McGraw-Hill School
TECHNOLOGY

Phonics CD-ROM Provides
extra phonics support.

interNET CONNECTION Research & Inquiry Ideas.

Visit www.mhschool.com

Fun in the Sun

Suggested Lesson Planner

READING AND LANGUAGE ARTS

- Phonological Awareness
- Phonics *review*
- Comprehension
- Vocabulary
- Beginning Reading Concepts
- Listening, Speaking, Viewing, Representing

DAY 1

Focus on Reading Skills

Develop Phonological Awareness, 234G–234H
"R is for Ribbon" and "The Lazy Little Lion" *Big Book of Phonics Rhymes and Poems,* 32, 45

 **Review Initial /r/r, /p/p, /l/l,** 234I–234
Practice Book, 234
Phonics/Phonemic Awareness Practice Book

 Phonics CD-ROM

 Read the Literature

Read *Allie's Adventure from A to Z* **Big Book,** 235A–235B
Shared Reading

Build Skills

☑ Positional Terms, 235C–235
Practice Book, 235

DAY 2

Focus on Reading Skills

Develop Phonological Awareness, 236A–236B
"Chicken Soup" *Big Book of Phonics Rhymes and Poems,* 42

 **Review Final /p/p,** 236C–236
Practice Book, 236
Phonics/Phonemic Awareness Practice Book

 **Phonics CD-ROM**

Read the Literature

Read *The Apple Pie Tree* **Big Book,** 237A–237B
Shared Reading

Build Skills

☑ Main Idea, 237C–237
Practice Book, 237

- Cross Curriculum

 Activity Language Arts, 235B

 Activity Science, 237B

- Writing

 Writing Prompt: Write your own story about a cat.

Journal Writing, 235B
Letter Formation, 234I

Writing Prompt: Write about a place in nature that you have been.

Journal Writing, 237B
Letter Formation, 236C

☑ = **Skill Assessed in Unit Test**

DAY 3

Every Time I Climb a Tree

Focus on Reading Skills

Develop Phonological Awareness, 238A–238B
"The Lazy Little Lion" and "Pease Porridge Hot" *Big Book of Phonics Rhymes and Poems,* 32, 41
 **Review /r/r, /p/p, /l/l,** 238C–238
Practice Book, 238
Phonics/Phonemic Awareness Practice Book

Phonics CD-ROM

Read the Literature

Read "Every Time I Climb a Tree"
Teacher Read Aloud, 239A–239B
Shared Reading
Read the Big Book of Real-Life Reading, 24–25
☑ Maps

Build Skills

☑ High-Frequency Words: *to, me, go, do,* 239C–239
Practice Book, 239

 Activity Social Studies, 239B

 Writing Prompt: Do you have a favorite place you like to visit? Write about it.

DAY 4

Fun in the Sun

Focus on Reading Skills

Develop Phonological Awareness, 240A–240B
"Making Mud Pies"
 **Review Blending with Short *u*,** 240C–240
Practice Book, 240
Phonics/Phonemic Awareness Practice Book

Phonics CD-ROM

Read the Literature

Read "Fun in the Sun" Decodable Story, 241/242A–241/242D

☑ Review *r, p, l, u;* Blending
☑ Compare and Contrast
☑ High-Frequency Words: *to, me, go, do*
☑ Concepts of Print

Build Skills

☑ Compare and Contrast, 243A–243
Practice Book, 243

 Activity Science, 241/242D

 Writing Prompt: What would you like to do at the pool? Write about it.

Letter Formation Practice Book, 241–242

DAY 5

Fun in the Sun

Ron's Radishes
by Ray Tanner
illustrated by Andrea Wallace

Focus on Reading Skills

Develop Phonological Awareness, 244A–244B
"Making Mud Pies"
 **Review Blending with Short *u, o, i,*** 244C–244
Practice Book, 244
Phonics/Phonemic Awareness Practice Book

Phonics CD-ROM

Read the Literature

Reread "Fun in the Sun" Decodable Story, 245A
Read "Ron's Radishes" Patterned Book, 245B
Guided Reading
☑ Review *r, p, l, u;* Blending
☑ Compare and Contrast
☑ High-Frequency Words: *to, me, go, do*
☑ Concepts of Print

Build Skills

☑ High-Frequency Words: *to, me, go, do,* 245C–245
Practice Book, 245

 **Activity** Science, 245B

 **Writing Prompt:** Draw a picture of something you like to wonder about.

Interactive Writing, 246A–246B

Develop Phonological Awareness

Listen

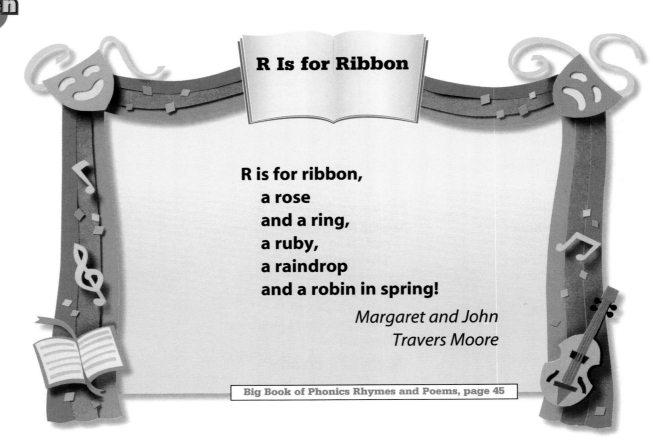

R Is for Ribbon

R is for ribbon,
  a rose
  and a ring,
  a ruby,
  a raindrop
  and a robin in spring!

*Margaret and John
Travers Moore*

Big Book of Phonics Rhymes and Poems, page 45

Objective: Review Initial /r/

IDENTIFY THE /r/ SOUND Read aloud the poem, exaggerating the initial /r/ sounds. Say the word *ribbon* and ask children what sound they hear at the beginning. Have children say the word with you . . . *r-r-r-ibbon*. Read the poem again and ask children to listen for other words that begin like *ribbon*.

> rose   ring   ruby
> raindrop   robin

PLAY A GAME Tell children that you will play a guessing game. Say, "I am thinking of something that begins with /r/. It is a kind of wet weather. What is it?" When children guess, have them repeat the answer with you, drawing out the initial /r/ sound. Continue play by giving clues such as these, but always begin by mentioning that the word begins with the sound of /r/:

- You use it in a yard to clean up leaves. *(rake)*
- It is an animal like a mouse. *(rat)*
- You use it in a game. You jump over it. *(rope)*
- It is a furry animal with long ears. *(rabbit)*

Objective: Review Initial /p/

IDENTIFY INITIAL P Ask children to listen carefully as you say the following sentence: "Patty and Peter packed a picnic." As you say the sentence, emphasize the initial /p/ sound. Then have children tell who the girl in the sentence is. Ask, "What sound do you hear at the beginning of *Patty*? Let's say the sound together." Then ask who the boy in the sentence is and repeat the procedure.

> **P-atty   P-eter**

PLAY A PICNIC GAME Repeat the sentence and this time ask children to tell what Patty and Peter did. Have them identify the sound at the beginning of *packed* and *picnic*. Then tell children that Patty and Peter only packed food that begins with the /p/ sound. Pose the following questions and have children say /p/ if the food has the /p/ sound.

- "Did Patty and Peter pack potatoes? peanuts? pears? peaches?"
- "Did Patty and Peter pack bananas? hot dogs?"

Read Together

From Phonemic Awareness to Phonics

Objective: Review Initial /l/ *L, l*

IDENTIFY THE LETTER Remind children that the letter *l* stands for the sound /l/. Display the Phonics Rhyme poem, "The Lazy Little Lion." Point to the letter in the upper left corner. Tell children that the letter is *l* and its sound is /l/.

READ THE POEM Read the poem through once and ask children to listen for the /l/ sound. Then read the poem again and point to each word. Exaggerate the words that begin with *l*.

LOOKING FOR L'S Have children repeat the poem title with

you, drawing out the initial /l/ sounds. Then ask a volunteer to come up and point to the letters in the title that make the /l/ sound at the beginning of the words. Continue, reading the poem line by line and inviting different children to find the *l*'s. If children notice that there are *l*'s in other parts of some words such as *little,* confirm that they are correct; the sound of /l/ can occur in other parts of a word as well as the beginning.

LI

The Lazy Little Lion

The lazy little lion likes
To rest and lie around.
He likes to lounge
In piles of leaves
Or sprawl out on the ground.

The lazy little lion naps
With other lions, too.
Lions love to sleep a LOT!
That's just what lions do.

Big Book of Phonics Rhymes and Poems, 32

OBJECTIVES

Children will:

- identify and discriminate among /r/R,r, /p/P,p, /l/L,l
- write and use letters R,r, P,p, L,l

....

MATERIALS

- letter cards from the Word Play Book

TEACHING TIP

INSTRUCTIONAL Have children line up. Show a letter card *r, p,* or *l* to the child on one end, and ask him or her to name the letter. If the child names the letter, the next person must say the sound of the letter, and the next person must say a word that begins with the letter. Children who pass go to the end of the line and try again.

ALTERNATE TEACHING STRATEGY

....

INITIAL /r/r, /p/p, /l/l

For a different approach to teaching this skill, see pages T24, T28, T31.

Review Initial /r/ r, /p/ p, /l/ l

> **TEACH**

Identify and Discriminate Among /r/r, /p/p, /l/l
Tell children they will review the sounds /r/, /p/, and /l/, and write the letters *R, r, P, p, L, l.* Set the letter cards for these letters in three places on the chalkboard ledge. Point to each, and ask children to say the sounds the letters make.

Write and Use R,r,P,p, L,l
Have children write both forms of the letters *r, p, l* on paper squares. Then read the following words, and have children hold up the square that shows the letter each word begins with: *pan, lad, rot, run, lap, pod.*

> **PRACTICE**

Complete the Practice Book Page
Read the directions on page 234 to the children, and make sure they clearly understand what they are being asked to do. Identify each picture, and complete the first item together. Then work through the page with children, or have them complete the page independently.

> **ASSESS/CLOSE**

Identify and Use R,r, P,p, L,l
Write the following sentences on the chalkboard, and read them aloud as you track print with your hand. Have children hold up the letter *r, p,* or *l* when they hear a word that begins with one of these letters: *Pat ran to the pond. Lin has a red pot.*

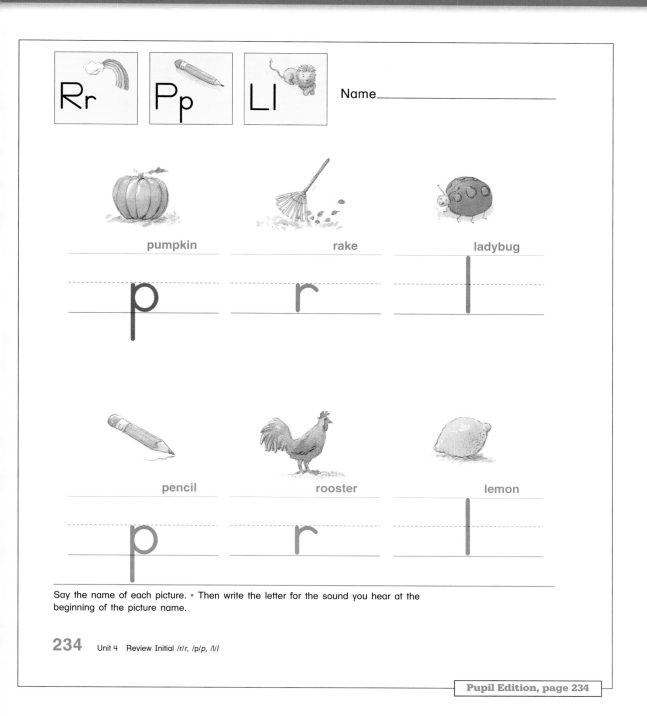

Rr Pp Ll Name_____

pumpkin	rake	ladybug
p	r	l

pencil	rooster	lemon
p	r	l

Say the name of each picture. • Then write the letter for the sound you hear at the beginning of the picture name.

234 Unit 4 Review Initial /r/r, /p/p, /l/l

Pupil Edition, page 234

ADDITIONAL PHONICS RESOURCES

Practice Book,
page 234
Phonics Workbook

McGraw-Hill School
TECHNOLOGY

Phonics CD-ROM
Activities for practice with Initial Letters

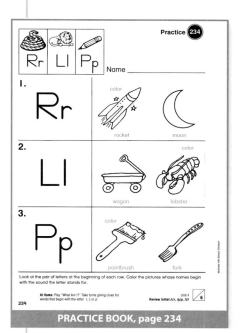

PRACTICE BOOK, page 234

Meeting Individual Needs for Phonics

EASY	ON-LEVEL	CHALLENGE	LANGUAGE SUPPORT
Give each child six strips of paper on which you have printed *R, r, P, p, L,* and *l*. Ask children to use crayons of three different colors and write both forms of a letter in the same color. Then have children point to letters at random and say the sound the letter makes.	**Use** letter cards *R, r, P, p,* and *L, l*. Show a capital and a lower-case form. Ask children to clap if they see both forms of the same letter. If not, they must write the other form of the letter that is being shown. Then ask children to name a word that begins with each letter.	**Show** pictures of objects that begin with *r, p,* and *l,* such as *rope, pan, rabbit, lips, picture, lamp*. Have children identify the sound each object's name begins with and write the letters that make the sounds on self-stick notes to use as labels for the pictures.	**Some** ESL children may have trouble distinguishing /r/ and /l/ sounds. Say pairs of words, and have children repeat the words and act out their meanings: *rabbit, rain, rip, lip, laugh, lion.*

234

OBJECTIVES

Children will:

- match letter cards with letters in the story
- use letters to recognize key words in the story

TEACHING TIP

INSTRUCTIONAL As children become familiar with letters and initial sounds, you may wish to make a word wall. Write a letter on an index card, and invite children to write words that begin with that sound.

Read the **Big Book**

Before Reading

Develop Oral Language   Read with children "The Alphabet Chant" on page 6–7 in the Big Book of Phonics Rhymes and Poems. Remind children that they have read a story about a kitten. Ask children to recall some of the things that Allie saw.

Set Purposes   Explain that children will use letters to name key words. They will also match letter cards with the letters in the book.

- Distribute two or three uppercase and lowercase letters to each child. As you read the story, children holding the letter in the story stand up and name the letter.

- Tell children that they will also think of other words that begin with the same initial letter.

Allie **jumps**!

A hole is no place for a **kitten**.

Allie's Adventure from A to Z, pages 12–13

During Reading

Read Together
- As you point to each letter, have children holding the letter cards stand up and identify them. Run your finger under each word in the story as you read. Have children repeat the words after you. *Concepts of Print*

- After you read page 3, emphasize the /b/ sound. Ask children for another word that starts with the same sound, and have children complete the sentence: *Allie sees a (ball)*. Continue through the story. *Phonics*

- After you read page 12, point to the exclamation point and identify it. Explain that this sentence should be read with an excited voice. Have children read the sentence with you. *Concepts of Print*

- After you read page 24–25, ask children: *Whose voice do you think Allie hears? Make Predictions*

Allie **jumps!**

Allie's Adventure from A to Z, page 12

After Reading

Literary Response
JOURNAL WRITING Ask children to think of another animal friend that Allie could meet on her adventure. Invite children to write and draw about that friend.

ORAL QUESTIONS Ask questions, such as:
- *What would Allie do with her new friend?*
- *Where would they go?*

ABC Activity
Have children sing "The Alphabet Song," on pages 2–3 in the Big Book of Phonics Rhymes and Poems, clapping hands for each letter. Clapping for each letter will help children distinctly say each letter. When children are ready, try two claps and two pats of thighs.

CENTER Activity

Cross Curricular: Language Arts

BUILDING A WORD For each child, provide construction paper shapes (circle, triangle, square, rectangle) in various colors. Have children choose a letter or two from "The Alphabet Chant" and write that letter on the front of their shape(s). Invite a child to recall a word beginning with that letter from the book and then ask other children to help him or her build that word with their letter shapes. Have children line up with their group in front of the class and then read their word aloud.

▶ **Kinesthetic/Interpersonal**

OBJECTIVES

Children will:
- identify positions

....

MATERIALS

- *Allie's Adventure from A to Z*

TEACHING TIP

INSTRUCTIONAL Give children a secret signal, such as "thumbs up," to use when they hear you say a positional term during the day.

Review Positional Terms

PREPARE

Review Positional Terms
Play a special game of "Hide and Seek." Hide an object in the classroom and give directions such as: *The book is inside a drawer. The cube is under a rug.* You may wish to have children hide an object and give clues to others.

TEACH

Identify Positions
Display the Big Book *Allie's Adventure from A to Z* and ask the children where the cow is. (inside the barn) Take a picture walk through the book, and have children look for examples of on, off; inside, outside; over, under; up, down.

PRACTICE

Show Positions
Read the directions on page 235 to the children, and make sure they clearly understand what they are asked to do. Identify each picture, and complete the first item. Then work through the page with children, or have them complete the page independently.

ASSESS/CLOSE

Review the Page
Check children's work on the Pupil Edition page. Note areas where children need extra help.

Name_____

1.

2.

3.

4.

1. Draw a circle around the person who is *on* the couch. Draw a line under the person who is *off* the couch.
2. Draw a circle around the dog that is *inside*. Draw a line under the dog that is *outside*. 3. Draw a circle around the bird that is *over* the tree. Draw a line under the bird that is *under* the tree. 4. Draw a circle around the kite that is *up*. Draw a line under the kite that is *down*.

Unit 4   Review Positional Terms   **235**

Pupil Edition, page 235

PRACTICE BOOK, page 235

ALTERNATE TEACHING
STRATEGY
....

POSITIONAL TERMS
For a different approach to teaching this skill, see pages T25, T29, and T33.

▶ **Visual/Auditory/ Kinesthetic**

Meeting Individual Needs for Beginning Reading Concepts

EASY	ON-LEVEL	CHALLENGE	LANGUAGE SUPPORT
Show picture cards, use position vocabulary and have children describe what they see. *(The bowl is on the table. The dog is outside. The bird is up in the sky.)*	**Use** index cards, and make cards that show opposites: off, on; inside, outside; over, under; up, down. Children place the cards face down and play a concentration memory game, matching opposites.	**Have** children take photographs to make a book that shows positional terms. Ask them to find areas in the classroom that illustrate on, off; inside, outside; up, down; over, under. Help children label the photographs.	**Play** a game of "Simon Says" using position vocabulary: *Simon says put your hands on your head. Put your finger under your chin. Simon says reach up.*

235

Develop Phonological Awareness

Listen

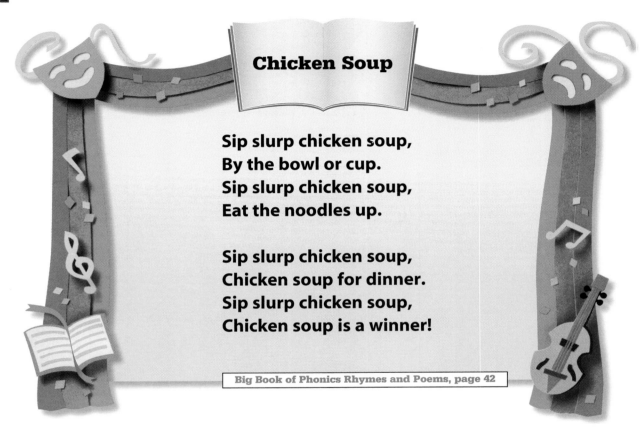

Chicken Soup

Sip slurp chicken soup,
By the bowl or cup.
Sip slurp chicken soup,
Eat the noodles up.

Sip slurp chicken soup,
Chicken soup for dinner.
Sip slurp chicken soup,
Chicken soup is a winner!

Big Book of Phonics Rhymes and Poems, page 42

Objective: Review Final /p/ *p*

INTRODUCE THE POEM Read the poem to the class, exaggerating the "sip slurp." Have children tell what the poem is about. Ask, "What sound do you hear at the end of *soup*?" Have children say the word with you, segmenting the sounds . . . *s-ou-p*. Emphasize the final /p/. Then read the poem again and ask children to listen for other words that end with /p/.

> sip   slurp   up   cup

USING THE SOUND Review the poem with children by asking questions that provide the opportunity for them to use words with final /p/. For example:

- What kind of food is this poem about? (*soup*)
- How do you eat it? (*by the bowl or cup*)
- What noise do you make? (*sip, slurp*)
- What do you do with the noodles? (*eat them up*)

Ask children to show how they use their lips to make the /p/ sound.

Objective: Review Initial /p/ *P, p*

PICK A PICTURE Collect pictures of items that end in /p/. For example:

Name each picture and emphasize the final sound. Ask children to repeat the words after you. Then have children take turns choosing a picture and naming the object. Ask the rest of the class to listen for the final /p/ sound.

PLAY THE SECRET SOUND GAME Ask children to listen to the final sound in the following set of words: *map, soup, pup*. Have children identify the /p/ sound. Give additional sets of words including other final sounds which children have learned. For example:

- hop, tap, soap; stop, drop, rip; rap, trap, up
- bed, head, said; man, pin, bun; rat, cut, bet

Read Together

From Phonemic Awareness to Phonics

Objective: Review Final /p/ *p*

IDENTIFY THE LETTER Review with children that the letter *p* stands for the sound /p/. Display the Phonics Rhyme poem and point out the letter in the upper right corner. Repeat the /p/ sound as you tell children that this is the letter *p*.

REREAD THE POEM As you reread the poem, point to each word. Draw children's attention to the letter *p* and the sound /p/ at the end of words.

FIND THE LETTERS Call on volunteers to come up and point to *p* as you say the lines of the poem. Have children tell where in the word they find the letter. Have them say the word to show where the /p/ sound occurs.

Pp

Chicken Soup

Sip slurp chicken soup,
By the bowl or cup.
Sip slurp chicken soup,
Eat the noodles up.

Sip slurp chicken soup,
Chicken soup for dinner.
Sip slurp chicken soup,
Chicken soup is a winner!

42

Big Book of Phonics Rhymes and Poems, page 42

OBJECTIVES

Children will:

- identify and review /p/ *p*
- write and use the letter *p*

MATERIALS

- letter cards from the Word Building Book

TEACHING TIP

INSTRUCTIONAL Write a word on the chalkboard, and cover it with a piece of paper. Give clues and have children guess the word that ends in /p/, for example: *opposite of bottom (top); where babies like to sit (lap); goes on a saucer (cup)*. When someone guesses the word, remove the paper and say the word aloud, asking children to repeat after you.

ALTERNATE TEACHING STRATEGY

. . . .

FINAL /p/ *p*

For a different approach to teaching this skill, see page T28.

▶ **Visual/Auditory/ Kinesthetic**

Review Final /p/ *p*

TEACH

Identify /p/ *p* Tell children they will review the sound /p/ at the end of a word and write the letter *p*. Write the letter, identify it, and have children say the sound with you. Ask them to say the sound /p/ and hold up their *p* letter cards when they hear *p* in these directions: *Sip from the top of the cup.*

Write and Use *p* Line up picture cards on the chalkboard ledge, some that show objects whose names end in *p* and some that do not. Ask children to write *p* on several large stick-on notes and place them on the pictures that show objects whose names end in /p/. Show, for example: *mop, pin, cap, pup, map, mat, cat.*

PRACTICE

Complete the Pupil Edition Page Read the directions on page 236 to the children, and make sure they clearly understand what they are being asked to do. Identify each picture, and complete the first item together. Work through the page with children, or have them complete the page independently.

ASSESS/CLOSE

Identify and Use *p* Ask children to place their *p* self-stick labels on classroom objects that end in /p/, such as: *map, top, cap, cup, mop, pup.* You may give them clues to help them identify the objects, such as: *Is there something in the room you could wear on your head?* (cap) But ask children to name the object before sticking the label on.

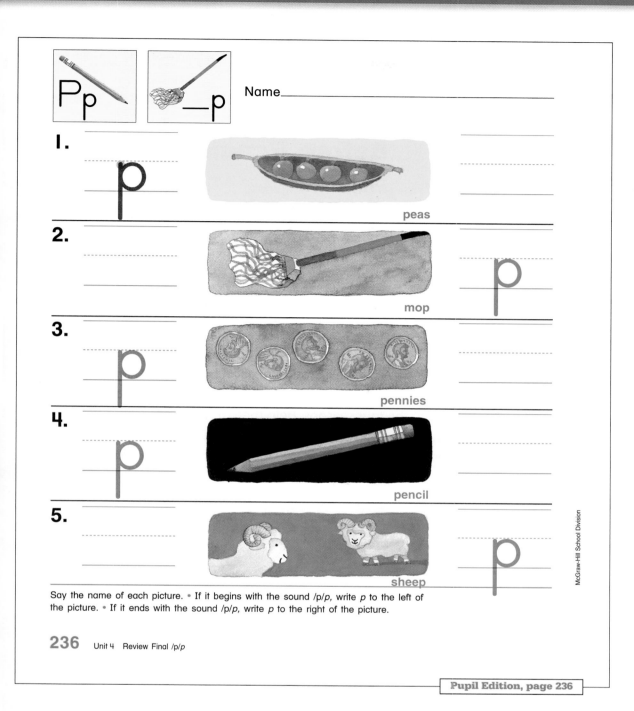

Pp   **_p**

Name_____

1. p

peas

2. p

mop

3. p

pennies

4. p

pencil

5. p

sheep

Say the name of each picture. • If it begins with the sound /p/p, write p to the left of the picture. • If it ends with the sound /p/p, write p to the right of the picture.

McGraw-Hill School Division

Pupil Edition, page 236

ADDITIONAL PHONICS RESOURCES

Practice Book, *page 236*
Phonics Workbook

McGraw-Hill School
TECHNOLOGY

Phonics CD-ROM
Activities for practice with Final Letters

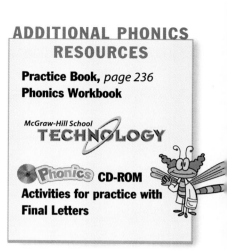

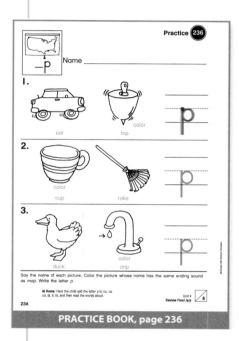

PRACTICE BOOK, page 236

Meeting Individual Needs for Phonics and Decoding

EASY	ON-LEVEL	CHALLENGE	LANGUAGE SUPPORT
Place these word cards on the chalkboard ledge: *tap, tan, sit, sap, dip, rip.* Point to each word and read it aloud. Ask children to raise their hands when they recognize a word that ends in *p* and to trace the letter *p* in the air with their fingers.	**Say** words that end in *p*, and ask children to say words that rhyme, such as: *mop (top, drop, stop); lap (map, nap, wrap); sip (hip, tip, drip).* Each time someone makes a rhyme, have children write *p* on a letter strip.	**Ask** children to complete the story using words that end in /p/, and say: *I went (up) the stairs. At the (top) I gave the door a (tap). A girl opened the door. She took my (cap) and scarf and gave me a hot (cup) of cocoa.*	**Have** children repeat the words and follow your gestures as you say and pantomime action words that end in *p*, such as: *hop, skip, jump, tap, step, drop.* Emphasize the final /p/ sound of each word. Children write *p* in the air for each word.

OBJECTIVES

- review words with initial /r/*r*
- review words with final /p/*p*
- identify the main idea of the story
- compare and contrast

MATERIALS

- *The Apple Pie Tree*

Read the Big Book

Before Reading

Develop Oral Language

PERFORM AN ACTION RHYME Display two apples, holding them aloft as though your arms were branches of a tree. Then have children repeat with you the apple finger play found on pages 201A–201B.

REVISIT THE LITERATURE Have children recall the title of the Big Book about apples. Ask them to re-tell *The Apple Pie Tree*.

Set Purposes

Have children determine a purpose for reading *The Apple Pie Tree* again. For example, they may want to read to compare and contrast the weather in the four seasons. Help them to recall how the different weather in each season affected how the apple tree looked. Ask children to describe how the apple tree looked during each of the four seasons.

The branches bend down low.
They are covered with
big, round apples.

The Apple Pie Tree, pages 22–23

During Reading

Read Together As you read *The Apple Pie Tree,* you may wish to pause before the mention of each new season, allowing time for children to name the season.

- As you read, point to each word as you say it to emphasize the one-to-one matching of the spoken word to the printed word. *Concepts of Print*

- Where appropriate, ask children to identify a word that shows either initial /r/r or final /p/p. *Phonemic Awareness*

- Have children compare and contrast the clothing worn by the girls throughout the seasons. *Compare and Contrast*

- After you finish the story, ask children to tell how the apples got from the tree to pie. *Main Idea*

My sister and I have a tree that grows the best part of apple pie.

Can you guess what that is?

The Apple Pie Tree, page 3

After Reading

Return to Purposes Discuss the purposes that children set before reading *The Apple Pie Tree.* Ask if their purposes were met. Revisit the Big Book as needed.

Literary Response **JOURNAL WRITING** Have children write about or draw their favorite parts of the story.

ORAL RESPONSE Have children share their journal entries with the class.

INFORMAL ASSESSMENT

IDENTIFY MAIN IDEA
HOW TO ASSESS
Children should identify the main idea of the cycle of the apple from blossoms to pie.

FOLLOW-UP If children have trouble identifying the main idea, tell two- or three-sentence stories.

CENTER Activity

Cross Curricular: Science

OUR FIVE SENSES Have children create a 5-page sense book (one page for each of the 5 senses). Ask them to draw or cut out magazine pictures of things that can be smelled, tasted, touched, heard, or seen. Have them paste the pictures in their books.

▶ **Bodily/Kinesthetic**

INQUIRY Ask children what else they would like to learn about their senses, such as what senses they use when they eat dinner.

 Help children log on to **www.mhschool.com/ reading,** where they can access links to various health sites.

OBJECTIVES

Children will:

- understand the main idea of a story

....

MATERIALS

- *The Apple Pie Tree*

TEACHING TIP

INSTRUCTIONAL Display some familiar books with straightforward titles and read the titles aloud. For example, you might use *Flower Garden* and *Peanut Butter and Jelly*. Ask children to tell what the books are about. Summarize by saying, "Yes, *Flower Garden* is about a girl and her father growing flowers." Confirm that children have been identifying the main idea of the story.

Review Main Idea

PREPARE

Review Main Idea
Ask children to recall the story *The Apple Pie Tree*. Reread the title and have children explain what it means. Talk about how the title helps readers understand what the story is about. Mention that a story title often contains the main idea of the story.

TEACH

Understand Main Idea
Remind children that the main idea tells what a story or passage is all about. Draw children's attention to details from the story, such as the bare tree in winter or adding cinnamon to the apple pie. Point out that these details are part of the story, but not what the whole story is about. Work with children to restate the main idea of *The Apple Pie Tree*.

PRACTICE

Complete the Pupil Edition Page
Read the directions on page 237 to children, and make sure they clearly understand what they are asked to do. Identify each picture, and complete the first item together. Then work through the page with children or have them complete the page independently.

ASSESS/CLOSE

Review the Page
Review how children complete the practice page and note any children who need additional work.

Name_____

1.    My cat ran to Dad.

   My pup ran to Pam.

2.    The cat can nap on the cot.

   The pup is in the mud.

3.    The pup can fit on the mat.

   The pup can fit in the cap.

Look at each picture. • Then read the sentences. • Draw a line under the sentence that tells what the picture is all about.

Unit 4   Review Main Idea   **237**

Pupil Edition, page 237

ALTERNATE TEACHING
STRATEGY
....
MAIN IDEA
For a different approach to teaching this skill, see page T26.

▶ **Visual/Auditory/Kinesthetic**

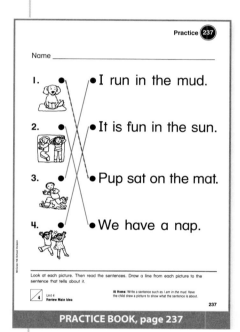

Practice 237

Name _____

1. • • I run in the mud.

2. • • It is fun in the sun.

3. • • Pup sat on the mat.

4. • • We have a nap.

Look at each picture. Then read the sentences. Draw a line from each picture to the sentence that tells about it.

Unit 4 Review Main Idea

At Home: Write a sentence such as *I am in the mud.* Have the child draw a picture to show what the sentence is about.

237

PRACTICE BOOK, page 237

Meeting Individual Needs for Comprehension

EASY	ON-LEVEL	CHALLENGE	LANGUAGE SUPPORT
Display objects that have related functions. For example, you might show a pencil, pen, and paper. Have children identify the items, then ask what the main idea of all the objects is. *(writing)* Repeat using other items, such as a crayon, paint jar, and easel.	**Show** children pictures of different people doing similar kinds of activities. For example, you might show athletes involved in different sports. Have children tell what the main idea of the pictures is. *(playing sports)* Repeat the activity using other subjects.	**Have** children draw or paint a picture showing some kind of scene. Ask children to explain what the main idea of their picture is. Or, children might display their pictures and have other class members identify the main idea.	**Use** the illustrations and text in the story to introduce or review the words for the seasons. Reread the passages that tell what happens in each season. Have children tell what they might do in each season.

Develop Phonological Awareness

Listen

The Lazy Little Lion
a poem

Pease Porridge Hot
a poem

The lazy little lion likes
To rest and lie around.
He likes to lounge in piles
   of leaves
Or sprawl out on the
   ground.
The lazy little lion naps
With other lions, too.
Lions love to sleep a LOT!
That's just what lions do.

Pease porridge hot,
Pease porridge cold,
Pease porridge in the pot,
Nine days old.
Some like it hot,
Some like it cold,
Some like it in the pot,
Nine days old.

Big Book of Phonics Rhymes and Poems, pages 32, 41

Objective: Focus on Syllables

READ THE POEM Read the poem "The Lazy Little Lion" several times, inviting children to join in.

IDENTIFY AND CLAP SYLLABLES Say the word *lazy* aloud. Repeat the word, clapping once for each syllable. Then say the title "The Lazy Little Lion" and have children clap out the syllables in the words.

> The   La/zy   Lit/tle   Li/on

SUBSTITUTE OTHER ANIMAL NAMES Invite children to name other animals. Substitute their suggestions for the word *Lion* in the title. Say the new titles aloud.

CLAP SYLLABLES AGAIN Repeat the new titles, having children clap once for each syllable.

Objective: Listen for /r/, /p/, and /l/

READ THE POEMS Read the poems, stressing words with /p/, /l/, and /r/. Say the sounds /p/, /l/, and /r/, and have children repeat them after you.

LISTEN FOR THE SOUND Sing the following song to the tune of "Do You Know the Muffin Man?"

> **Do you hear a /p/ in *pet*?**
> **A /p/ in *pet*? A /p/ in *pet*?**
> **Do you hear a /p/ in *pet*?**
> **Then say the word right now!**

Pause for children to either remain silent or repeat the word.

> **pig mop bed pan**
> **pie dog cap**

If children hear the sound /p/ in the word, encourage them to tell where they hear it: at the beginning or at the end.

SING AGAIN Have children sing the song again, this time listening for words that begin with /l/.

> **lid race light**
> **ladder stop lot**

Repeat the song with words that begin with /r/.

> **rabbit rope wagon**
> **rip fun ring**

Read Together

From Phonemic Awareness to Phonics

Objective: Associate /p/ *P, p*; /l/ *L, l*; and /r/ *R, r*

IDENTIFY THE LETTERS
Display the Big Book of Phonics Rhymes and Poems, pages 32 and 41. On each page, point to the letters, identify them, and say the sound they stand for.

REREAD THE POEMS Reread the poems, tracking the print and emphasizing the words with initial or final /p/, initial /r/, or initial /l/.

FIND WORDS WITH *P, p, L, l,* and *r* Write the letters *P, p, L, l,* and *r* on cards, and have children match them with letters in words in the poems.

Ll

The Lazy Little Lion

The lazy little lion likes
To rest and lie around.
He likes to lounge
In piles of leaves
Or sprawl out on the ground.

The lazy little lion naps
With other lions, too.
Lions love to sleep a LOT!
That's just what lions do.

32

Pease Porridge Hot

Pease porridge hot,
  Pease porridge cold,
Pease porridge in the pot,
  Nine days old.
Some like it hot,
  Some like it cold,
Some like it in the pot,
  Nine days old.

41

Big Book of Phonics Rhymes and Poems, pages 32, 41

OBJECTIVES

Children will:

- identify and discriminate among /r/R,r, /p/P,p, and /l/L,l
- write and use letters R,r, P,p, and L,l

MATERIALS

- letter cards from the Word Building Book

TEACHING TIP

INSTRUCTIONAL Give children a selection of tactile letters R, r, L, l, P, and p. Lead a discussion about how the capital letters are alike and how they are different, and have children sort for capital and lowercase forms. Then have children sort the letters into three groups of same letters.

ALTERNATE TEACHING STRATEGY

LETTERS /r/r, /p/p, /l/l
For a different approach to teaching this skill, see page T24, T28, T31.

▶ **Visual/Auditory/Kinesthetic**

Review /r/r, /p/p, /l/l

TEACH

Identify and Discriminate Among /r/R,r, /p/P,p, and /l/L,l

Tell children they will review the sounds /r/, /p/, and /l/ and write the letters R,r P,p, L,l. Write both forms of each letter on three different parts of the chalkboard. Say the sounds with the children. Ask children to point to the letter that each of the following words begins with: *lid, lip, rip, rod, pod, pot*. Repeat the words, and ask them to listen for words that end with the sound /p/ and the letter *p*. Tell children to tap on their tables each time they hear a word that ends in *p*.

Write and Use R,r, P,p, and L,l

Give each child three index cards, and have them write capital *R, P, L* on one side of each card and lowercase *r, p, l* on the reverse side. Point to any children whose first names begin with one of these three letters, or say names aloud and have children show the capital letter each name begins with. Show pictures or point to objects, and continue the game using lowercase *r, p, l*. Be sure to include some pictures and objects that end with the letter *p*.

PRACTICE

Complete the Pupil Edition Page

Read the directions on page 238 to the children, and make sure they clearly understand what they are being asked to do. Identify each picture, and complete the first item together. Then work through the page with children or have them complete the page independently.

ASSESS/CLOSE

Identify and Use R,r, P,p, L,l

Show the following word cards, one at a time: *lit, lap, pop, pad, Pam, rot, ran, Lin, lad, Ron, pod*. Have children point to the letter each word begins with and place it on the chalk ledge beneath that letter. Then ask children to identify the two words that end with *p*.

Name_____

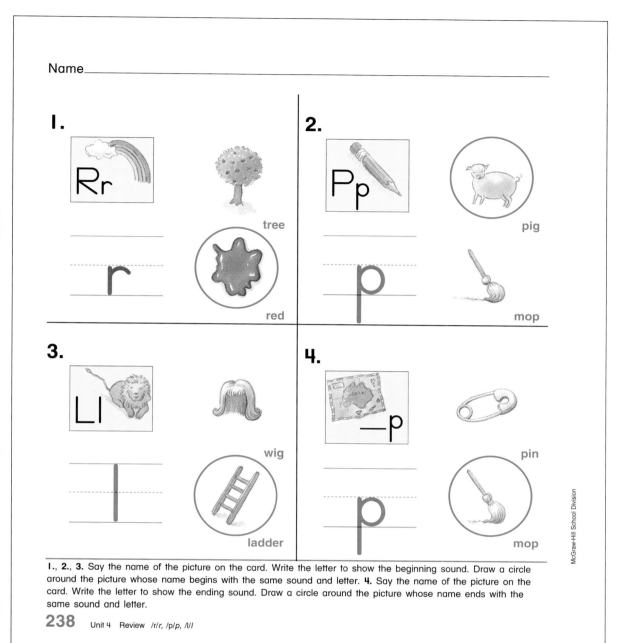

1. Rr — tree — r — red

2. Pp — pig — p — mop

3. Ll — wig — l — ladder

4. map — _p — pin — p — mop

1., 2., 3. Say the name of the picture on the card. Write the letter to show the beginning sound. Draw a circle around the picture whose name begins with the same sound and letter. 4. Say the name of the picture on the card. Write the letter to show the ending sound. Draw a circle around the picture whose name ends with the same sound and letter.

238 Unit 4 Review /r/r, /p/p, /l/l

McGraw-Hill School Division

Pupil Edition, page 238

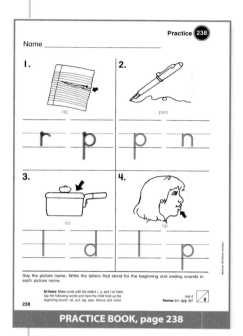

ADDITIONAL PHONICS RESOURCES

Practice Book, *page 238*
Phonics Workbook

McGraw-Hill School
TECHNOLOGY

Phonics CD-ROM
Activities for practice with Initial Letters

Practice **238**

Name_____

1. rip — r p

2. pen — p n

3. lid — l d

4. lip — l p

Say the picture name. Write the letters that stand for the beginning and ending sounds in each picture name.

At Home: Make cards with the letters r, p, and l on them. Say the following words and have the child hold up the beginning sound: rat, pull, leg, pear, lettuce, and robot.

238 Unit 4 Review /r/r, /p/p, /l/l

PRACTICE BOOK, page 238

Meeting Individual Needs for Phonics

EASY	ON-LEVEL	CHALLENGE	LANGUAGE SUPPORT
Form a circle and play "Pass the Hat." Put pictures of objects whose names begin with r, p, or l in the hat. Children pass the hat along until you raise your hand. Then the child holding the hat pulls out a picture and identifies whether its name begins with r, p, or l.	**Form** a circle, and pass a hat into which children have put letters r, p, and l written on slips of paper. Each child pulls out a letter and says a word that begins with that letter. If children can't think of a word, they can pass and try again on their next turn.	**Play** "Categories" and ask children to name places, food, household items, classroom objects, animals, articles of clothing, and so forth that begin with the letters r, p, or l. Keep a running list of all the words the children can think of.	**Help** ESL children practice distinguishing the initial sounds /r/ and /l/ by having them sing "Do the Hokey-Pokey." This will also reinforce their recognition of parts of the body and their use of *right, left*. Emphasize the initial r and l as you sing the song.

Teacher Read Aloud

 **Listen**

Every Time I Climb a Tree
by David McCord

Every time I climb a tree
Every time I climb a tree
Every time I climb a tree
I scrape a leg
Or skin a knee
And every time I climb a tree
I find some ants
Or dodge a bee
And get the ants
All over me

And every time I climb a tree
Where have you been?
They say to me
But don't they know that I
   am free
Every time I climb a tree?
I like it best

To spot a nest
That has an egg
Or maybe three

And then I skin
The other leg
But every time I climb a tree
I see a lot of things to see
Swallows rooftops and TV
And all the fields and farms
   there be
Every time I climb a tree
Though climbing may be good
   for ants
It isn't awfully good for pants
But still it's pretty good for me
Every time I climb a tree

Oral Comprehension

LISTENING AND SPEAKING Review with children the poem "Every Time I Climb a Tree." Remind them that the child in the poem describes how it feels to look at things from close-up and from far away.

Ask children to name the images they like best in the poem, and share what they find appealing about them. What do they think is the best part of seeing the world from a tree?

Activity Have children choose their favorite images from the poem and draw pictures to match. You can have them make a caption of descriptive words for what they have drawn.

▶ **Spatial**

Real-Life Reading

Can you follow the footsteps?
Start at **X**.

24

25

Big Book of Real-Life Reading, pages 24–25

Objective: Read a Map

REVIEW THE PAGE Ask children why they think maps are important. Have them name maps they have seen at home or in school. How is a bus map different from a road map?

FOLLOW-UP ACTIVITY Guide children to create maps of their own rooms at home. Ask them to try to remember major objects in the room, and where each object is located. You can have them color-code furniture, clothes, and toys.

CENTER Activity

Cross Curricular: Social Studies

MAP TIME Provide children with a simple map of their own town. The map should focus on one street they all know, a main street next to their school or near a public playground. Have them:

• label the map, using words and/or pictures, to indicate important buildings

• include special places on the street, such as an ice cream parlor, movie house, toy store, or book shop

• write a sentence describing the street—for example, whether the street is busy, quiet, pretty, or plain

▶ **Interpersonal/Spatial/Linguistic**

OBJECTIVES

Children will:
- review high-frequency words *to, me, go, do*

MATERIALS
- word cards from the Word Building Book

TEACHING TIP

MANAGEMENT Some children may not be able to complete the worksheets without additional support. You may wish to have these children work with a partner to complete this part of the lesson.

Review *to, me, go, do*

PREPARE

Listen to Words

Tell children that you will be reviewing the words *to, me, go,* and *do.* Read each of the following sentences aloud and ask children to listen carefully.

1. Let's <u>go to</u> the tree.

2. Will you come with <u>me</u>?

3. We will <u>do</u> something fun.

Tell children that you will read the sentences another time. As you read, have children raise their hands when they hear one of the high-frequency words.

TEACH

Model Reading the Word in Context

Pass out the word cards from the Word Building Book so that each child has a set of the high-frequency words. Display each card and pronounce the word. Ask children to listen for each high-frequency word as you read the sentences again. Have children raise their hands when they hear a word.

Identify the Words

Write the three sentences on chart paper. Reread each sentence, tracking the print as you read. Ask children to hold up the correct word card when they hear each high-frequency word. Remind children that more than one word might be in a sentence. Call on volunteers to come up and circle the words in the sentences.

PRACTICE

Complete the Pupil Edition Page

Read the directions on page 239 to the children, and make sure they clearly understand what they are asked to do. Complete the first item together. Then work through the page with children or have them complete the page independently.

ASSESS/CLOSE

Review the Page

Go over children's pages and note any children who need additional support.

Name_____

1. (do)   that   to   my

2. me   we   is   (to)

3. go   you   said   (me)

4. have   has   for   (go)

Read the words. **1.** Draw a circle around the word *do*. **2.** Draw a circle around the word *to*. **3.** Draw a circle around the word *me*. **3.** Draw a circle around the word *go*.

Unit 4   Review *to, me, go, do*   **239**

Pupil Edition, page 239

ALTERNATE TEACHING STRATEGY

HIGH-FREQUENCY WORDS: *to, me, go, do*

For a different approach to teaching this skill, see page T27.

▶ **Visual/Auditory/ Kinesthetic**

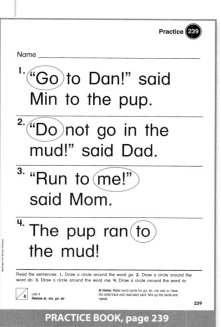

Practice 239

Name _____

1. ("Go) to Dan!" said Min to the pup.

2. ("Do) not go in the mud!" said Dad.

3. "Run to (me!") said Mom.

4. The pup ran (to) the mud!

Read the sentences. 1. Draw a circle around the word *go*. 2. Draw a circle around the word *do*. 3. Draw a circle around the word *me*. 4. Draw a circle around the word *to*.

At Home: Make word cards for *go, do, me,* and *to.* Have the child trace and read each card. Mix up the cards and repeat.

Unit 4
Review *to, me, go, do*

239

PRACTICE BOOK, page 239

Meeting Individual Needs for Vocabulary

EASY	ON-LEVEL	CHALLENGE	LANGUAGE SUPPORT
Write the heading "About Me" on sheets of drawing paper. Then have children draw pictures to illustrate the heading. Set aside time for children to share their pictures and tell about themselves. Have the rest of the class identify the word *me* in the title.	**Fold** sheets of drawing paper in half and write the headings "Things to Do" and "Places to Go" on the two parts. Have children draw several small pictures to illustrate each heading. When children present their pictures to the class, have them point to the high-frequency words.	**Give** children the following clues and have them hold up the word card that identifies each high-frequency word. 1. It sounds like the number 2. *(to)* 2. It is another word for I. *(me)* 3. The boys _____ to the store. *(go)*	**Give** children practice in subject/verb agreement using the verbs *go* and *do*. Ask children to repeat these sentences with you paying attention to the high-frequency words: *We go to lunch. The principal goes to lunch. The boys do their homework. That girl does her homework.*

Develop Phonological Awareness

Making Mud Pies
a poem

Find a lot of sand.
Add a cup of water.
Make a lot of mud pies,
And sell them for a quarter.
After mud pies have baked in
the sun,
Run into the lake and have
some fun!

Objective: Listen for Syllables

READ THE POEM Encourage children to listen closely as you read the poem "Making Mud Pies." Ask children what the poem is about.

> making   mud   pies

CLAP FOR SYLLABLES Read the title of the poem aloud, clapping once for each syllable. Repeat the title and invite children to clap out the syllables. Have children identify the word in the title that has two syllables.

LISTEN AND CLAP Reread the poem slowly. have children clap out syllables in each of the words.

NAME OTHER PLACES Ask children where the people in the poem ran after mud pies baked in the sun. *(lake)* Say the word *lake* and have children clap out the syllable. Invite children to suggest other place names.

> ocean pool sprinkler house

Repeat each of their suggestions and have them clap to determine the number of syllables in each word.

SUBSTITUTE PLACES Reread the poem "Making Mud Pies," substituting the new places for the word *lake* in the poem.

Objective: Blending with Short *u*

LISTEN FOR THE SOUND Have children listen as you read the poem "Making Mud Pies." Say the word *mud* and emphasize the /u/ sound. Then say the word *sun* and determine that both words have the same medial sound. Have children repeat the words with you. Then read each line of the poem slowly. Children hold up their hands each time they hear a word with the /u/ sound.

> cup mud mud
> sun run fun

RECOGNIZE THE SOUND Say the following words. Children clap if the word has the medial/u/ sound.

> cup hat run
> bag fun net bun

BLENDING SOUNDS Tell children you are going to say all of the sounds in a word. Say /m/-/u/-/d/. Then have children repeat the sounds with you to determine the word *mud*. Then tell children to listen as you say the sounds of the following words. Ask for a volunteer to blend and say the word.

> nut bun hut pup run

IDENTIFY WORDS WITH /u/ Tell children you will say two words and have them repeat the word that has the /u/ sound. Say *cup* and *rat*. Continue with the following words.

> net/bug bat/run
> cup/sit nut/car

Read Together

From Phonemic Awareness to Phonics

Objective: Identify Word Endings

LISTENING FOR RHYMING WORDS Read the last two lines of the poem "Making Mud Pies," stressing the rhyming words. Ask children to name the words that rhyme and write them. (sun, fun)

IDENTIFY THE LETTERS Invite a volunteer to circle the letters in the words that are the same and identify them. Ask children to say the sounds these letters stand for.

NAME OTHER RHYMING WORDS Invite children to name other words that rhyme with *sun*

and *fun*. Write their suggestions on the board, circling the letters *un* to show that these words also have the same ending letters.

> bun run spun

IDENTIFY OTHER WORD ENDINGS Write the word *hum* on the board as you demonstrate its meaning. Say the word aloud. Invite children to suggest words that rhyme with *hum*. Write their responses on the board. Help children see that these words all end with the letters *um*.

SORT THE WORDS Write all the *um* words and *un* words on index cards. Have children sort the cards into rhyming families.

OBJECTIVES

Children will:

- identify /u/*u*
- blend and read short *u* words
- write short *u* words
- review /l/*l*, /p/*p*, /r/*r*, /f/*f*, /k/*c*, /t/*t*, /m/*m*, /s/*s*, /d/*d*, and /n/*n*

MATERIALS

- letter cards from the Word Building Book

TEACHING TIP

INSTRUCTIONAL Display the following pictures and ask children to sort them to show objects whose names have /u/ in the middle: *sun, cat, cup, mop, nut, lid.*

ALTERNATE TEACHING STRATEGY

....

BLENDING SHORT *u*

For a different approach to teaching this skill, see page T32.

▶ **Visual/Auditory/ Kinesthetic**

Review Blending with short *u*

TEACH

Identify *u* as the Symbol for /u/

Tell children that today they will be reading and writing words with the letter *u* that stands for the sound /u/.

- Display the *u* letter card and say /u/. Have children repeat the sound /u/ after you as you point to the *u* card.

BLENDING Model and Guide Practice

- Place a *t* letter card to the right of the *u* card. Blend the sounds together and have children repeat after you: *ut.*

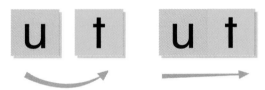

- Place a *c* letter card before the *ut* cards. Blend the sounds in the word to read *cut.* Have children repeat after you.

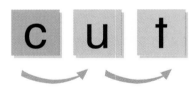

Use the Word in Context

- Invite children to use *cut* in a sentence, perhaps talking about how people make things like clothing, pictures, or puppets.

Repeat the Procedure

- Use the following words to continue modeling and for guided practice with short *u*: *mud, fun, nut, pup, run, sun, cup.*

PRACTICE

Complete the Pupil Edition Page

Read aloud the directions on page 240 to the children, and make sure they clearly understand what they are being asked to do. Identify each picture, and complete the first item together. Then work through the page with children, or have them complete the page independently.

ASSESS/CLOSE

Write Short *u* Words

Observe children as they complete page 240. Then display letter cards *l, p, r, f, c, t, m, s, d, n* and have children choose four of the letters to write two words with short *u* in the middle.

Name_____

1. s u n   sun

2. n u t   nut

3. p u p   pup

4. c u p   cup

Blend the sounds and say the word. • Write the word. • Draw a circle around the picture that goes with the word.

McGraw-Hill School Division

Pupil Edition, page 240

ADDITIONAL PHONICS RESOURCES

Practice Book, *page 240*
Phonics Workbook

McGraw-Hill School
TECHNOLOGY

Phonics CD-ROM
Activities for practice with Blending and Segmenting

Practice 240

Name_____

1. u p   up

2. c u p   cup

3. n u t   nut

4. m u d   mud

Blend the sounds and say the word. Write the word. Draw a line under the picture that goes with the word.

At Home: Write *up* in the air and blend the sounds as you write. Continue with *mud* and *cup*. Use the words in sentences.

240   Unit 4 Review Blending with Short *u*   8

PRACTICE BOOK, page 240

Meeting Individual Needs for Phonics

EASY	ON-LEVEL	CHALLENGE	LANGUAGE SUPPORT
Ask children to sort the following word cards for words that have the sound /u/ in the middle, and those that have another sound in the middle: *nap, nut, nod, sip, sat, sun.* Have children blend and read the short *u* words and use each word in a sentence.	**Pronounce** each letter distinctly as you say the word *sun.* Ask children to name the first, middle, and last letters, and write them on the chalkboard. Repeat with *cut* and *pup.*	**On** the chalkboard write the word *fin.* Invite children to change the i to a *u* to make a new word. *(fun)* Have children read the new word aloud. Continue with the words *cot, mad, pop,* and *not.*	**Ask** children to hold up the *u* letter card when they hear the sound /u/, and say: *That pup is not having fun in the sun.* Invite children to talk about safe ways to have fun in the sun, with or without a pet.

240

Guided Instruction

BEFORE READING

PREVIEW AND PREDICT Take a brief **picture walk** through the book, focusing on the illustrations.

- *Who is the story about? Where is it taking place?*

- *What do you think will happen in the story?*

- *Do you think the story will be realistic or make-believe? Why?*

SET PURPOSES Ask children to think about what they might want to find out about the story. As volunteers think of some questions, you may wish to compile a class list for reference as children read the story.

TEACHING TIP

To put book together:
1. Tear out the story page.
2. Cut along dotted line.
3. Fold each section on fold line.
4. Assemble book.

MANAGEMENT Some children may not be ready to read this story successfully. You may wish to tape record the story and have these children listen to the story and read along at their own level.

Fun in the Sun

"I have my fan," said Mom to me.

3

McGraw-Hill School Division

Mom sat in the sun.

2

McGraw-Hill School Division

Dad sat in the sun.

4

Guided Instruction

DURING READING

☑ **Blending with Short *u***

☑ **Compare and Contrast**

☑ **Concepts of Print**

☑ **High-Frequency Words:** *to, me, go, do*

(1) CONCEPTS OF PRINT Model how to run your finger from left to right under each word as you read the title page.

(2) BLENDING WITH SHORT *u* Have children point to the word on page 2 that contains the letter *u*. Ask children to blend the sounds to read the word *s u n sun*.

(3) HIGH-FREQUENCY WORDS Have children locate the words *to* and *me* on page 3.

(4) COMPARE AND CONTRAST Ask children to compare the sentences on pages 4 and 2. Have them find the words that are different. (Mom/Dad)

LANGUAGE SUPPORT

ESL Point out the word *fan* on page 3. Make sure children understand that a fan of this type is used to cool someone off. Help children fold a piece of paper to form a fan.

Guided Instruction

DURING READING

5 **USE ILLUSTRATIONS** Ask children how the girl in the story might be feeling. (excited and anxious)

6 **USE ILLUSTRATIONS** Point out the sign on the fence shown on page 6. Explain that the word *Exit* always means "the way out of a place" and that this is important safety information for people to know in many situations.

7 **MAKE INFERENCES** Ask children to look at page 7 and ask them why Dad might like to wear a cap in the sun. Then ask why Dad and Mom might like to wear sunglasses. (Both help protect them from the sun's rays.)

8 **COMPARE AND CONTRAST** Have children compare how Mom and Dad look at the beginning of the story and how they look at the end of the story.

COMPARE AND CONTRAST
HOW TO ASSESS Have children show or tell about something that is the same and something that is different in the story. (girl is in pool/parents are not in the pool; all of them are wet)

FOLLOW UP Have children use several pages of the story to point out words that are the same and words that are different by one or two letters. (*sun/fun; fun/fan; sat/sun;* and so on)

"I have my cap," said Dad to me.

5

"Can I go and have a dip?" I said.

7

I sat in the sun.

6

Mom and Dad do not have fun in the sun.

8

Guided Instruction

AFTER READING

RETURN TO PREDICTIONS AND PURPOSES
Ask children if their predictions about the story were correct. Ask if they were surprised at the end of the story.

RETELL THE STORY Have children work together to retell the story. Children can use their books to check the sequence of the story.

LITERARY RESPONSE To help children respond to the story, ask:

- How did the girl have fun at the pool?

- Did Mom and Dad have fun at the pool? Why, or why not?

Invite children to tell a different ending for the story.

CENTER Activity

Cross Curricular: Science

SUN SPOTS Have children place classroom objects such as crayons, erasers, cubes, and paper clips on dark construction paper in direct sunlight. Have them put the papers in direct sunlight. Have them remove the objects at the end of the day. Ask what happened to the paper, and have them circle spots that are lighter than others.

▶ **Logical/Mathematical**

OBJECTIVES

Children will:

- compare and contrast to understand a story

MATERIALS

- *Fun in the Sun*

TEACHING TIP

INSTRUCTIONAL Ask children what they do in the summer to keep cool. Then ask what they do in the winter to keep warm. Compare the lists.

Review Compare and Contrast

PREPARE

Recall the Story Ask children to recall the story *Fun in the Sun*. Ask who the characters are, and where the story takes place. Help children make a list of ways they might stay cool in summer. Compare what the girl does to stay cool to the list that the children made. Ask: *What is the same? What is different?*

TEACH

Compare and Contrast Reread the story together. Then have them compare how the girl felt and how Mom and Dad felt. Ask: *Did the girl have fun? Did Mom and Dad have fun?*

PRACTICE

Complete the Pupil Edition Page Read the directions on page 243 to the children, and make sure they clearly understand what they are asked to do. Identify each picture, and complete the first item together. Then work through the page with children or have them complete the page independently.

ASSESS/CLOSE

Review the Page Review children's work, and note children who are experiencing difficulty.

Name_____

1.

2.

3.

Look at the two bicycles at the top of the page. • Then look at the pictures along the left side of the page. • Under each bicycle, put a ✔ on the line if the bicycle has that part. • Put an ✘ on the line if the bicycle does not have that part.

Unit 4   Review Compare and Contrast   **243**

Pupil Edition, page 243

ALTERNATE TEACHING STRATEGY

COMPARE AND CONTRAST

For a different approach to the teaching this skill, see page T30.

▶ **Visual/Auditory/ Kinesthetic**

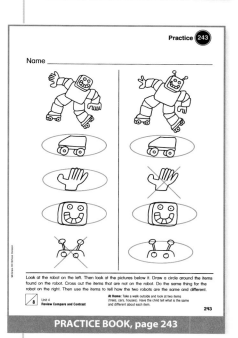

Look at the robot on the left. Then look at the pictures below it. Draw a circle around the items found on the robot. Cross out the items that are not on the robot. Do the same thing for the robot on the right. Then use the items to tell how the two robots are the same and different.

At Home: Take a walk outside and look at two items (trees, cars, houses). Have the child tell what is the same and different about each item.

Unit 4   Review Compare and Contrast   243

PRACTICE BOOK, page 243

Meeting Individual Needs for Comprehension

EASY	ON-LEVEL	CHALLENGE	LANGUAGE SUPPORT
Divide a sheet of chart paper into halves. On one side, have children draw pictures of what they like to do at a pool. On the other side, have them draw pictures of what they like to do at the beach. Compare the results.	**Give** each child a sheet of drawing paper, and label one side *summer* and the other side *winter*. Have children draw or find pictures of clothes that they wear in each season. Compare the information.	**Invite** children to think of a tree that they are familiar with. Children may choose a tree near their homes or near school. Talk with children about how the tree looks during each season, emphasizing how it is alike and different.	**Invite** children to find two classroom books. Compare and contrast by asking questions such as: *Are the books about the same things? Do they both have pictures? Do they both have words? Do they have the same number of pages?*

Develop Phonological Awareness

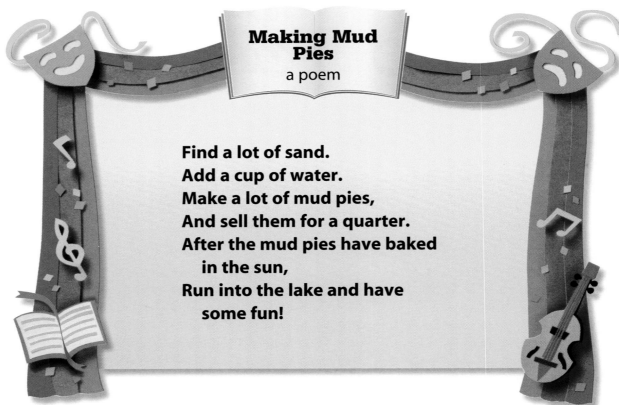

Making Mud Pies
a poem

Find a lot of sand.
Add a cup of water.
Make a lot of mud pies,
And sell them for a quarter.
After the mud pies have baked
  in the sun,
Run into the lake and have
  some fun!

Objective: Focus on Words in Context

READ THE POEM Have children sit in a circle. Read the poem "Making Mud Pies." Repeat several times, encouraging children to join in on familiar words.

LISTEN FOR DETAILS Say the following sentence: *The children like to make mud pies.* Ask: *What do the children like to make?*

> mud   pies

REPEAT WORDS IN CONTEXT Reread the poem line by line, omitting the last word in the sentence. Have children fill in the last word. Repeat this activity a few times until children feel comfortable reciting the missing words.

> Find a lot of _____.

REPEAT THE SENTENCE Say the sentence again. Encourage children to repeat it after you. Then choose seven children and assign each one a word of the sentence. Have children stand in a left-to-right line and say their words in order. Repeat several times, increasing the tempo until the sentence flows smoothly.

> The children like to make mud pies.

COUNT THE WORDS Ask a volunteer to count the number of words in the sentence by counting the children in line. Repeat the activity with the sentence *I like mud pies.* Have children compare the number of words.

> I like mud pies.

Objective: Blending with Short *u*, *o*, and *i*

LISTEN AND BLEND Read the fifth line of the poem "Making Mud Pies," segmenting the sounds in the word *sun*. Invite children to repeat the segmented sounds and have them determine that there are three sounds.

> /s/-/u/-/n/

Say the segmented sounds again. Have children take one step forward for each sound. Repeat several times, gradually increasing the speed until the word is blended smoothly. Then repeat with other words from the poem.

> **fun   lot   cup   mud   run**

BLEND THE SOUNDS Set out several pie tins. Encourage children to listen carefully as you say a word slowly. Have a volunteer place one pie tin on the chalkboard ledge for each sound in the word. Repeat the segmented word several times, gradually increasing the speed until the word is blended smoothly. Have the vol-

unteer point to the tins as the sounds are blended. Be sure the volunteer starts at the left.

> **nut   top   pot   lid   rod   cot   mop**

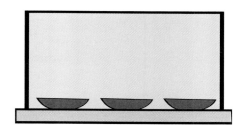

PRACTICE BLENDING Provide each child with several connecting cubes. Have them set out one cube for each sound they hear in the segmented words you say aloud. Have them point to the cubes as they blend the sounds and determine the word.

> **rod   cot   mop   rip   fit   sit   rim**

From Phonemic Awareness to Phonics

Objective: Associate Sounds with Letters

LISTEN FOR A RHYMING WORD Read the first line of the poem "Making Mud Pies." Ask: *What word rhymes with* rot? Write the words *lot* and *rot* on the chalkboard.

> **rot   lot**

IDENTIFY THE LETTERS Invite a volunteer to circle the letters in the words that are the same. Then identify the letters. Ask children to say the sound each letter stands for.

NAME OTHER RHYMING WORDS Invite children to name other words that rhyme with *lot* and *rot*. Write their responses on the chalkboard. Have a volunteer circle the ending letters that are the same in all the words.

> **not   dot   tot   cot**
> **pot   got   hot   jot**

MORE RHYMING WORDS Have children suggest rhyming words for *dim, tin,* and *cut.* Work on one rhyming family at a time. Write their suggestions on the chalk-

board. Circle the ending letters to show that all the words that rhyme have the same ending letters.

> **him Jim Kim rim Tim slim**
> **bin fin pin chin shin skin**
> **spin but hut nut shut**

SORT RHYMING WORDS Write all the words from the chalkboard on index cards, one word per card. Shuffle the cards. Have children work together to sort the cards into rhyming families.

OBJECTIVES

Children will:

- identify /u/u, /o/o, /i/i
- blend and read short *u, o, i* words
- write short *u, o, i* words
- review /l/l, /p/p, /r/r, /f/f, /k/c, /t/t, /m/m, /s/s, /d/d, and /n/n

MATERIALS

- letter cards from the Word Building Book

TEACHING TIP

INSTRUCTIONAL Have children work with a partner and repeat the sounds /u/, /o/, /i/. Tell them to use a mirror to watch their mouths closely. Then lead a discussion about how the shape of the mouth is similar or different with each sound.

ALTERNATE TEACHING STRATEGY

BLENDING SHORT *u, o, i*
For a different approach to teaching this skill, see Unit 2, page T32; Unit 3, page T30; Unit 4, page T32.

▶ **Visual/Auditory/ Kinesthetic**

Review Blending with short *u, o, i*

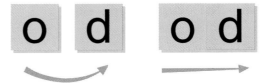

TEACH

Identify *u, o, i* as Symbols for /u/, /o/, /i/
Tell children they will continue to read words with *u, o, i*.

- Display the *o* letter card and say /o/. Have children repeat the sound /o/.

BLENDING Model and Guide Practice
- Place the *d* card after the *o* card. Blend the sounds together and have children repeat after you.

- Place an *n* card before *o*. Blend the sounds to read *nod*.

Use the Word in Context
- Ask children to use *nod* in a sentence. Encourage them to give a direction, such as: *When you hear a short* u *sound, nod your head.*

Repeat the Procedure
- Use the following words to continue modeling and for guided practice with short *u, o, i: sip, cut, pod, lid, fin, mop, run.*

PRACTICE

Complete the Pupil Edition Page
Read aloud the directions on page 244. Identify each picture, and complete the first item together. Then work through the page with children, or have them complete the page independently.

ASSESS/CLOSE

Build Short *u, o, i* Words
Observe children as they complete page 244. Then have them use *l, p, r, f, c, t, m, s, d, n* letter cards to build short *u, o,* and *i* words.

Name_____

1. (fin) fan

   fin

2. (Mom) mud

   Mom

3. rip (run)

   run

4. (dot) dig

   dot

Draw a circle around the word that names the picture. • Say the word. • Then write the word.

244   Unit 4   Review Blending with Short *u, o, i*

McGraw-Hill School Division

Pupil Edition, page 244

ADDITIONAL PHONICS RESOURCES

Practice Book, *page 244*
Phonics Workbook

McGraw-Hill School
TECHNOLOGY

Phonics **CD-ROM**
Activities for practice with Blending and Segmenting

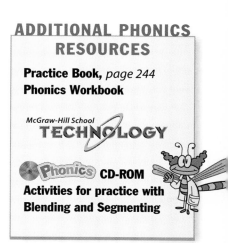

Practice **244**

Name_____

1. fun fin

   fun

2. Mom mop

   Mom

3. rut run

   run

4. top tip

   tip

Look at the picture. Read the words. Draw a line under the word that goes with the picture. Write the word.

At Home: Write *fin.* Ask the child to change *fin* to *fun.* Take turns. Change *fun* to *run* and change *fun* to *sun.*

244   Review Blending with Short *a, e, i*   Unit 4   8

PRACTICE BOOK, page 244

Meeting Individual Needs for Phonics

EASY	ON-LEVEL	CHALLENGE	LANGUAGE SUPPORT
Have children sort pictures of objects with medial *u, o, i,* such as: *fin, cot, sun, mop, lid, nut.* Ask them to name the object, saying the middle sound of each word. After children have sorted the pictures, write each word on the chalkboard. Ask children to underline the medial vowel.	**Form** a circle with children and pass a bag containing slips of paper on which you have written words, such as: *sun, tip, pot, top, fit, tin, dot, run, cup.* Each child takes a slip of paper, reads the word aloud, and then uses the words in a sentence.	**Have** children work in small groups to build words with *u, o,* and *i* in the middle and *l, p, r, f, c, t, m, s, d, n* as the first or last letter. Then have groups read their words and write them on the chalkboard. Compare each group's list. Children can make a chart showing all their words.	**Help** children get extra practice with blending short *u, o, i* words. Write on the chalkboard and say *-up;* then write and say words in that rhyming family, such as *cup, pup.* Repeat, using *-ut, -un, -ot, -od, -ip, -it.* Have children blend and read each word after you.

Reread the Decodable Story

☑ **Blend with Short *u***

☑ **Compare and Contrast**

☑ **High-Frequency Words:** *to, me, go, do*

☑ **Concepts of Print**

Fun in the Sun

Guided Reading

SET PURPOSES Have children discuss what their purpose is for rereading the story. Children may have unanswered questions about the story.

REREAD THE BOOK As you reread the story, keep in mind any problems children experienced during the first reading. Be alert to any misconceptions children may have about the story.

• **HIGH-FREQUENCY WORDS** Help children with any words they may have forgotten. Have them repeat aloud phrases such as "to me" (pages 3 and 5) and use these words in original sentences.

• **CONCEPTS OF PRINT** Have children look through their story to find the page with the question. (page 7) Ask how they can tell it is a question. (question mark at the end) Have volunteers practice reading this page aloud with their voices raised appropriately at the question mark.

• **MAKE INFERENCES** Ask children to look again at page 8 and think about how Mom and Dad feel, and tell why. Ask volunteers to tell about a time they may have been splashed with water.

RETURN TO PURPOSES Ask children if they found out what they needed to know from the story. Ask if they have any unanswered questions.

LITERARY RESPONSE Ask children to draw a picture or write a list of things they might take to a pool or beach. Invite children to share their work.

TEACHING TIP

MANAGEMENT Some groups of children may enjoy role playing the action of the three characters in the story. You may wish to reread the story with a small group of children who had difficulties during the first reading of the story or who are not ready to read independently.

INFORMAL **ASSESSMENT**

BLENDING

HOW TO ASSESS Write the following rhyming words on the chalkboard: *run, fun, sun.* Ask children to blend the sounds and read the word.

FOLLOW UP For those children who are experiencing difficulty, work with them individually to blend short *u* words.

Read the Patterned Book

Self-Selected Reading

UNIT SKILLS REVIEW

☑ **Phonics**

☑ **Comprehension**

☑ **High-Frequency Words**

Help children self-select a Patterned Book to read and apply phonics and comprehension skills.

Ron's Radishes
by Ray Tanner
illustrated by Andrea Wallace

Guided Reading

SET PURPOSES Have children choose one of the patterned books to reread. Have them find the pattern.

READ THE BOOK Remind children to run their fingers under each word in the story as they read. You may wish to pause during the story to ask these questions.

- Name the letters that I point to. (*Answers will vary.*)

- Which words show short *u* blended with other letters? Short *o*? Short *i*? (*Answers will vary.*) *Phonics and Decoding*

- What is the main idea of this page? (*Answers will vary.*) *Main Idea*

- How is this page like the one before it? How is it different? (*Answers will vary.*) *Compare and Contrast*

- Which of these words can you find on the page: *to, me, go, do*? (*Answers will vary.*) *High-Frequency Words*

- Look at the picture. Name something that is *under* something else. Name something that is *on* something else. (*Answers will vary.*) *Concepts of Print*

RETURN TO PURPOSES Have children share the patterns they discovered in their books. Use these prompts.

- Which words did you see repeated in the sentences in your pattern?

- Make up a new sentence with your pattern.

LITERARY RESPONSE Have children who read different books work in pairs to compare their books. Have them talk about these questions.

- How were the main ideas the same or different?

- Did the stories take place inside or outside?

Have children share what they discovered by comparing their stories.

☑ **Phonics and Decoding**

- Initial /r/*r*, /p/*p*, /l/*l*, /u/*u*

- Final /p/*p*

- Medial /u/*u*

- Blending with Short *a, i, o, u*

☑ **Comprehension**

- Main Idea

- Compare and Contrast

☑ **Vocabulary**

- High-Frequency Words: *to, me, go, do*

CENTER Activity

Cross Curricular: Science

KINDER-GARDEN Start a classroom garden either indoors or outside with the children. Help them plant and label various seeds such as carrot, tomato, and cucumber. Children can take turns for the daily upkeep of the plants. Have a veggie feast at "harvest time."

▶ **Logical/ Interpersonal**

OBJECTIVES

Children will:

- review high-frequency words *to, me, go, do.*

MATERIALS

- word cards from the Word Building Book
- *Fun in the Sun*

TEACHING TIP

INSTRUCTIONAL

Mention to children that the high-frequency word *to* is not the same as the word for the numeral *two*. Point out that although the words sound the same, they look different when you read them because they are spelled in different ways.

Review *to, me, go, do*

PREPARE

Listen to the Words
Say aloud the following sentences emphasizing the underlined high-frequency words. Ask children to listen to the sentences and then repeat each high-frequency word with you after the sentence is finished.

1. What can we <u>do</u>?

2. Will you play with <u>me</u>?

3. We can <u>go to</u> the playground.

TEACH

Model Reading the Word in Context
Read the decodable story "Fun in the Sun" in the Pupil Edition. Ask children to listen for and identify the high frequency words.

Identify the Words
Provide children with word cards from the Word Building Book for the high-frequency words. Read the sentences from the story that have these words. Point to each word as you read. Ask children to hold up the correct word card when they hear the word. Then read each sentence again and have children place a stick-on note below each word.

Review the High-Frequency Words
Pronounce each high-frequency word plus the words *I* and *my* and have children hold up the corresponding word card. Ask children to repeat the word with you.

PRACTICE

Complete the Pupil Edition Page
Read the directions on page 245 to the children, and make sure they clearly understand what they are asked to do. Complete the first item together. Then work through the page with children or have them complete the page independently.

ASSESS/CLOSE

Review the Page
Observe children's work on page 245 and note any children who are experiencing difficulty.

Name_____

1.	go	my	do	(go)	to
2.	me	we	go	my	(me)
3.	to	(to)	do	the	is
4.	do	I	a	to	(do)

Say the first word in the row. • Draw a circle around the word where you see it in the same row.

Unit 4   Review *to, me, go, do*   **245**

Pupil Edition, page 245

ALTERNATE TEACHING STRATEGY

HIGH-FREQUENCY WORDS: *to, me, go, do*

For a different approach to teaching this skill, see page T27.

▶ Visual/Auditory/ Kinesthetic

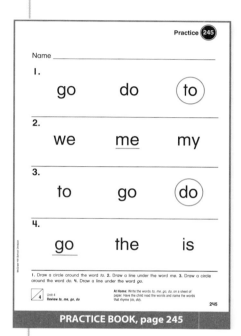

Practice **245**

Name _____

1.
go   do   (to)

2.
we   me   my

3.
to   go   (do)

4.
go   the   is

1. Draw a circle around the word *to*. 2. Draw a line under the word *me*. 3. Draw a circle around the word *do*. 4. Draw a line under the word *go*.

Unit 4
Review *to, me, go, do*

At Home: Write the words *to, me, go, do,* on a sheet of paper. Have the child read the words and name the words that rhyme (*to, do*).

245

PRACTICE BOOK, page 245

Meeting Individual Needs for Vocabulary

EASY	ON-LEVEL	CHALLENGE	LANGUAGE SUPPORT
Review the high-frequency words with children. Then reread the story "Fun in the Sun" to them. Have children hold up their word cards from the Word Building Book each time they hear one of the high-frequency words.	**Hold** up one of the word cards for the high-frequency words. Ask a volunteer to use the word in a sentence. Have other children tell what the word is. Repeat until all the children have had a turn.	**Have** children select a classroom book and find a match for each of the word cards for the high-frequency words. Have children mark the words they find with stick-on notes.	**Ask** children to think of words that rhyme with *to* and *do*. If necessary, give other examples such as *you*. List children's rhyming words on a chart pad. Then work with children to make up simple rhymes.

245

Interactive Writing

Write Character Dialogue

Prewrite

LOOK AT THE STORY PATTERN Reread the story *Allie's Adventures from A to Z.* Talk about the pattern of the story: every page of the story has a letter of the alphabet. Allie sees something that begins with the sound of that letter. Then make a list of the characters in the story.

Draft

WRITE DIALOGUE Explain that children are going to write words that one of the characters might be thinking of saying in the story.

- Have children think of a character and an event in the story. Talk about what the character might be thinking or saying.

- Children dictate their ideas to you as you write on the chalkboard.

- Show examples of cartoon speaking and thought balloons. Suggest that children use this format. Have each child choose a character, draw a picture of the character, and write the dialogue.

Publish

CREATE THE BOOK Bind the pages together to make a book. Volunteers may create a book cover.

Presentation Ideas

MAKE PUPPETS Have children make simple craft stick puppets to show the characters in the story. Children can draw on small sheets of paper and tape the paper to the sticks.

▶ **Representing/Viewing**

ACT OUT THE DIALOGUE Have children read their dialogue and act out the scene with puppets.

▶ **Representing/Speaking**

Meeting Individual Needs for Writing

EASY	ON-LEVEL	CHALLENGE
Write Dialogue Revisit the story, and have children choose another section for which to write dialogue. Help them write it, and then read the dialogue together.	**Descriptive Words** Have children write words that describe one of the characters in the story. Make a list of words.	**Journal Entry** Have children pretend to be Allie and write a journal entry about something she might do during the day.

Wrap Up
the Theme

I Wonder
*We can make discoveries about the wonders of nature
in our own backyard.*

REVIEW THE THEME Read the theme statement to children. Engage them in a conversation about some of the nature discoveries they have made during the past few weeks.

READ THE POEM Read the poem "Shell" aloud. Try to bring in a conch shell and pass it around so that children can have the experience of "hearing the water sound."

SHELL

When it was time
for Show and Tell,
Adam brought a big
   pink shell.

He told about
the ocean roar
and walking on the
   sandy shore.

And then he passed
the shell around.
We listened to the
   water sound.

And that's the first
   time
I could hear
the wild waves
   calling to my ear.

Myra Cohn Livingston

AUDIO
Student Listening Library

DISCUSS THE POEM Before rereading "Shell," ask children to listen for words that give clues about where Adam found the shell. Ask why the beach is a good place to find shells.

LOOKING AT GENRE: NONFICTION (INFORMATIONAL STORIES) The Literature Big Books *The Apple Pie Tree* and *Nature Spy* are stories that contain information about nature. Discuss how some books may have fictional characters but may also contain valuable information that children can learn from.

Research *and Inquiry*

Theme Project: The Life and Travels of an Apple

GROUP **Give the Presentation** Display all the murals in the classroom. Work with each group as they practice telling about their mural. Then invite another class to hear the presentations. Follow up with an apple-eating celebration.

Draw Conclusions Encourage questions from the visiting class. Ask the visitors to tell what they

learned about apples. Create a list of conclusions from their feedback.

Ask More Questions Ask children how they would like to expand their research about apples. Some suggestions for topics include Foods You Can Make with Apples and Caring for an Apple Tree. Encourage each group to research and present its findings in an imaginative way.

HIGH-FREQUENCY WORDS

GROUP Display the word cards *to, me, go, do.* Track print as you read each word with children. Ask them to point to the word that makes sense in this sentence: *Can you ____ this?* After they identify the word *do,* play a game in which you make a gesture, or other physical movement, and then ask: *Can you do this?* Have children imitate your movement.

Unit Review

You Are IT!
to

Tap the Sap
me

Nap in a Lap
go

Mud Fun
do

Fun in the Sun
review: *to, me, go, do*

✓ SKILLS & STRATEGIES

Phonics and Decoding
☑ Initial /r/r, /p/p, /l/l, /u/u
☑ Final /p/p
☑ Medial /u/u
☑ Blending with Short *a, i, o, u*

Comprehension
☑ Main Idea
☑ Compare and Contrast

Vocabulary
☑ High-Frequency Words: *to, me, go, do*

Beginning Reading Concepts
☑ On, Off
☑ Inside, Outside
☑ Over, Under
☑ Up, Down

McGRAW-HILL READING

UNIT Assessment

UNIT 4 ASSESSMENT

Assessment
Follow-Up

Use the results of the informal and formal assessment opportunities in the unit to help you make decisions about future instruction.

SKILLS AND STRATEGIES	Alternate Teaching Strategies
Phonics and Decoding	
Initial /r/r, /f/f, /p/p, /l/l, /u/u	Unit 3 T32, T24, T28, T31, T32
Final /p/p, Medial /u/u	T28, T32
Blending with Short a, i, o, u	Unit 1 T32, Unit 2 T32, Unit 3 T30, T32
Comprehension	
Main Idea	T26
Compare and Contrast	T30
Vocabulary	
High-Frequency Words: to, me, go, go, the, that, you, I, and	T27
Beginning Reading Concepts	
On, Off	T25
Inside, Outside	T29
Over, Under; Up, Down	T33
Writing	
Letter Formation	T34

McGraw-Hill School
TECHNOLOGY

 CD-ROM Provides extra phonics support.

 Research & Inquiry Ideas.
Visit www.mhschool.com

Cover Illustration: Mary Jane Begin

The publisher gratefully acknowledges permission to reprint the following copyrighted material:

"Aekyung's Dream" by Min Paek. Copyright © 1978, 1988 by Children's Book Press.

"Amazing Grace" by Mary Hoffman. Text copyright © 1991 by Mary Hoffman. Illustrations copyright © 1991 by Caroline Binch. Used by permission of Dial Books for Young Readers.

"Annie's Pet" by Barbara Brenner. Text copyright © 1989 by Bank Street College of Education. Used by permission of Bantam Books, a division of Bantam Doubleday Dell Publishing Group, Inc.

ANY KIND OF DOG by Lynn Whisnant Reiser. Copyright © 1992 by Lynn Whisnant Reiser. Reprinted by permission of William Morrow & Company.

THE APPLE PIE TREE by Zoe Hall. Text copyright ©1996 by Zoe Hall. Illustrations copyright ©1996 by Shari Halpern. Reproduced by permission of Scholastic Inc.

"Beehive" from A CHILDREN'S SEASONAL TREASURY compiled by Betty Jones. Copyright © 1971 by Dover Publishing, Inc. Reprinted by permission of Dover Publishing, Inc.

THE CHICK AND THE DUCKLING by Mirra Ginsburg. Text copyright © 1972 by Mirra Ginsburg. Illustration copyright © 1972 by Jose Aruego. Reprinted by permission of Simon & Schuster Children's Publishing Division.

"Cinderella" is primarily based on the version by Charles Perrault, in THE BLUE FAIRY BOOK, edited by A. Lang (1889) and incorporates elements of the Brothers Grimm version, translated by L. Crane (1886), as well as details from the retelling by F. Baker and A. Thorndike in EVERYDAY CLASSICS: THIRD READERS (1920).

"Clay" from A SONG I SANG TO YOU by Myra Cohn Livingston. Copyright © 1958, 1959, 1965, 1967, 1969, 1984 by Myra Cohn Livingston. Used by permission of Marian Reiner for the author.

"The Clever Turtle" retold by Margaret H. Lippert from CHILDREN'S ANTHOLOGY. Copyright © 1988 by Macmillan Publishing Company, a division of Macmillan Inc.

THE EARTH AND I by Frank Asch. Copyright © 1994 by Frank Asch. Reprinted by permission of Harcourt Brace & Company.

THE ENORMOUS CARROT by Vladimir Vagin. Copyright © 1998 by Vladimir Vagin. Reproduced by permission of Scholastic Inc.

"Every Time I Climb a Tree" from FAR AND FEW by David McCord. Copyright © 1929, 1931, 1952 by David McCord. Reprinted by permission of Little, Brown & Company.

"50 Simple Things Kids Can Do to Save the Earth" from 50 SIMPLE THINGS KIDS CAN DO TO SAVE THE EARTH by The EarthWorks Group. Copyright © 1990 by John Javna.

"Five Little Seeds" from THIS LITTLE PUFFIN compiled by Elizabeth Matterson. Copyright © 1969 by Puffin Books. Reproduced by permission of Penguin Books. Reprinted by permission.

FLOWER GARDEN by Eve Bunting. Text copyright ©1994 by Eve Bunting, illustrations copyright ©1994 by Kathryn Hewitt. Reprinted by permission of Harcourt Brace & Company.

"The Hare and the Tortoise" from THE FABLES OF AESOP by Aesop, retold by Joseph Jacobs (c. 1900).

"Helping" from WHERE THE SIDEWALK ENDS by Shel Silverstein. Copyright © 1974 by Evil Eye Music, Inc. Reprinted by permission of HarperCollins Publishers.

"Hill of Fire" from HILL OF FIRE by Thomas P. Lewis. Text copyright © 1971 by Thomas P. Lewis. Used by permission of Harper & Row Publishers, Inc.

"How Many Spots Does a Leopard Have?" from HOW MANY SPOTS DOES A LEOPARD HAVE AND OTHER STORIES by Julius Lester. Copyright © 1989 by Julius Lester. Reprinted by permission of Scholastic Inc.

"It Could Always Be Worse" by Margot Zemach. Copyright © 1976 by Margot Zemach. Reprinted by permission of Farrar, Straus & Giroux, Inc.

"A Kite" from READ-ALOUD RHYMES FOR THE VERY YOUNG. Copyright © 1986 by Alfred A. Knopf, Inc.

"Learning" from POETRY PLACE ANTHOLOGY by M. Lucille Ford. Copyright © 1983 by Instructor Publications, Inc.

"The Legend of the Bluebonnet" by Tomie dePaola. Copyright © 1983 by Tomie dePaola. Used by permission of The Putnam Publishing Group.

"Little Brown Rabbit" from THIS LITTLE PUFFIN compiled by Elizabeth Matterson. Copyright © 1969 by Puffin Books. Reprinted by permission of Penguin Books Ltd.

"The Little Engine That Could" by Watty Piper. Copyright © 1930, 1945, 1954, 1961, 1976 by Platt & Munk, Publishers. Used by permission of Platt & Munk, Publishers, a division of Grosset & Dunlap, Inc., which is a member of the Putnam & Grosset Group, New York.

"The Little Red Hen" from WHAT YOUR KINDERGARTNER NEEDS TO KNOW edited by E. D. Hirsch, Jr., and John Holdren. Copyright © 1996 by The Core Knowledge Foundation. Used by permission of Delta Books, a division of Bantam Doubleday Dell Publishing Group, Inc.

"The Little Turtle" from COLLECTED POEMS by Vachel Lindsay. Copyright © 1920 by Macmillan Publishing Co., Inc., renewed 1948 by Elizabeth C. Lindsay.

"Making Friends" from NATHANIEL TALKING by Eloise Greenfield. Text copyright © 1988 by Eloise Greenfield. Illustrations copyright © by Jan Spivey Gilchrist. Used by permission of Writers and Readers Publishing, Inc., for Black Butterfly Children's Books.

"Mary Had a Little Lamb" from WHAT YOUR KINDERGARTNER NEEDS TO KNOW edited by E. D. Hirsch, Jr., and John Holdren. Copyright © 1996 by The Core Knowledge Foundation. Used by permission of Delta Books, a division of Bantam Doubleday Dell Publishing Group, Inc.

"Morning Verse" from THE KINDERGARTEN SERIES. Copyright ©1983 by Wynstone Press. Reprinted by permission of Wynstone Press.

NATURE SPY by Shelley Rotner and Ken Kreisler. Text copyright © 1992 by Shelley Rotner and Ken Kreisler. Illustrations copyright © 1992 by Shelley Rotner. Reprinted by permission of Simon & Schuster Children's Publishing Division.

PEANUT BUTTER AND JELLY by Nadine Bernard Westcott. Copyright ©1987 by Nadine Bernard Westcott. Reprinted by permission of Dutton Children's Books, a division of Penguin Books USA Inc.

PRETEND YOU'RE A CAT by Jean Marzollo, illustrated by Jerry Pinkney. Text copyright © 1990 by Jean Marzollo. Paintings copyright © 1990 by Jerry Pinkney. Reprinted by permission of Dial Books for Young Readers, a division of Penguin Putnam Inc.

"Shell" from WORLDS I KNOW AND OTHER POEMS by Myra Cohn Livingston. Copyright © 1985 by Myra Cohn Livingston. Reprinted by permission of Margaret K. McElderry Books, an imprint of Simon & Schuster Children's Publishing Division.

SHOW AND TELL DAY by Anne Rockwell. Text copyright © 1997 by Anne Rockwell. Illustrations copyright © 1997 by Lizzy Rockwell. Reprinted by permission of HarperCollins Publishers.

"The Squeaky Old Bed" from CROCODILE! CROCODILE! STORIES TOLD AROUND THE WORLD by Barbara Baumgartner. Text copyright © 1994 by Barbara Baumgartner. Illustrations copyright © by Judith Moffatt. Used by permission of Dorling Kindersley.

"The Three Little Pigs" by Joseph Jacobs from TOMIE DEPAOLA'S FAVORITE NURSERY TALES. Illustrations copyright © 1986 by Tomie dePaola. Used by permission of the Putnam Publishing Group.

"Tommy" from BRONZEVILLE BOYS AND GIRLS by Gwendolyn Brooks. Copyright © 1956 by Gwendolyn Brooks Blakely.

"The Town Mouse and the Country Mouse" retold and illustrated by Lorinda Bryan Cauley. Copyright © 1984 by Lorinda Bryan Cauley. Used by permission of G.P. Putnam's Sons.

Untitled from JUNE IS A TUNE THAT JUMPS ON A STAIR by Sarah Wilson. Copyright © 1992 by Sarah Wilson. Used by permission of Simon & Schuster Books for Young Readers.

"The Velveteen Rabbit; or, How Toys Become Real" from WHAT YOUR KINDERGARTNER NEEDS TO KNOW edited by E. D. Hirsch, Jr., and John Holdren. Copyright © 1996 by The Core Knowledge Foundation. Used by permission of Delta Books, a division of Bantam Doubleday Dell Publishing Group, Inc.

WARTHOGS IN THE KITCHEN by Pamela Duncan Edwards. Text ©1998 by Pamela Duncan Edwards. Illustrations ©1998 by Henry Cole. Reprinted by Hyperion Books for Children.

"Whistling" from RAINY RAINY SATURDAY by Jack Prelutsky. Copyright © 1980 by Jack Prelutsky. Used by permission of William Morrow & Company.

WHITE RABBIT'S COLOR BOOK by Alan Baker. Copyright © 1994 by Alan Baker. Reprinted by permission of Larousse Kingfisher Chambers, Inc.

"Winnie the Pooh" from WINNIE-THE-POOH by A. A. Milne. Copyright © 1926 by E.P. Dutton, renewed 1954 by A. A. Milne.

"Winter Days in the Big Woods" from LITTLE HOUSE IN THE BIG WOODS by Laura Ingalls Wilder. Copyright © 1932 by Laura Ingalls Wilder, renewed 1959 by Roger L. MacBride. Illustrations copyright © 1994 by Reneé Graef. Used by permission of HarperCollins Publishers.

"Wonderful World" from POETRY PLACE ANTHOLOGY by Eva Grant. Copyright © 1983 by Instructor Publications, Inc.

"Yesterday's Paper" by Mabel Watts from READ-ALOUD RHYMES FOR THE VERY YOUNG. Copyright © 1986 by Alfred A. Knopf, Inc.

Backmatter Contents

"Every Time I Climb a Tree"
by David McCord

Every time I climb a tree
Every time I climb a tree
Every time I climb a tree
I scrape a leg
Or skin a knee
And every time I climb a tree
I find some ants
Or dodge a bee
And get the ants
All over me

And every time I climb a tree
Where have you been?
They say to me
But don't they know that I am free
Every time I climb a tree?
I like it best
To spot a nest
That has an egg
Or maybe three

And then I skin
The other leg
But every time I climb a tree
I see a lot of things to see
Swallows rooftops and TV
And all the fields and farms there be
Every time I climb a tree
Though climbing may be good for ants
It isn't awfully good for pants
But still it's pretty good for me
Every time I climb a tree

Hill of Fire
by Thomas P. Lewis

The farmer in this story thinks nothing ever happens in his village community—until something big happens in his own field. In 1943 there really was a "hill of fire" in a small village in Mexico, and people had to leave their homes because of it. After the farmer moved to his new village, do you think he still complained that nothing ever happened? Why or why not?

Once there was a farmer who lived in Mexico. He lived in a little village in a house which had only one room. The farmer was not happy.

"Nothing ever happens," he said.

The people in the village thought the farmer was foolish. "We have everything we need," they said. "We have a school, and a market, and a church with an old bell that rings on Sunday. Our village is the best there is."

"But nothing ever happens," said the farmer.

Every morning, when the farmer woke up, the first thing he saw was the roof of his little house. Every morning for breakfast he ate two flat cakes of ground corn. His wife had made them the night before. He put honey over the cakes, and drank cinnamon tea from a clay mug.

"Nothing ever happens," he said.

It was still dark and the farmer got ready to leave for the field. His son Pablo was still asleep.

"Perhaps today," said his wife, "something will happen."

"No," said the farmer. "Nothing will."

The farmer led his ox away and did not look back.

At night the farmer returned. He fed his ox. Then he sat down by the fire. Pablo played with five smooth stones. He threw the stones at a hole he had dug in the earth.

"See, Papa!" said Pablo. "I got one in!"

But the farmer was tired. He did not answer. Every day was the same.

One morning the farmer woke up very early. He pulled on his woolen shirt. He took his big hat from a peg on the wall.

"I must go to the field early," he said. "The plowing is not done. Soon it will be time to plant the corn."

All morning the farmer worked in his field. The ox helped him. When there was a big rock in the way, the ox stopped and lay down. The farmer pushed the rock away.

"Tst-tst!" said the farmer.

The ox looked at the farmer. Then the ox got up and pulled again.

Late in the morning, when the sun was high, Pablo came to the field.

"Pablo!" said the farmer. "Why are you not in school?"

"There is no school today, Papa," said Pablo. "I have come to help you plow."

The farmer smiled. He reached into his pocket, and gave the boy a small wooden toy.

"A bull!" cried Pablo.

The farmer had made it for his son during the hot time of the day when he rested from his work.

Pablo helped the farmer plow the field. The ox pulled, and the plow turned up the soil. Suddenly the plow stopped. The farmer and his son pushed, and the ox pulled, but the plow did not move. It sank into the earth. It went down, down, down, into a little hole.

The little hole became a bigger hole. There was a noise deep under the ground, as if something big had growled. The farmer looked. Pablo looked. The ox turned its head. White smoke came from the hole in the ground.

"Run!" said the farmer. "Run!"

There was a loud CRACK, and the earth opened wide. The farmer ran, Pablo ran, and the ox ran too. Fire and smoke came from the ground. The farmer ran all the way to the village.

He ran inside the church and rang the old bell. The other farmers came from their fields. People came out of their houses.

"Look!" said the farmer. "Look there!"

That night no one slept. Everyone watched the fire in the sky. It came from where the farmer's field had been. There was a loud BOOM, and another, and another.

Hot lava came out of the earth. Steaming lava spread over the ground, through the trees. It came toward the farmer's house. It came toward the village. Pieces of burning stone flew in the air. The earth was coughing. Every time it coughed, the hill of fire grew bigger.

In a few days the hill was as big as a mountain. And every few minutes there was a loud BOOM. Squirrels and rabbits ran, and birds flew away from the fire. People led their burros and their oxen to safety. Pieces of burning ash flew everywhere. The farmer and his neighbors put wet cloths over their noses to keep out the smoke.

Some of the people went close to the steaming lava. They carried big crosses. They prayed for the fire to stop. The farmer and Pablo watched from the side of a hill.

When the booming stopped and the fires grew smaller, the farmer's house was gone. The school was gone. The market was gone. Half the village was gone.

One day some men in uniform came in cars and trucks.

"So you are the one with the plow that opened up the earth," they said to the farmer. They laughed. "You are lucky to be alive, amigo."

The soldiers looked at the village.

"Everyone must go!" the captain said. "It is not safe to live here any longer."

The farmer and his wife and Pablo and all the people of the village went with the soldiers. They rode away in the trucks.

The farmer found a new house. It was bigger than the one they lived in before. It was not far from the old one. But it was far enough away to be safe from El Monstruo, which means "The Monster." That is the name the people gave to the great volcano.

The people made a new village. They made a new school and a new market.

They had a great fiesta because now they were safe. At the fiesta the band played, and the people danced and clapped their hands.

People from the city came in a bus to see El Monstruo. The people of the village sold them oranges and melons and hot dogs and corn cakes to eat.

Now the farmer had a new field. Every morning he woke up early. It was still dark, and El Monstruo glowed in the sky. Every morning for breakfast he ate two flat cakes of ground corn. His wife had made them the night before. The farmer went to his new field. His ox went with him, just as before.

Sometimes Pablo brought the children of the village to see the farmer. From the field they could see the volcano smoking, like an old man smoking his pipe.

"Can you make another hill of fire?" the children said.

"No, my friends, no, no," said the farmer. He laughed. "One hill of fire is enough for me."

The Clever Turtle
a Hispanic folk tale retold by Margaret H. Lippert

Wheet-weedle-whoo, wheet-weedle-whoo, wheet-wheet-wheet-whoo. Every day, Turtle sat by the Amazon River and played her flute. All the birds and animals loved to listen to her play.

One day, a man walking through the forest heard her beautiful music. Wheet-weedle-whoo, wheet-weedle-whoo, wheet-wheet-wheet-whoo.

He stopped to listen. When he saw that a turtle was playing the flute, he thought about dinner.

"Turtle soup would be a treat tonight," he thought. So he picked Turtle up and carried her home.

He put Turtle into a cage made of branches and closed the lid. "Don't let the turtle out of the cage," he said to his children. "Tonight we will have turtle soup." Then the father picked up his hoe and went to work in the garden. The children played in the yard.

Turtle did not want to be made into soup. She started to play her flute. Wheet-weedle-whoo, wheet-weedle-whoo, wheet-wheet-wheet-whoo. The children stopped their game and listened.

"Turtle is playing the flute!" they shouted.

"I can dance as well as I can play," called Turtle. "I can even play and dance at the same time. If you open the lid you can watch me." The children opened the lid, and Turtle started to dance.

Wheet-weedle-whoo. Crash-bam. Wheet-weedle-whoo. Crash-bam. Turtle's shell banged against the sides of the cage as she danced.

The children laughed and clapped.

Turtle danced for a while, then she stopped. "I am stiff from dancing in this little cage," she said. "I need to stretch my legs. Let me go for a short walk. Then I will dance some more for you."

The children wanted to see Turtle dance again. They lifted Turtle out of the cage. "Don't go far," they said. Turtle walked around and around the yard. She walked closer and closer to the forest. Then she crawled under some leaves and disappeared.

The children looked and looked for Turtle. "Turtle! Turtle!" they called. But there was no answer. "Father will be angry," they said. "What can we do now?"

The children found a big smooth stone and painted it to look like a turtle. Then they put the painted stone in Turtle's cage. "It is dark in the cage," they said. "Father will think that the turtle is still in there."

When the father came home, he lit a fire and put some water in a pot. "Bring me the turtle," he said. The children brought the painted stone and threw it in the pot. CRASH! "The shell is hard," said the father. "But the meat will be soft when it is cooked."

After some time, the father decided the soup must be ready. He spooned the painted stone out of the pot. The stone fell onto his dish and broke it.

The father looked at the silent children. "You let the turtle go," he said. "Now we have nothing to eat tonight. But tomorrow is another day. In the morning I will try to find the turtle."

The next day the father walked into the forest. He looked and looked for Turtle. Then he got tired and went home. Do you think he ever found Turtle again?

How Many Spots Does a Leopard Have

an African folktale retold by Julius Lester

One morning Leopard was doing what he enjoyed doing most. He was looking at his reflection in the lake. How handsome he was! How magnificent was his coat! And, ah! The spots on his coat! Was there anything in creation more superb?

Leopard's rapture was broken when the water in the lake began moving. Suddenly Crocodile's ugly head appeared above the surface.

Leopard jumped back. Not that he was afraid. Crocodile would not bother him. But then again, one could never be too sure about Crocodile.

"Good morning, Leopard," Crocodile said. "Looking at yourself again, I see. You are the most vain creature in all of creation."

Leopard was not embarrassed. "If you were as handsome as I am, if you had such beautiful spots, you, too, would be vain."

"Spots! Who needs spots? You're probably so in love with your spots that you spend all your time counting them."

Now there was an idea that had not occurred to Leopard. "What a wonderful idea!" he exclaimed. "I would very much like to know how many spots I have." He stopped. "But there are far too many for me to count myself."

The truth was that Leopard didn't know how to count. "Perhaps you will count them for me, Crocodile?"

"Not on your life!" answered Crocodile. "I have better things to do than count spots." He slapped his tail angrily and dove beneath the water.

Leopard chuckled. "Crocodile doesn't know how to count, either."

Leopard walked along the lakeshore until he met Weasel. "Good morning, Weasel. Would you count my spots for me?"

"Who? Me? Count? Sure. One-two-three-four."

"Great!" exclaimed Leopard. "You can count."

Weasel shook his head. "But I can't. What made you think that I could?"

"But you just did. You said, 'One-two-three-four.' That's counting."

Weasel shook his head again. "Counting is much more difficult than that. There is something that comes after four, but I don't know what it is."

"Oh," said Leopard. "I wonder who knows what comes after four."

"Well, if you ask at the lake when all the animals come to drink, you will find someone who can count."

"You are right, Weasel! And I will give a grand prize to the one who tells me how many spots I have."

"What a great idea!" Weasel agreed.

That afternoon all the animals were gathered at the lake to drink. Leopard announced that he would give a magnificent prize to the one who could count his spots.

Elephant said he should be first since he was the biggest and the oldest.

"One-two-three-four-five-six-seven-eight-nine-ten," Elephant said very loudly and with great speed. He took a deep breath and began again. "One-two-three-four-five-si-"

"No! No! No!" the other animals interrupted. "You've already counted to ten once."

Elephant looked down his long trunk at the other animals. "I beg your pardon. I would appreciate it if you would not interrupt me when I am counting. You made me forget where I was. Now, where was I? I know I was somewhere in the second ten."

"The second ten?" asked Antelope. "What's that?"

"The numbers that come after the first ten, of course. I don't much care for those 'teen' things, thirteen, fourteen, and what have you. It is eminently more sensible to count ten twice and that makes twenty. That is multiplication."

None of the other animals knew what Elephant was talking about.

"Why don't you start over again?" suggested Cow.

Elephant began again and he counted ten twice and stopped. He frowned and looked very confused. Finally he said, "Leopard has more than twenty spots."

"How many more than twenty?" Leopard wanted to know.

Elephant frowned more. "A lot." Then he brightened. "In fact, you have so many more spots than twenty that I simply don't have time to count them now. I have an important engagement I mustn't be late for." Elephant started to walk away.

"Ha! Ha! Ha!" laughed Mule. "I bet Elephant doesn't know how to count higher than twenty."

Mule was right.

"Can you count above twenty?" Leopard asked Mule.

"Who? Me? I can only count to four because that's how many legs I have."

Leopard sighed. "Can anyone count above twenty?" he asked plaintively.

Bear said, "Well, once I counted up to fifty. Is that high enough?"

Leopard shrugged. "I don't know. It might be. Why don't you try and we will see."

Bear agreed. "I'll start at your tail. One-two-three-four-five-six . . . . Hm. Is that one spot or two spots?"

All the animals crowded around to get a close look. They argued for some time and finally agreed that it should only count as one.

"So, where was I?" asked Bear.

"Five," answered Turkey.

"It was six, you turkey," said Chicken.

"Better start again," suggested Crow.

Bear started again and got as far as eleven. "Eleven. That's a beautiful spot right there, Leopard."

"Which one?" Leopard wanted to know.

"Right there. Oh, dear. Or was it that spot there? They're both exquisite. My, my. I don't know where I left off counting. I must start again."

Bear counted as far as twenty-nine this time and then stopped suddenly. "Now, what comes after twenty-nine?"

"I believe thirty does," offered Turtle.

"That's right!" exclaimed Bear. "Now, where did I leave off?"

"You were still on the tail," offered Lion.

"Yes, but was that the twenty-ninth spot, or was it this one here?"

The animals started arguing again.

"You'd better start again," suggested Cow.

"Start what again?" asked Rabbit who had just arrived.

The animals explained to Rabbit about the difficulty they were having in counting Leopard's spots.

"Is that all?" Rabbit said. "I know the answer to that."

"You do?" all the animals, including Leopard, exclaimed at once.

"Certainly. It's really quite simple." Rabbit pointed to one of Leopard's spots. "This one is dark." He pointed to another. "This one is light. Dark, light, dark, light, dark, light." Rabbit continued in this way until he had touched all of Leopard's spots.

"It's simple," he concluded. "Leopard has only two spots—dark ones and light ones."

All the animals remarked on how smart Rabbit was, all of them, that is, except Leopard. He knew something was wrong with how Rabbit counted, but unless he learned to count for himself, he would never know what it was.

Leopard had no choice but to give Rabbit the magnificent prize.

What was it?

What else except a picture of Leopard himself!

Annotated Workbooks

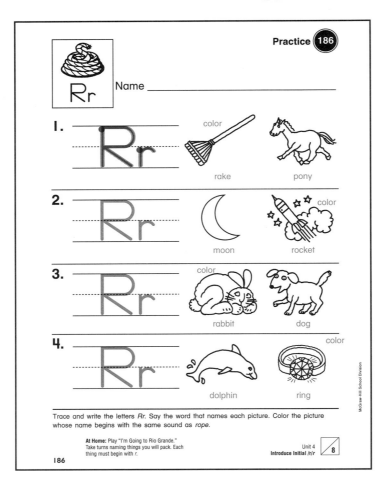

Practice 186

Name _____

1. Rr   color — rake   pony

2. Rr   moon   color — rocket

3. Rr   color — rabbit   dog

4. Rr   dolphin   color — ring

Trace and write the letters *Rr*. Say the word that names each picture. Color the picture whose name begins with the same sound as *rope*.

At Home: Play "I'm Going to Rio Grande." Take turns naming things you will pack. Each thing must begin with *r*.

Unit 4
Introduce Initial /r/ 8

186

Practice 187

Name _____

color

color

color

color

Look at the picture. Color the items that are *on* the tree. Draw a circle around the things that are *off* the tree.

9 Unit 4
Introduce On, Off

At Home: Place common objects on a table and on the floor. Together, talk about the items that are on the table and those that are off.

187

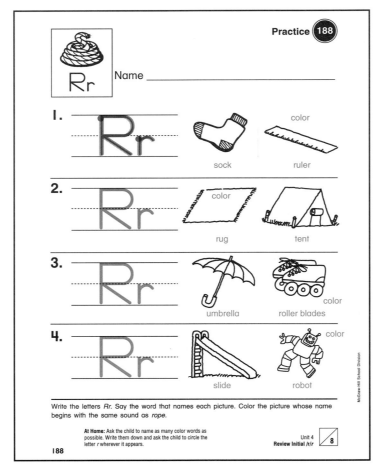

Practice 188

Rr   Name _____

1. Rr   sock   color — ruler

2. Rr   color — rug   tent

3. Rr   umbrella   color — roller blades

4. Rr   slide   color — robot

Write the letters *Rr*. Say the word that names each picture. Color the picture whose name begins with the same sound as *rope*.

At Home: Ask the child to name as many color words as possible. Write them down and ask the child to circle the letter *r* wherever it appears.

Unit 4
Review Initial /r/ 8

188

Practice 189

Name _____

1.   •   • Sam is sad.

2.   •   • Min is a cat.

3.   •   • I ran to Mom.

4.   •   • Nat is a man.

Look at each picture. Then read the sentences. Draw a line from each picture to the sentence that tells about it.

4 Unit 4
Introduce Main Idea

At Home: Say a sentence such as: *Lisa won the race.* Have the child draw a picture to show the idea.

189

Annotated Workbooks

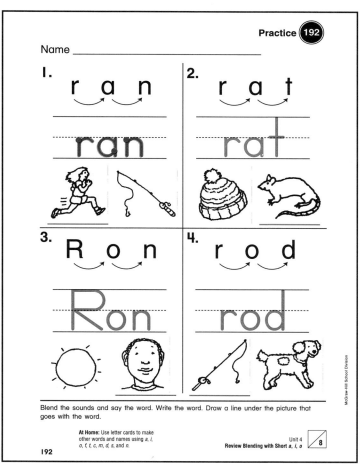

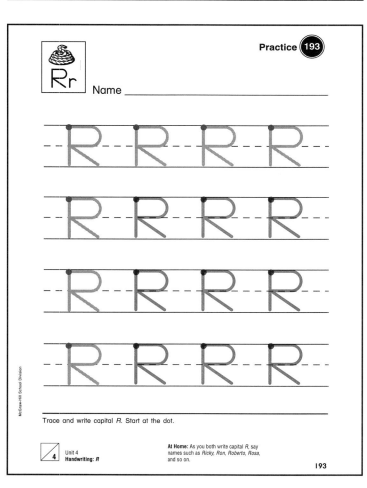

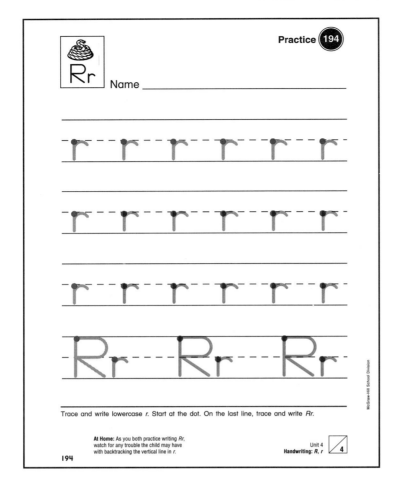

Name _____

r r r r r r

r r r r r r

r r r r r r

Rr   Rr   Rr

Trace and write lowercase *r*. Start at the dot. On the last line, trace and write *Rr*.

At Home: As you both practice writing *Rr*, watch for any trouble the child may have with backtracking the vertical line in *r*.

Unit 4
Handwriting: R, r 4

194

Name _____

1. ● ● Sid did not fit.

2. ● ● Ron ran to Tom.

3. ● ● The cat ran.

4. ● ● Tam is mad.

Look at each picture. Then read the sentences. Draw a line from each picture to the sentence that tells about it.

4 Unit 4
Review Main Idea

At Home: Together, pick a picture from a photo album. Have the child say a sentence that tells what the picture is about.

195

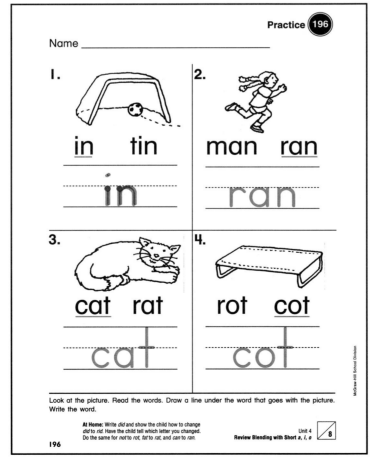

Name _____

1. in   tin

in

2. man   ran

ran

3. cat   rat

cat

4. rot   cot

cot

Look at the picture. Read the words. Draw a line under the word that goes with the picture. Write the word.

At Home: Write *did* and show the child how to change *did* to *rid*. Have the child tell which letter you changed. Do the same for *not* to *rot*, *fat* to *rat*, and *can* to *ran*.

Unit 4
Review Blending with Short a, i, o 8

196

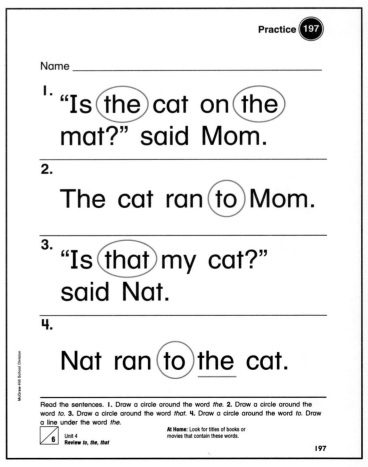

Name _____

1. "Is (the) cat on (the) mat?" said Mom.

2. The cat ran (to) Mom.

3. "Is (that) my cat?" said Nat.

4. Nat ran (to) the cat.

Read the sentences. 1. Draw a circle around the word *the*. 2. Draw a circle around the word *to*. 3. Draw a circle around the word *that*. 4. Draw a circle around the word *to*. Draw a line under the word *the*.

6 Unit 4
Review to, the, that

At Home: Look for titles of books or movies that contain these words.

197

Tap the Sap • PRACTICE

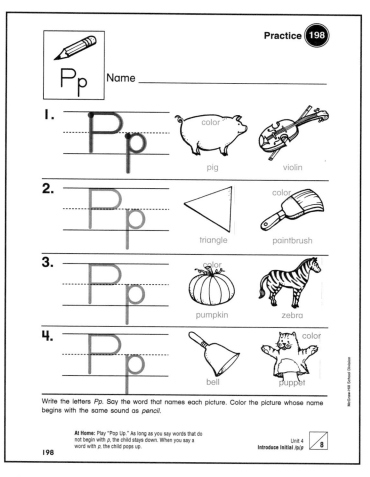

Pp Name _____

1.
pig   violin

2.
triangle   paintbrush

3.
pumpkin   zebra

4.
bell   puppet

Write the letters *Pp*. Say the word that names each picture. Color the picture whose name begins with the same sound as *pencil*.

At Home: Play "Pop Up." As long as you say words that do not begin with *p*, the child stays down. When you say a word with *p*, the child pops up.

Unit 4
Introduce Initial /p/p   8

198

Name _____

1.

2.

3.

Look at the picture on the left. Draw a circle around the picture on the right that shows something you would find inside the building. Draw a line under the picture on the right that shows something you would find outside the building.

6   Unit 4
Introduce Inside, Outside

At Home: Take a walk around the block. Have the child choose a building. Take turns naming what might be inside the building. Would it have an elevator? Do people work there?

199

_p Name _____

cup   sock   mop

p

cap   top   pot

p   p

Say the name of each picture. Write the letter *p* under each picture that has the same ending sound as *map*.

At Home: Take turns saying the name of something that ends with the sound the letter *p* stands for.

Unit 4
Introduce Final /p/p   6

200

Name _____

Look at the bear on the left. Then look at the pictures below it. Draw a circle around the items found on the bear. Cross out the items that are not on the bear. Do the same thing for the bear on the right. Then use the items to tell how the two bears are the same and different.

8   Unit 4
Introduce Compare and Contrast

At Home: Have child compare his or her clothing with another person's clothing. Help child see similarities and differences in pants, shirts, shoes and so on.

201

Tap the Sap • PRACTICE

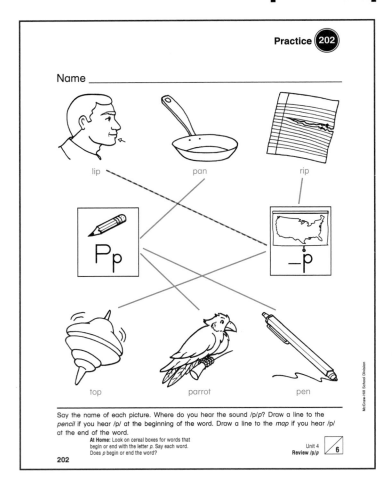

Practice 202

Name _____

lip   pan   rip

Pp   _p

top   parrot   pen

Say the name of each picture. Where do you hear the sound /p/p? Draw a line to the *pencil* if you hear /p/ at the beginning of the word. Draw a line to the *map* if you hear /p/ at the end of the word.

At Home: Look on cereal boxes for words that begin or end with the letter *p*. Say each word. Does *p* begin or end the word?

Unit 4
Review /p/p   6

202

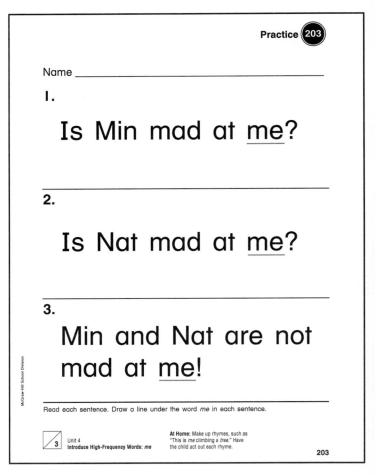

Practice 203

Name _____

1.

Is Min mad at <u>me</u>?

2.

Is Nat mad at <u>me</u>?

3.

Min and Nat are not mad at <u>me</u>!

Read each sentence. Draw a line under the word *me* in each sentence.

3   Unit 4
Introduce High-Frequency Words: *me*

At Home: Make up rhymes, such as "This is *me* climbing a *tree*." Have the child act out each rhyme.

203

Practice 204

Name _____

1. P a m   **Pam**
2. r i p   **rip**
3. t o p   **top**
4. p i n   **pin**

Blend the sounds and say the word. Write the word. Draw a line under the picture that goes with the word.

At Home: Together, write words that begin and end with the same letters. Take turns using some of the words in sentences.

Unit 4
Review Blending with Short *a, i, o*   8

204

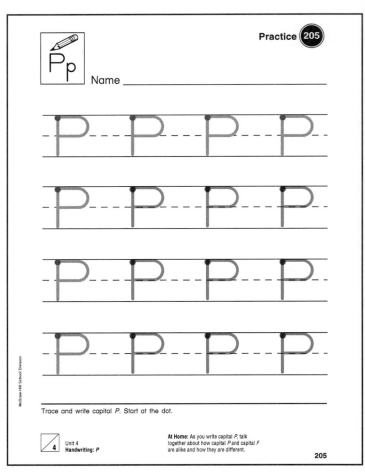

Practice 205

Pp   Name _____

P P P P
P P P P
P P P P
P P P P

Trace and write capital *P*. Start at the dot.

4   Unit 4
Handwriting: *P*

At Home: As you write capital *P*, talk together about how capital *P* and capital *F* are alike and how they are different.

205

T12   *Annotated Workbooks*

Tap the Sap • PRACTICE

Pp

Name _____

p p p p p p p

p p p p p p

p p p p p p

Pp Pp Pp

Trace and write lowercase p. Start at the dot. On the last line, trace and write Pp.

At Home: Take turns saying "P is for Peter" (or pickle, Pam, and so on). If a name is said, write capital P. If an object is said, write lowercase p.

206

Unit 4
Handwriting: P, p   4

Name _____

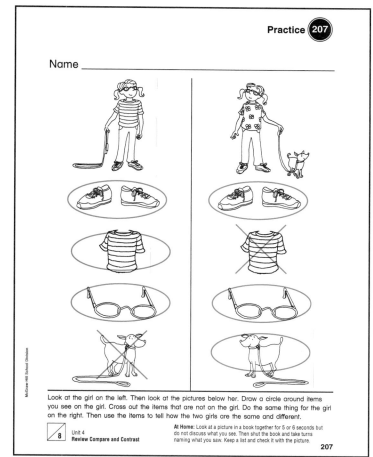

Look at the girl on the left. Then look at the pictures below her. Draw a circle around items you see on the girl. Cross out the items that are not on the girl. Do the same thing for the girl on the right. Then use the items to tell how the two girls are the same and different.

8 Unit 4
Review Compare and Contrast

At Home: Look at a picture in a book together for 5 or 6 seconds but do not discuss what you see. Then shut the book and take turns naming what you saw. Keep a list and check it with the picture.

207

Name _____

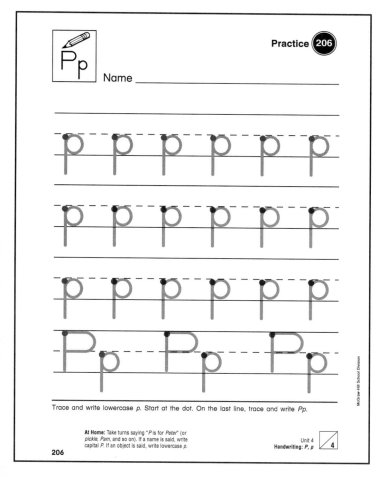

1. pin tan
    pin

2. man map
    man

3. cat cot
    cot

4. pan nap
    nap

Look at the picture. Read the words. Draw a line under the word that goes with the picture. Write the word.

At Home: Together, use letter cards to make the word cot. Then change the o to a to make the word cat. Change the vowels in the words pin and tin to make pan and tan.

208

Unit 4
Review Blending with Short a, i, o   8

Name _____

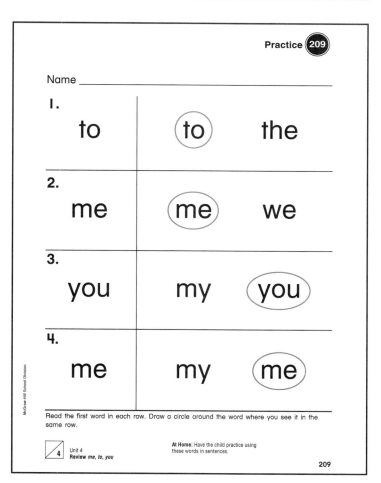

1. to   (to)   the

2. me   (me)   we

3. you   my   (you)

4. me   my   (me)

Read the first word in each row. Draw a circle around the word where you see it in the same row.

4 Unit 4
Review me, to, you

At Home: Have the child practice using these words in sentences.

209

Nap in a Lap • PRACTICE

Practice 210

Ll Name _____

1.
color
puppet   lamp

2.
color
lion   mitt

3.
color
lock   cow

Write the letters *Ll*. Say the word that names each picture. Color the picture whose name begins with the same sound as *lion*.

At Home: Play an *L* game. Give clues such as (lettuce): *What is green, is in a salad, and begins with l?*

Unit 4
Introduce Initial /l/   6

210

Practice 211

Name _____

1.
color

2.
color

3.
color

Color the picture that shows *over*. Draw a line under the picture that shows *under*.

6 Unit 4
Introduce Over, Under

At Home: Find and talk about items over or under another item, such as a chair or a table.

211

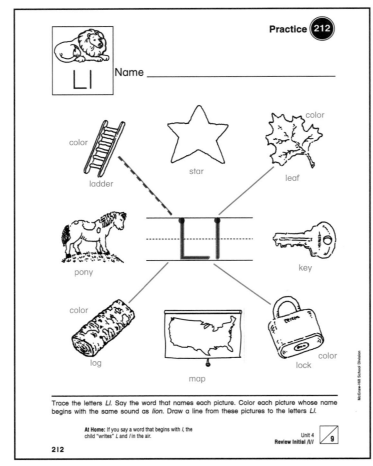

Practice 212

Ll Name _____

color
ladder

star

color
leaf

pony

Ll

key

color
log

map

color
lock

Trace the letters *Ll*. Say the word that names each picture. Color each picture whose name begins with the same sound as *lion*. Draw a line from these pictures to the letters *Ll*.

At Home: If you say a word that begins with *l*, the child "writes" *L* and *l* in the air.

Unit 4
Review Initial /l/   9

212

Practice 213

Name _____

1.   ● ●Ron is mad.

2.   ● ●I have a dip.

3.   ● ●The lid can fit.

4.   ● ●I have a nap.

Look at each picture. Then read the sentences. Draw a line from each picture to the sentence that tells about it.

4 Unit 4
Review Main Idea

At Home: Read a story together. Have the child say the main idea of the story: "This story is about ____."

213

T14 *Annotated Workbooks*

Practice **214**

Name _____

1.
l
p
ladder

2.
l
p
pot

3.
l
p
lamb

4.
l
p
puppet

5.
l
p
cap

6.
l
p
mop

1–4. Say the name of each picture. Draw a circle around the letter that stands for the sound you hear at the beginning of each picture name. 5–6. Say the name of each picture. Draw a circle around the letter that stands for the sound you hear at the end of each picture name.

At Home: Play "Rhyme Time." Say *cap* and ask for words that rhyme. Do the same with *mop, cup, lip.*

Unit 4
Review /l/l, /p/p 6

214

Practice **215**

Name _____

1. "Can we go in?" said Dan.

2. "We can go in." said Mom.

3. "Can the cat go in?" said Pam.

4. "The cat can go in," said Mom.

Read each sentence. Draw a line under the word *go* in each sentence.

4 Unit 4
Introduce High-Frequency Words: *go*

At Home: Use *go* in questions and answers, such as *Can I go to the park? You can go to the park.*

215

Practice **216**

Name _____

1. l i t
lit

2. l i p
lip

3. f a n
fan

4. r o d
rod

Blend the sounds and say the word. Write the word. Draw a line under the picture that goes with the word.

At Home: Write *not* and *dot*. Have the child change *dot* to *lot* and tell how it was done. Do the same for *dad* to *lad, did* to *lid,* and *tap* to *lap.*

Unit 4
Review Blending with Short *a, i, o* 8

216

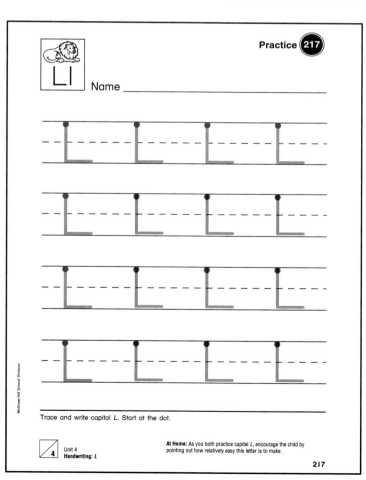

Practice **217**

Ll   Name _____

Trace and write capital *L*. Start at the dot.

4 Unit 4
Handwriting: *L*

At Home: As you both practice capital *L*, encourage the child by pointing out how relatively easy this letter is to make.

217

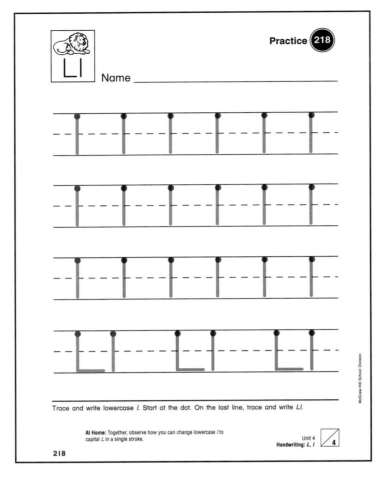

Practice 218

Ll   Name _____

Trace and write lowercase *l*. Start at the dot. On the last line, trace and write *Ll*.

At Home: Together, observe how you can change lowercase *l* to capital *L* in a single stroke.

Unit 4
Handwriting: L, l /4

218

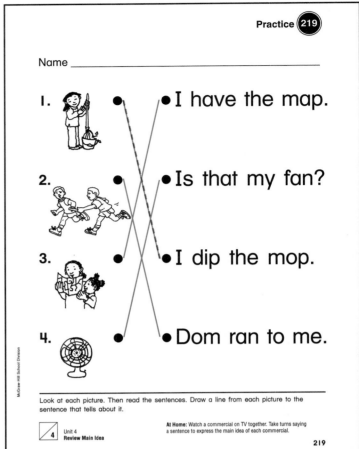

Practice 219

Name _____

1. •   •I have the map.

2. •   •Is that my fan?

3. •   •I dip the mop.

4. •   •Dom ran to me.

Look at each picture. Then read the sentences. Draw a line from each picture to the sentence that tells about it.

/4 Unit 4
Review Main Idea

At Home: Watch a commercial on TV together. Take turns saying a sentence to express the main idea of each commercial.

219

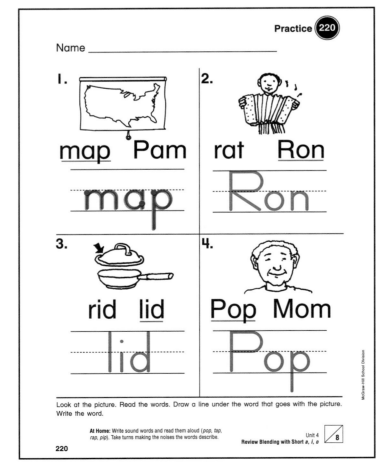

Practice 220

Name _____

1. map Pam

   map

2. rat Ron

   Ron

3. rid lid

   lid

4. Pop Mom

   Pop

Look at the picture. Read the words. Draw a line under the word that goes with the picture. Write the word.

At Home: Write sound words and read them aloud (*pop, tap, rap, pip*). Take turns making the noises the words describe.

Unit 4
Review Blending with Short a, i, o /8

220

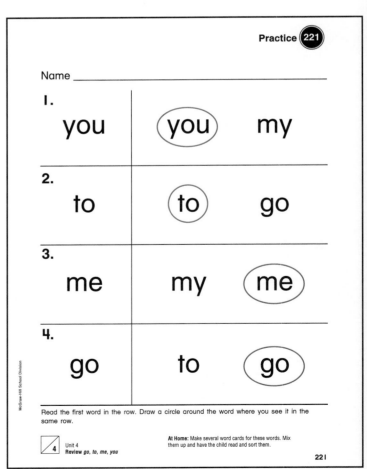

Practice 221

Name _____

1. you   (you)   my

2. to   (to)   go

3. me   my   (me)

4. go   to   (go)

Read the first word in the row. Draw a circle around the word where you see it in the same row.

/4 Unit 4
Review go, to, me, you

At Home: Make several word cards for these words. Mix them up and have the child read and sort them.

221

Mud Fun • PRACTICE

Uu

Name _____

1.

color
vase
under

2.

color
umpire
mitt

3.

astronaut
color
up

Write the letters *Uu*. Say the word that names each picture. Color the picture whose name begins with the same sound as *umbrella*.

At Home: Play "Jack-in-the-Box." When you say a word that begins with /u/, such as *up*, the child jumps up.

Unit 4
Introduce Initial /u/*u* 6

222

Name _____

color
color
color
color
color

Look at the picture. Draw a circle around the things in the picture that are up in the air. Color the things that are down on the ground.

10 Unit 4
Introduce Up, Down

At Home: Name some things that are up (books on shelves, etc.) and some things that are down (rugs, grass, etc.).

223

_u_

Name _____

u

ham
color
pup
color
rug
sock
mug
color
tub
color
cat
hug
color

Write the letter *u*. Say the word that names each picture. Listen for the sound in the middle of the word. Color each picture whose name has the same middle sound as *sun*.

At Home: Play "Rhyme Time." Say *sun* and ask for words that rhyme. Do the same for *nut* and *rug*.

Unit 4
Introduce Medial /u/*u* 9

224

Name _____

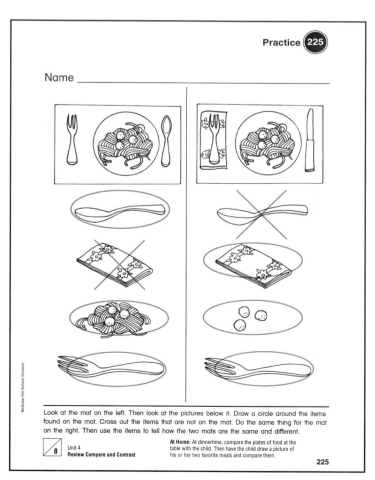

Look at the mat on the left. Then look at the pictures below it. Draw a circle around the items found on the mat. Cross out the items that are not on the mat. Do the same thing for the mat on the right. Then use the items to tell how the two mats are the same and different.

8 Unit 4
Review Compare and Contrast

At Home: At dinnertime, compare the plates of food at the table with the child. Then have the child draw a picture of his or her two favorite meals and compare them.

225

T17

Mud Fun • PRACTICE

Say the name of the picture. Where do you hear the sound /u/u? Draw a circle around the first u if it is the beginning sound (as in *umbrella*). Draw a circle around the second u if it is the middle sound (as in *sun*).

At Home: Take turns saying words that begin with *under* (*underneath, underwater,* and so on). Point out that they begin with the letter *u.*

Unit 4
Review /u/u

9

226

Practice 226

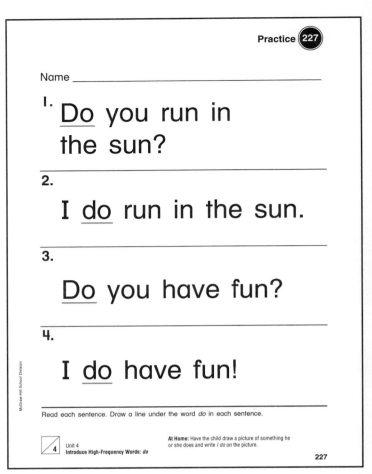

Read each sentence. Draw a line under the word *do* in each sentence.

Unit 4
Introduce High-Frequency Words: *do*

At Home: Have the child draw a picture of something he or she does and write *I do* on the picture.

227

Practice 227

Blend the sounds and say the word. Write the word. Draw a line under the picture that goes with the word.

At Home: Ask the child to write words you say: *up, cup, pup.* Ask which one names something that can wag its tail.

Unit 4
Introduce Blending with Short *u*

8

228

Practice 228

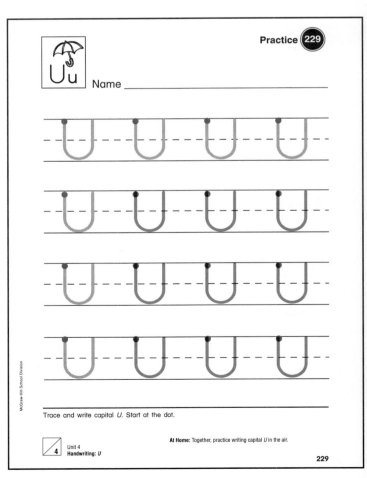

Trace and write capital *U.* Start at the dot.

Unit 4
Handwriting: *U*

At Home: Together, practice writing capital *U* in the air.

229

Practice 229

T18 *Annotated Workbooks*

Mud Fun • PRACTICE

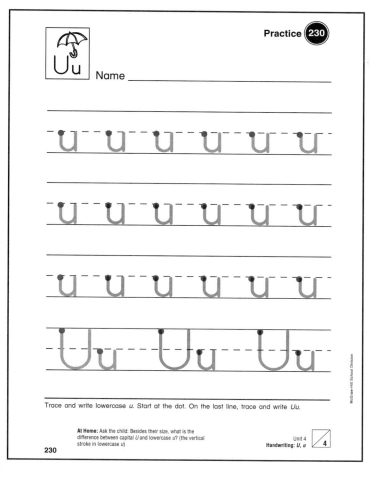

Uu Name _____

u u u u u u

u u u u u u

u u u u u u

Uu Uu Uu

Trace and write lowercase *u*. Start at the dot. On the last line, trace and write *Uu*.

At Home: Ask the child: Besides their size, what is the difference between capital *U* and lowercase *u*? (the vertical stroke in lowercase *u*)

Unit 4
Handwriting: U, u 4

230

Name _____

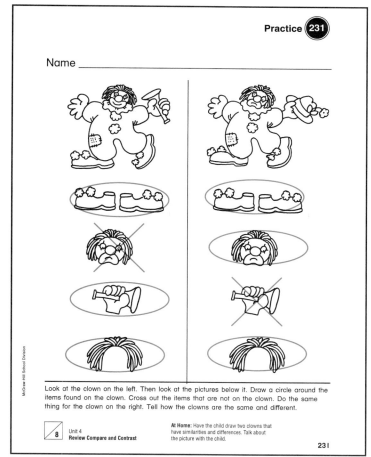

Look at the clown on the left. Then look at the pictures below it. Draw a circle around the items found on the clown. Cross out the items that are not on the clown. Do the same thing for the clown on the right. Tell how the clowns are the same and different.

8 Unit 4
Review Compare and Contrast

At Home: Have the child draw two clowns that have similarities and differences. Talk about the picture with the child.

231

Name _____

1. cut cup

cup

2. rod pod

rod

3. nut cut

cut

4. mop top

mop

Look at the picture. Read the words. Draw a line under the word that goes with the picture. Write the word.

At Home: Say some of the following words. Have the child point "up" if the word has the sound that *u* stands for: *up, cup, fun, pat, sun, mud, bag, pup.*

Unit 4
Review Blending with Short u, o 8

232

Name _____

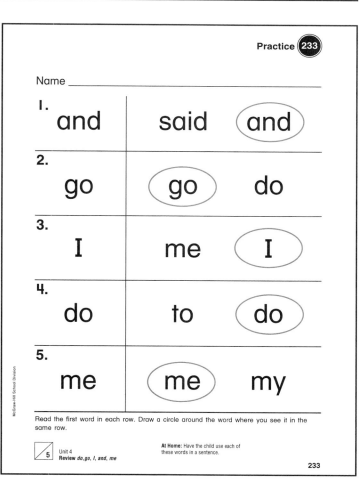

1.	and	said	(and)
2.	go	(go)	do
3.	I	me	(I)
4.	do	to	(do)
5.	me	(me)	my

Read the first word in each row. Draw a circle around the word where you see it in the same row.

5 Unit 4
Review do, go, I, and, me

At Home: Have the child use each of these words in a sentence.

233

T19

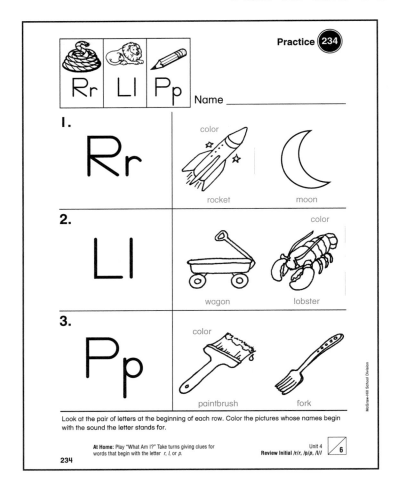

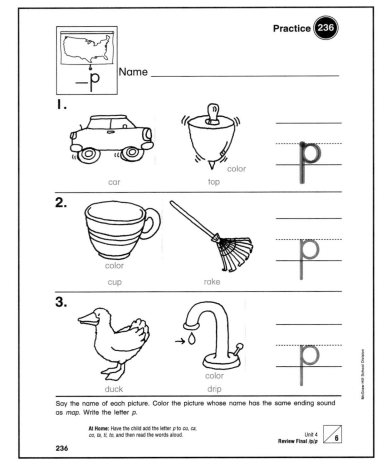

Fun in the Sun • PRACTICE

Name _____

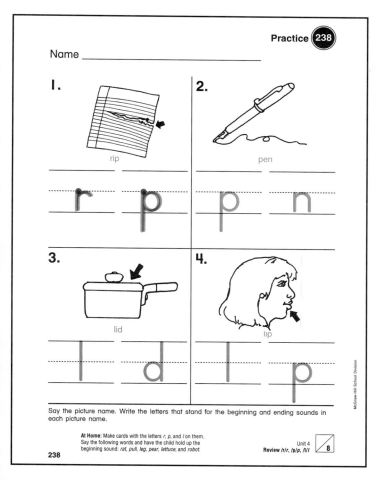

1.
rip

r | p

2.
pen

p | n

3.
lid

l | d

4.
lip

l | p

Say the picture name. Write the letters that stand for the beginning and ending sounds in each picture name.

At Home: Make cards with the letters *r, p,* and *l* on them. Say the following words and have the child hold up the beginning sound: *rat, pull, leg, pear, lettuce,* and *robot.*

Unit 4
Review /r/r, /p/p, /l/l

8

238

Name _____

1. "Go to Dan!" said Min to the pup.

2. "Do not go in the mud!" said Dad.

3. "Run to me!" said Mom.

4. The pup ran to the mud!

Read the sentences. 1. Draw a circle around the word *go.* 2. Draw a circle around the word *do.* 3. Draw a circle around the word *me.* 4. Draw a circle around the word *to.*

4 Unit 4
Review *to, me, go, do*

At Home: Make word cards for *go, do, me,* and *to.* Have the child trace and read each card. Mix up the cards and repeat.

239

Name _____

1.
u p

up

2.
c u p

cup

3.
n u t

nut

4.
m u d

mud

Blend the sounds and say the word. Write the word. Draw a line under the picture that goes with the word.

At Home: Write *up* in the air and blend the sounds as you write. Continue with *mud* and *cup.* Use the words in sentences.

Unit 4
Review Blending with Short *u*

8

240

Name _____

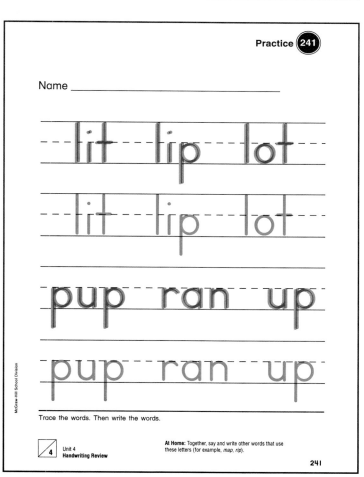

lit lip lot

lit lip lot

pup ran up

pup ran up

Trace the words. Then write the words.

4 Unit 4
Handwriting Review

At Home: Together, say and write other words that use these letters (for example, *map, rip*).

241

Practice **242**

Name _____

Run to Pat.

Run to Pat.

Mud is fun!

Mud is fun!

Trace the words in the sentence. Then write the words.

At Home: Make sure that the child is holding his/her pencil
comfortably and correctly.

Unit 4
Handwriting Review / 4

242

Practice **243**

Name _____

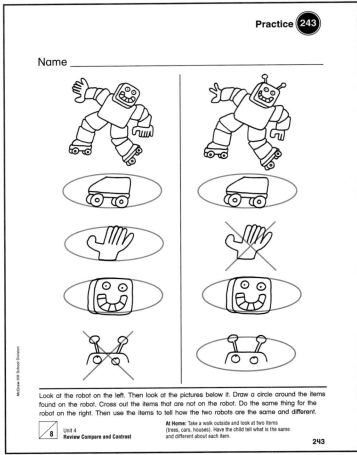

Look at the robot on the left. Then look at the pictures below it. Draw a circle around the items
found on the robot. Cross out the items that are not on the robot. Do the same thing for the
robot on the right. Then use the items to tell how the two robots are the same and different.

8 / Unit 4
Review Compare and Contrast

At Home: Take a walk outside and look at two items
(trees, cars, houses). Have the child tell what is the same
and different about each item.

243

Practice **244**

Name _____

1. fun fin
    fun

2. Mom mop
    Mom

3. rut run
    run

4. top tip
    tip

Look at the picture. Read the words. Draw a line under the word that goes with the picture.
Write the word.

At Home: Write *fin*. Ask the child to change *fin* to *fun*.
Take turns. Change *fun* to *run* and change *fun* to *sun*.

Unit 4
Review Blending with Short u, o, i / 8

244

Practice **245**

Name _____

1.
   go   do   (to)

2.
   we   me   my

3.
   to   go   (do)

4.
   go   the   is

1. Draw a circle around the word *to*. 2. Draw a line under the word *me*. 3. Draw a circle
around the word *do*. 4. Draw a line under the word *go*.

4 / Unit 4
Review to, me, go, do

At Home: Write the words *to, me, go, do*, on a sheet of
paper. Have the child read the words and name the words
that rhyme (*to, do*).

245

Initial *r*

OBJECTIVES Children will apply letter/sound associations for *r*. They will identify words that begin with *r*.

Alternate Activities

Visual

R RIBBONS

Materials: red ribbon or strips of red construction paper, markers, pictures or objects whose names begin with *r*, masking tape

Have children write *r* on a ribbon and label a picture or object whose name begins with *r*.

- Gather other pictures and objects whose names begin with *r*.

- Give each child a ribbon or strip of red construction paper. Point out that *red* and *ribbon* both begin with *r*.

 Have children label their red ribbon *r*.

- Invite them to use masking tape to attach their *r* ribbon to a picture or object whose name begins with r.

- Invite each child to share the name of their object or picture as you lead children in singing a variation of a round. Have each child sing the name of the object or picture to the tune of "Row, Row, Row Your Boat." ▶**Linguistic**

Auditory

RICE

Materials: unsweetened crisp rice cereal, napkins

Children will listen to a list of words and respond by moving a piece of rice cereal to a napkin if the word begins with *r*.

- Give each child two napkins, one with a small pile of rice cereal.

- Say a list of words, some that begin with *r*, and some that do not.

- Tell children to move a piece of the rice cereal to the clean napkin when they hear a word that begins with *r*, as in *rice*. ▶**Bodily/Kinesthetic**

Kinesthetic

RAINBOW ROAD

Materials: large sheets of colored butcher paper, markers

Children will blend sounds as they walk along a path of letters to read words that begin with *r*.

- On large sheets of colored butcher paper, write letters children can blend to form words that begin with *r*, such as r*an, rat, rod, rid*. Allow space between each letter to create a path for children to walk along.

- Set up letters to create a "rainbow road" of colors. Point out that *rainbow* and *road* both begin with *r*.

- Have pairs of children take turns walking along a path, saying each letter's sound to blend and read the words. ▶**Bodily/Kinesthetic**

 **CD-ROM**

On, Off

Alternate Activities

Visual

SWITCHING OFF AND ON

 Materials: construction paper, markers

ONE Children will create light switch covers that are labeled *off* and *on*.

- Give each child a pre-cut light switch cover made of construction paper.

- Have a volunteer demonstrate turning the lights off and on. Ask children to notice the position of the switch when the lights are off and when they are on.

WRITING On the chalkboard, write the words *off* and *on*. Have children create a design for their switch cover that includes the labels. Children may wish to dictate other words, phrases, or sentences for you to record. ▶**Spatial**

Auditory

SIMON SAYS ON/OFF

Children will respond to directions that include *off* and *on*.

GROUP

- Lead children in playing *Simon Says.* In each direction, include *on* or *off.* For example, *Simon says put your hands on your head. Take your hands off your head.*

- Have volunteers take turns being Simon and giving directions to classmates. ▶**Interpersonal**

Kinesthetic

OFF/ON GAME

GROUP **Materials:** butcher paper, construction paper, scissors, tape, paper plate, paper arrow, brad

Children will use the words *on* and *off* as they play a game.

- Choose four colors of construction paper. Cut four large circles of each color. Tape the circles in rows to a large sheet of butcher paper.

- Use a paper plate to create a spinner. Divide the plate into four sections with a drawing to represent left hand, left foot, right hand, right foot. Within each section, show each color. Attach a paper arrow with a brad to complete the spinner.

- Spin the arrow for children. As each child takes a turn, have the child use the words *off* and *on* to describe his or her movements, such as *I'm taking my left hand* off *green and putting it* on *yellow.* ▶**Bodily/Kinesthetic**

Main Idea

 **OBJECTIVES** Children will identify the main idea in several stories.

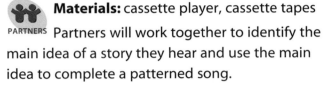

Auditory

MAIN IDEA IN A SONG

Materials: cassette player, cassette tapes

PARTNERS Partners will work together to identify the main idea of a story they hear and use the main idea to complete a patterned song.

- Have pairs of children listen to a brief story, either one you read aloud or a story on tape. Assign a different story to each pair of children.

- Have partners discuss what the story was about.

- Ask pairs to complete a song about the story to a familiar tune. For example, the following words can be sung to the tune of "Twinkle, Twinkle, Little Star."

  Listen, listen, to this tale

  It is about a _____ who _____.

- Invite pairs to share with classmates the title of their book and their song. ▶**Musical**

Kinesthetic

MAIN IDEA TABLEAU

 Materials: magazine pictures, props featured in magazine pictures

GROUP

Children will work in groups to portray the main idea of a magazine picture.

- Gather several magazine pictures.

- Organize the class into small groups, and give each group a picture. Have the groups discuss what the picture is mainly about.

- Have each group arrange themselves and props to show the main idea of the picture.

- Have groups show the picture, discuss the action or scene, and answer questions their classmates ask. ▶**Bodily/Kinesthetic**

Visual

MAIN IDEA HEAD BANDS

Materials: sentence strips, stapler or tape, ONE markers or crayons, construction paper, scissors

Children will dictate the main idea of a story and use art materials to create a head band.

- Lead children in a discussion about a story you have recently read together, or introduce a new story.

 Give each child a sentence strip about 18 WRITING inches long. Have children write or dictate a sentence that tells about the main idea of the story.

- Ask children to draw or cut and paste shapes onto the sentence strip to show the main idea.

- Tape or staple the strips to create head bands for children to wear while they reread or discuss the story. ▶**Intrapersonal**

High-Frequency Words
to, me, go, do

☑OBJECTIVES Children will practice reading the high-frequency words *to, me, go,* and *do*.

Alternate Activities

Visual

BOOKWORM PULL-THROUGHS

ONE **Materials:** oak tag, marker, paper, scissors

Children will make a pull-through game to practice reading high-frequency words.

- Make an oak tag bookworm or other character cutout for each child. Cut two slits in the cutout. Give each child a strip of paper or oak tag that is the same width as the slits.

- **WRITING** Write the high-frequency words *to, me, go, do* on the chalkboard. Have children write the words on their strips of paper.

- Show children how to feed the paper strip through the slits in the character cutout to reveal one word at a time.

- Have children use their strips to practice reading the words. ▶**Spatial**

Kinesthetic

HOPSCOTCH WITH WORDS

GROUP **Materials:** chalk, stone or other marker

Children will play a variation of *Hopscotch* and read high-frequency words.

- In an outdoor area, draw a *Hopscotch* grid with four squares. In each square, write a high-frequency word: *me, to, go, do.*

- Have groups of children take turns playing the game. Children must read the word in the box where his or her stone lands and then hop to that box. ▶**Bodily/Kinesthetic**

Auditory

ROUND ROBIN STORY

PARTNERS **Materials:** index cards, markers

Children will incorporate high-frequency words into an oral story.

- Write the high-frequency words *me, to, go,* and *do* on individual index cards, and give pairs of children each a set of the cards.

- Have the pairs turn the cards face down. Have one child begin the story with a story starter, such as *One day, something strange happened on the way to school.*

- Have partners take turns turning over a card and using the high-frequency word in a sentence that continues the story.

- Have children return the cards to the pile and play until they feel their story is complete.

- Invite partners to share their stories with the rest of the class. ▶**Linguistic**

Initial and Final /p/ p

OBJECTIVES Children will apply letter/sound associations for /p/ p. They will identify words that begin or end with p.

Alternate Activities

Auditory

TONGUE TWISTERS

Materials: p letter cards

Children will make letter/sound associations as they say tongue twisters. Partners will collaborate on an original tongue twister that uses the repeated sound of p.

- Lead children in saying "Peter Piper."

  Peter Piper picked a peck of pickled peppers.

  If Peter Piper picked a peck of pickled peppers,

  How many pickled peppers did Peter Piper pick?

- Give children p letter cards. Have them raise their cards when they hear a word that begins with p.

- Lead children in brainstorming additional words that begin with p. Encourage pairs of children to incorporate some of those words in a sentence to make a tongue twister.

- Invite pairs to share their tongue twisters with classmates. ▶Linguistic

Visual

PICNIC PUZZLES

Materials: paper plates, magazine pictures of foods whose names begin with p, scissors, glue, markers

Children will match puzzle pieces of foods that begin with p with their labels.

- Gather magazine pictures of foods whose names begin with p, such as *pizza, pineapple, pear* and *pie.*

- On one half of a paper plate, glue a picture. On the other half, write p and the object's label.

- Cut apart the picture and label in a way that creates a unique puzzle with only one match.

- Mix the puzzle pieces for children to assemble. When children complete each puzzle, ask them to say the object's name and point to the letter that stands for its beginning sound. ▶Spatial

Kinesthetic

WORD GROUPS

Materials: construction paper, hole punch, yarn, markers

Small groups of children will wear letter necklaces and arrange themselves to build words. Other children will blend the sounds to read the words.

- Organize children into groups of three. Give each child a "letter necklace" (construction paper with a letter; holes punched and yarn tied to make a necklace). Arrange the letters so the group can spell words that begin or end with p.

- Have groups arrange themselves so they spell a word from left to right when facing the class.

- Have the class blend the sounds to read the words. ▶Bodily/Kinesthetic

 CD-ROM

Inside, Outside

✓BJECTIVES Children will discriminate between inside and outside as they respond to directions.

Alternate Activities

Kinesthetic

HOKEY POKEY

GROUP Children will apply the concepts of *inside* and *outside* as they play a traditional musical circle game.

- Have children form a circle. Point out areas that are inside the circle and those that are outside the circle.

- Lead children in singing the "Hokey Pokey" and performing the moves. You may wish to begin with your right hand and invite children to suggest other body parts to continue the song. ▶**Musical**

Visual

IN AND OUT

PARTNERS **Materials:** large plastic play hoop or masking tape, index cards, markers, various classroom objects

Pairs of children will arrange objects to match a scene drawn on a card you give them.

- Create a set of cards that show various classroom objects, including children, inside or outside a circle. For example, the cards might include a stick-figure child standing in the circle, a pencil placed outside the circle, a book placed inside the circle, and so on.

- Make a large masking-tape circle on the floor, or use a plastic hoop.

- Provide children with the objects depicted in the drawings on the cards. Have pairs work together to arrange the objects to create a scene that matches the drawing. ▶**Spatial**

Auditory

INSIDE/OUTSIDE GAME

ONE Children will share examples to demonstrate *inside* and *outside*.

- Review the concepts of inside and outside with children. Stand inside an area, such as the reading center. Describe your position with an oral sentence, such as *I am inside the reading center.* Then change your position and describe it, such as *I am outside the reading center.*

- Encourage children to think of and demonstrate other examples. If children need help, you might whisper some suggestions, such as standing inside/outside a closet, inside/outside a big box, or putting a small object inside/outside a cup. ▶**Bodily/Kinesthetic**

Compare and Contrast

OBJECTIVES Children will compare and contrast different people and objects. They will sort objects based on similarities and differences.

Alternate

Auditory

COMPARE CHARACTERS

 Materials: two large plastic play hoops

Children will participate in a discussion to compare and contrast two characters from literature. They will assist in completing a Venn diagram.

* Tape together two large plastic hoops to create a three-dimensional Venn diagram. Set the hoops on the chalk rail. Alternatively, draw a large Venn diagram on the chalkboard or on chart paper.

* Identify two characters in stories children have recently read.

* Label each circle with one character's name. Label the area where the circles intersect *Both*. Explain to children that a Venn diagram can be used to tell how people or objects are the same and different.

* Lead children in discussing how the characters are alike and different, and record their responses in the appropriate places on the diagram.
  ▶**Spatial**

Visual

MAKE THEM THE SAME

Materials: construction paper, scissors

Children will manipulate geometric shapes to make two different patterns the same.

* Cut a variety of geometric shapes from construction paper. Make a pattern by arranging four colored shapes in a row. Beneath that row, create the same pattern with one exception.

* Have children identify how the pattern in the second row is different from that in the first row. Have a volunteer replace the shape so the two patterns are identical.

* Have pairs of children work together. Have one partner create a new pattern in one row and duplicate it with one exception in the second row. Have the other partner replace one shape to make the two patterns the same. Then have partners switch roles. ▶**Logical/Mathematical**

Kinesthetic

SHOE SORT

Children will compare and contrast shoes in the classroom, sorting them by category.

* Have children stand in a circle and notice all the different types of shoes. Discuss how the shoes are alike. (They are worn to protect the feet.) Then discuss differences in color and style.

* Have children choose a criterion, such as color or style. Ask them to arrange themselves in groups by category. For example, children with black shoes will stand together. ▶**Interpersonal**

Initial *l*

 OBJECTIVES Children will apply letter/sound associations for *l*. They will identify words that begin with *l*.

Alternate Activities

Visual

TOWERING L

 Materials: boxes or blocks, self-stick notes, crayons, markers

Children will build a tower in the shape of the letter *l*. They will attach pictures and labels to the tower.

- Have children use stacks of boxes or blocks to build a tower resembling the letter *l*.

 Give each child a self-stick note. Ask children to draw a picture of something that begins with *l*. Help children label their drawings.

- Invite children to share their drawings and attach them carefully to the tower. ▶**Interpersonal**

Auditory

DID YOU EVER SEE AN L WORD?

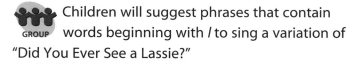 Children will suggest phrases that contain words beginning with *l* to sing a variation of "Did You Ever See a Lassie?"

- Lead children in singing "Did You Ever See a Lassie?" Guide them to realize that *lassie* begins with *l*.

- Tell children that you want to sing a new version of the song that uses more words that begin with *l*. Provide several examples, such as *lick a lollipop, lose a letter,* or *lie on the lawn*. Encourage children to suggest additional phrases. Sing the new phrases to the tune of "Did You Ever See a Lassie?" ▶**Musical**

Kinesthetic

L LADDERS

 **Materials:** index cards, markers, step ladder or paper ladder

Children will blend sounds to read words that begin with *l* as they "climb" a ladder.

- On index cards, write words beginning with *l*, such as *lip, lid, lit, lap,* and *lot*. Attach each card to the rung of a step ladder. Alternatively, you may wish to attach labels to a playground ladder, or one you draw on butcher paper.

- Have children blend the sounds to read the words as they climb up and down the ladder. ▶**Bodily/Kinesthetic**

Phonics CD-ROM

T31

Initial and Medial Short *u*

✓BJECTIVES Children will apply letter/sound associations for short *u*. They will identify words that have short *u* in the initial and medial positions.

Alternate Activities

Visual

POP-UPS

 Materials: construction paper, scissors, crayons or markers

Children will create a pop-up page with illustrations of words containing the short *u* sound.

- For each child, prepare a pop-up card. Fold a piece of construction paper in half across the width. Two inches from the top of the page, make a two-inch cut toward the fold. Cut an arch, similar to a quarter circle, to the top of the page. Open the card. Press the half circle down into the card. When reopened, it's a pop-up.

Have children open the card and label the half-circle pop-up *u*. Have children draw pictures whose names contain the short *u* sound in the initial and medial positions. ▶Spatial

Auditory

RHYME WITH SHORT *U*

 Children will identify words with the short *u* sound in the initial and medial positions in a finger play.

- Share the following words and movements:

We had no umbrella as we walked to the bus.
(swing arms by your side)

Suddenly the rain started pouring on us!
(flutter fingers down in front of you)

Let's get an umbrella to hold up high.
(pretend to hold handle of umbrella)

If we stand under it, then we will be dry.
(pretend to flick rain from each shoulder)

- Repeat each line. Ask volunteers to identify words that contain the short *u* sound. Have children tell whether they hear the sound at the beginning or in the middle of the word. ▶Bodily/Kinesthetic

Kinesthetic

UNDER THE UMBRELLA

Materials: umbrella, yarn, paper clips, index cards, markers

Partners will take turns selecting word cards for each other to blend and read.

- Prepare an umbrella prop by tying three pieces of yarn to spokes on an umbrella. At the end of each piece of yarn, tie a paper clip.

- On index cards, write words with the short *u* sound in the initial or medial positions, for example, *up, us, cup, mud, sun, fun, run* and *cut.*

- Have partners take turns choosing three cards and attaching them to the clips hanging from the umbrella. Have the partner who chose the words stand under the open umbrella. The other partner blends the sounds to read the words. Have children switch roles. ▶Linguistic

 **CD-ROM**

Over, Under, Up, Down

OBJECTIVES Children will distinguish *over, under, up,* and *down* as they respond to directions.

Alternate Activities

Auditory

UNDER/OVER FINGER PLAY

GROUP Children will explore the concepts of *over, under, up,* and *down* as they perform a finger play.

- Share the following words and movements with children:

  Under the water, down deep,
  (point hand down as if diving into water)

  What kinds of animals might you see?
  (raise hands and tilt head)

  Over the water, up in the air,
  (gesture toward sky)

  What kinds of animals might like it there?
  (raise hands and tilt head)

- Repeat each line and have children echo after you.

- Invite children to suggest what kinds of animals they might see in each place mentioned in the finger play. ▶**Musical**

Kinesthetic

LIMBO BEAT

GROUP **Materials:** wooden stick or string
Children will explore the concepts of *over, under, up,* and *down* as they play a traditional *Limbo* game.

- Have two volunteers hold the string or bar. Lead children in a discussion about things in the room that are *over* the line and things that are *under* the line. Point out that to describe an object's position, children can tell someone to look *up* or *down.*

- Demonstrate for children how you can step *over* or go *under* the bar.

- Guide children in playing *Limbo*. Have them bend backward to go under the bar. After everyone has had a turn, lower the bar. If someone touches the bar, he or she is out of the game.
  ▶**Bodily/Kinesthetic**

Visual

I SPY

PARTNERS Children will give each other clues about objects using the position words *over, under, up,* and *down.*

- Model for children playing the game *I Spy* using the position words *over, under, up,* and *down* in the clues.

- Have pairs of children play the game in the classroom or on the playground. ▶**Spatial**

Writing Readiness

Before children begin to write, fine motor skills need to be developed. Here are examples of activities that can be used:

- **Simon Says** Play Simon Says using just finger positions.
- **Finger Plays and Songs** Sing songs such as "Where Is Thumbkin" or "The Eensie, Weensie, Spider" or songs that use Signed English or American Sign Language.
- **Mazes** Use or create mazes, especially ones that require moving the writing instruments from left to right.

The Mechanics of Writing

POSTURE

- Chair height should allow for the feet to rest flat on the floor.
- Desk height should be two inches above the elbows.
- There should be an inch between the child and the desk.
- Children sit erect with the elbows resting on the desk.
- Letter models should be on the desk or at eye level.

PAPER POSITION

- **Right-handed children** should turn the paper so that the lower left-hand corner of the paper points to the abdomen.

- **Left-handed children** should turn the paper so that the lower right-hand corner of the paper points to the abdomen.

- The nondominant hand should anchor the paper near the top so that the paper doesn't slide.
- The paper should be moved up as the child nears the bottom of the paper. Many children won't think of this.

The Writing Instrument Grasp

For handwriting to be functional, the writing instrument must be held in a way that allows for fluid dynamic movement.

FUNCTIONAL GRASP PATTERNS

- **Tripod Grasp** The writing instrument is held with the tip of the thumb and the index finger and rests against the side of the third finger. The thumb and index finger form a circle.

- **Quadrupod Grasp** The writing instrument is held with the tip of the thumb and index finger and rests against the fourth finger. The thumb and index finger form a circle.

INCORRECT GRASP PATTERNS

- **Fisted Grasp** The writing instrument is held in a fisted hand.

- **Pronated Grasp** The instrument is held diagonally within the hand with the tips of the thumb and index finger but with no support from other fingers.

- **Five-Finger Grasp** The writing instrument is held with the tips of all five fingers.

- **Flexed or Hooked Wrist** Flexed or bent wrist is typically seen with left-handed writers but is also present in some right-handed writers.

- To correct wrist position, have children check their writing posture and paper placement.

TO CORRECT GRASPS

- Have children play counting games with an eye dropper and water.
- Have children pick up small objects with a tweezer.
- Do counting games with children picking up small coins using just the thumb and index finger.

Evaluation Checklist

Formation and Strokes

- ☑ Does the child begin letters at the top?
- ☑ Do circles close?
- ☑ Are the horizontal lines straight?
- ☑ Do circular shapes and extender and descender lines touch?
- ☑ Are the heights of all upper-case letters equal?
- ☑ Are the heights of all lower-case letters equal?
- ☑ Are the lengths of the extenders and descenders the same for all letters?

Directionality

- ☑ Do the children form letters starting at the top and moving to the bottom?
- ☑ Are letters formed from left to right?

Spacing

- ☑ Are the spaces between letters equidistant?
- ☑ Are the spaces between words equidistant?
- ☑ Do the letters rest on the line?
- ☑ Are the top, bottom and side margins on the paper even?

Write the Alphabet
Trace and write the letters.

Trace and write the letters.

C C C

c c c

D D D

d d d

Trace and write the letters.

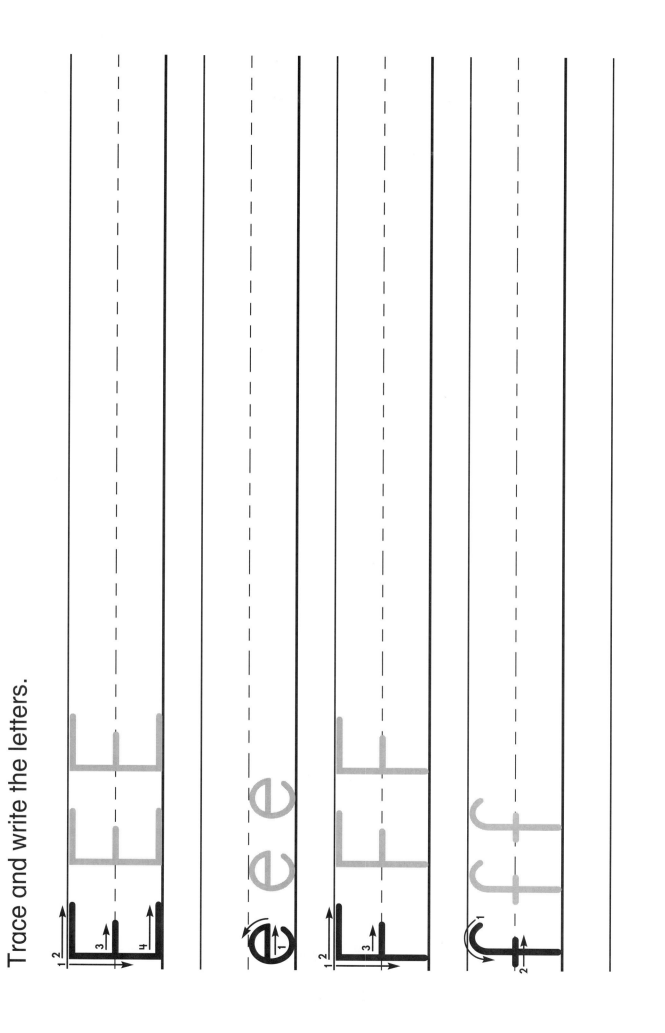

Trace and write the letters.

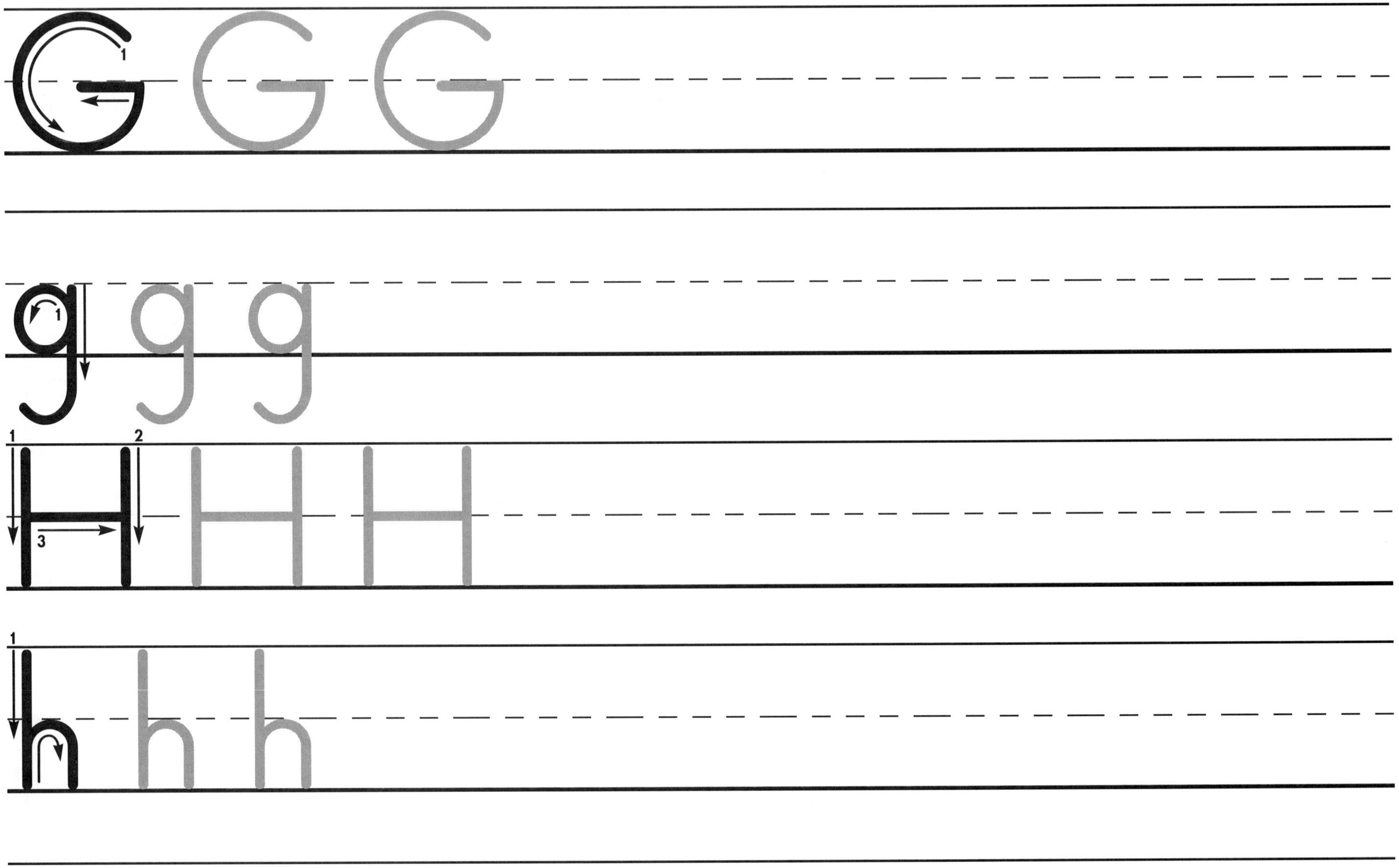

G G G

g g g

H H H

h h h

Trace and write the letters.

Trace and write the letters.

Trace and write the letters.

Trace and write the letters.

O O O

o o o

P P P

p p p

Trace and write the letters.

Q

q

R

r

Trace and write the letters.

S S S

s s s T T T

t t t

Trace and write the letters.

U u u

u u u

V v v

v v v

Trace and write the letters.

Trace and write the letters.

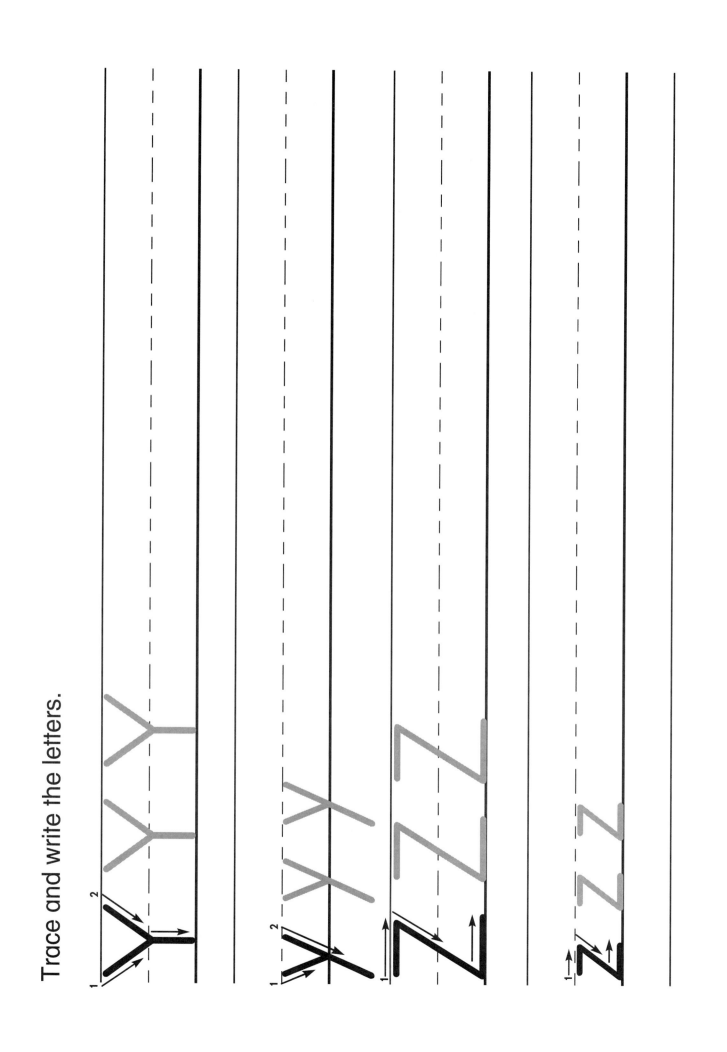

The Apple Pie Tree

BY Zoe Hall

ILLUSTRATED BY

Shari Halpern

The
Apple Pie
Tree

BY Zoe Hall
ILLUSTRATED BY Shari Halpern

McGraw-Hill
School Division
New York   Farmington

My sister and I have a tree that grows the best part of apple pie.

Can you guess what that is?

3

Apples!
And every year,
we watch our apple tree grow.

In winter, our apple tree
is brown and bare.

But in spring,
leaves grow
on every branch.

Look! Two robins
are building a nest
in our tree.

Tiny pink flower buds
appear on the branches.
The robins chirp loudly,
guarding their eggs.

T49

Just when the flower buds open, baby robins break through the eggshells.

Now our tree is covered with blossoms.
And the baby robins begin to grow feathers.

When breezes blow,
the petals fall to the ground.
Mama and Papa Robin
teach their little birds to fly.

Some days it rains,
and the wind blows hard.
But our apple tree is strong.
And the robins are safe
in the branches.

Small green apples grow
where the blossoms used to be.

Soon it is summer.
The apples get bigger and bigger...

The little robins have grown up.
But they visit every day.

The branches bend down low.
They are covered with
big, round apples.

Now it is autumn.
The apples are red and ready to be picked!
We fill our basket to the brim.

Mom and Dad help us
peel the apples, cut them up,
and pile them into a pie shell.
Then we sprinkle cinnamon
and sugar over the top.

Mom puts the pan in the oven.

At last, the pie is cooked
and ready to be eaten.

Our tree has grown an apple pie!
It smells so good!

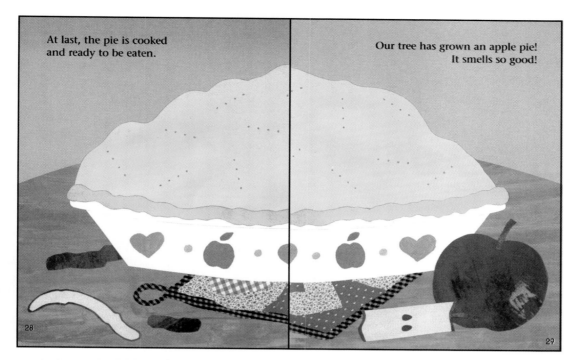

28

29

And it tastes delicious!

There's nothing as good
as an apple pie
you grew yourself.

30

31

How bees help our apples grow:

1. Inside each flower are tiny stems, some tipped with yellow **pollen**, and some with sticky tops. **Nectar** deep inside smells sweet.

2. The bright petals and sweet nectar attract bees. **Pollen** collects on the bees' bodies.

3. As the bees fly from flower to flower, **pollen** clings to the sticky tops. This is called **pollination**.

4. The petals fall off, and the base of the flower begins to swell. This is the beginning of an **apple**.

This is how we make our apple pie!

1. **Make the pie crust:** Mix 2 cups all-purpose flour and 1 teaspoon salt in a large bowl. Cut up ⅔ cup butter into small pieces and mix in. Sprinkle ⅓ cup ice water on top and mix till the dough makes a loose ball. Cut in half. Roll out one half on a floured board to form a circle 12 inches across, ⅛ inch thick. Gently place in a 9-inch pie pan. Roll out remaining dough the same way and cover with a towel.

2. **Fill the pie:** Peel 6 to 8 apples and cut them up, removing the centers. Put the slices into the pie pan. Sprinkle 1 teaspoon cinnamon and ½ cup sugar over the slices.

3. **Close the pie:** Place the second circle of dough over the apples. Pinch the edges together, and trim off the extra dough. Make small holes in the top.

4. **Bake** at 400° for 50 minutes. Serve and eat. Yum!

32

NATURE SPY

written by SHELLEY ROTNER and KEN KREISLER
photographs by SHELLEY ROTNER

McGraw Hill

NATURE SPY

written by SHELLEY ROTNER and KEN KREISLER
photographs by SHELLEY ROTNER

 McGraw-Hill School Division
New York   Farmington

I like to go outside—to look around and discover things.

7

To take a really close look, even closer

8

and closer.

9

My mother says I'm a curious kid. She calls me a nature spy.

10

Sometimes I look so closely, I can see the lines on a shiny green leaf.

11

or one small acorn on a branch,

12

or seeds in a pod.

13

I notice the feathers of a bird,

14

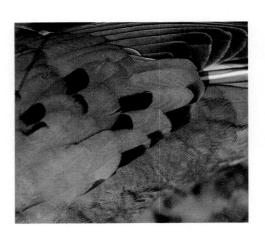

15

or the golden eye of a frog.

16

17

When you look closely, things look so different—
like the bark of a tree or an empty hornet's nest,

18

the seeds of a sunflower, or even a rock.

19

Sometimes there's a pattern, like ice on a frozen pond,

20

or a spider's web, or a butterfly's wing.

21

Everything has its own shape, color,

22

and size.

23

Look closely at a turtle's shell,

24

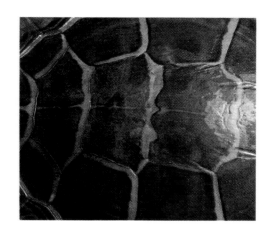

25

or a dog's fur.

26

27

or even raspberries.

28

or kernels of corn.

29

No matter where you look, up, down

30

or all around,

31

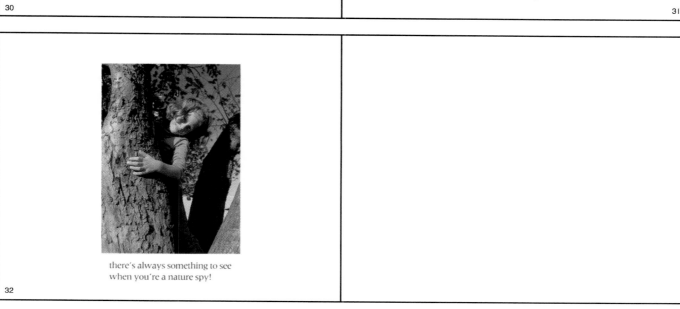

there's always something to see
when you're a nature spy!

32

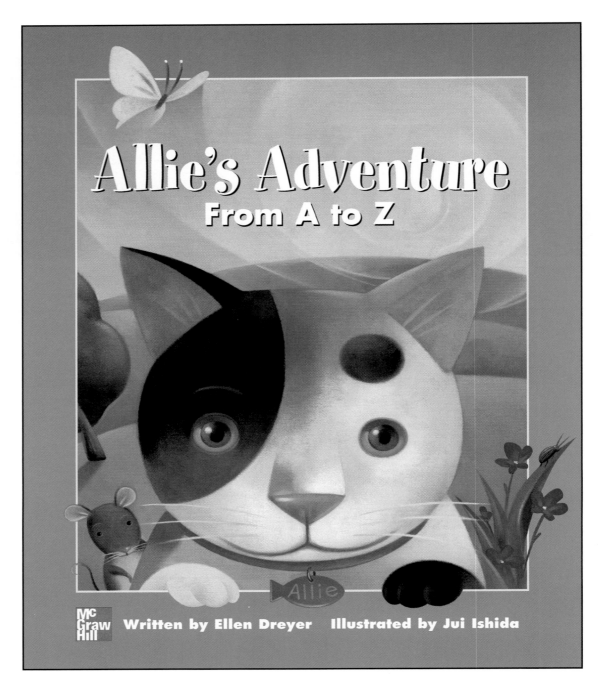

Allie sees a **cow**.

Allie sees a **door**.

Allie sees some **eggs**.

Allie sees lots of **feathers**.

Allie pushes the **gate**.

Allie sees a **hole**.

Allie sees an **insect**.

Allie **jumps**!

A hole is no place for a **kitten**.

Allie sees some **lettuce**.

Allie does not see the **mouse**.

Allie sees a tiny **nose**.

She puts her paw **on** the nose.

The mouse runs past the **pumpkins!**

The mouse is very **quick**.

Allie needs a **rest**!

Allie curls up in a **sunny** spot.

She is very **tired**.

Allie wakes **up**.

She hears a **voice**.

Allie **walks** toward the voice.

Allie is **excited**.

A boy is **yelling** her name.

Zack missed Allie.

Selection Titles	Honors, Prizes, and Awards
 **SHOW AND TELL DAY** by **Anne Rockwell**	**Author/Ilustrator Anne Rockwell,** winner of American Booksellers' Award Pick of the List for *Boats* (1985) and *Cars* (1986); National Science Teachers Association Award for Outstanding Science Trade Book for Children (1988) for *Trains*
 **CHICK AND THE DUCKLING** by **Mirra Ginsburg** Illustrated by **Jose Aruego and Ariane Dewey**	**Illustrators: Jose Aruego and Ariane Dewey,** winners of Boston Globe-Horn Book Honor (1974) for *Herman the Helper*
 **FLOWER GARDEN** by **Eve Bunting** Illustrated by **Kathryn Hewitt**	**Author: Eve Bunting,** winner of ALA Notable Book (1990), IRA-CBC Children's Choice, IRA-Teachers' Choice, School Library Journal Best Book (1989) for *The Wednesday Surprise;* Mark Twain Award (1989) for *Sixth Grade Sleepover;* ALA Notable (1990) for *Wall;* ALA Notable (1992) for *Fly Away Home;* Edgar Allen Poe Juvenile Award (1993) for *Coffin on a Case;* ALA Notable, Caldecott Medal (1995) for *Smoky Night;* Booklist Editors' Choice (1995) for *Spying on Miss Müller;* ALA Notable, Booklist Editors' Choice (1997) for *Train to Somewhere;* National Council for Social Studies Notable Children's Book Award (1998) for *Moonstick,* and *I Am the Mummy Heb-Nefert,* and *On Call Back Mountain;* Young Reader's Choice Award (1997) for *Nasty Stinky Sneakers* **Illustrator: Kathryn Hewitt,** winner of Association of Booksellers for Children, Children's Choice Award (1998) for *Lives of the Athletes: Thrills, Spills (And What the Neighbors Thought);* ALA Notable (1994) Boston Globe-Horn Book Honor (1993) for *Lives of the Musicians: Good Times, Bad Times (and What the Neighbors Thought)*
 **PRETEND YOU'RE A CAT** by **Jean Marzolla** Illustrated by **Jerry Pinkney**	**Author: Jean Marzolla,** winner of 1998 Association of Booksellers for Children, Children's Choice Award for *I Spy Little Book* **Illustrator: Jerry Pinkney,** winner of Coretta Scott King Award, ALA Notable, Christopher Award (1986) for *Patchwork Quilt;* Newbery Medal, Boston Globe-Horn Book Honor (1977) for *Roll of Thunder, Hear My Cry;* Boston Globe-Horn Book Honor (1980) *Childtimes: A Three Generation Memoir;* Coretta Scott King Award (1987) for *Half a Moon and One Whole Star;* ALA Notable (1988) for

Selection Titles	Honors, Prizes, and Awards

 **PRETEND YOU'RE A CAT (CONTINUED)**
by *Jean Marzolla*
Illustrated by *Jerry Pinkney*

Tales of Uncle Remus: The Adventures of Brer Rabbit; ALA Notable, Caldecott Honor, Coretta Scott King Award (1989) for *Mirandy and Brother Wind;* ALA Notable, Caldecott Honor, Coretta Scott King Honor (1990) for *Talking Eggs: A Folktale for the American South;* Golden Kite Award Book (1990) for *Home Place;* ALA Notable (1991) for *Further Tales of Uncle Remus: The Misadventures of Brer Rabbit, Brer Fox . . .;* ALA Notable (1993) for *Back Home;* ALA Notable, Boston Globe-Horn Book Award, Caldecott Honor (1995) for *John Henry;* ALA Notable, Blue Ribbon, Booklist Editors' Choice (1997) for *Sam and the Tigers;* ALA Notable, Christopher Award, Coretta Scott King Award, Golden Kite Honor Book (1997) for *Minty: A Story of Young Harriet Tubman;* Aesop Prize (1997) for *The Hired Hand;* National Council for Social Studies Notable Children's Book Award (1998) for *The Hired Hand* and *Rikki-Tikki-Tavi* (also Children's Choice Award, Association of Booksellers for Children, and Booklist Editors' Choice, 1998); Rip Van Winkle Award (1998); 1998 Hans Christian Andersen nominee

 **ANY KIND OF DOG**
by *Lynn Reiser*

Author/Illustrator: *Lynn Reiser,* winner of ALA Notable (1995) for *The Surprise Family*

 **THE EARTH AND I**
by *Frank Asch*

Author/Illustrator: *Frank Asch,* winner of American Book Award Pick of the List Award (1997) for *Barnyard Animals*

Trade Books

 Additional fiction and nonfiction trade books related to each selection can be shared with children throughout the unit.

Look Book
Tana Hoban (Greenwillow, 1997)

Nature photographs are first viewed through a cut-out hole, and then in their entirety, to challenge young nature enthusiasts.

When the Wind Stops
Charlotte Zolotow, illustrated by Stefano Vitali (HarperCollins, 1995)

In answer to her son's many questions, a mother explains that in nature an end is also a beginning.

Zoo in the Sky: A Book of Animal Constellations
Jacqueline Mitton, illustrated by Christina Balit (National Geographic, 1998)

Simple descriptions and shiny illustrations provide an introduction to astronomy for youngsters.

My Backyard Garden
Carol Lerner (Morrow, 1998)

Young readers are provided with details on how to start their own vegetable gardens.

My Spring Robin
Anne F. Rockwell, illustrated by Harlow and Lizzy Rockwell (Macmillan, 1989)

While searching for a robin in her backyard, a child discovers many interesting plants and creatures.

Planting a Rainbow
Lois Ehlert (Harcourt Brace Jovanovich, 1988)

A mother and child plant a rainbow of flowers in the family garden.

Technology

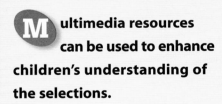 **M**ultimedia resources can be used to enhance children's understanding of the selections.

 Where Do Animals Go in Winter? (National Geographic) Video, 17 min. Children learn about animal behaviors, appearances, and needs in this award-winning film.

 Where Does It Come From? (National Geographic) Video, 15 min. This award-winning film explains how raw materials are processed and used, from pizza to paper.

Backyard Birds (National Geographic) Video, 15 min. One family observes both the migratory and non-migratory birds attracted to their backyard bird feeder.

 Backyard Bugs (National Geographic) Video, 15 min. This multiple-award-winning film introduces children to the numerous creatures that live in neighborhoods and backyards.

Subtheme: Wonders of Nature

Fireflies, Fireflies Light My Way
Jonathan London, illustrated by Linda Messier (Viking, 1996)

Rhyming text features fireflies and other creatures in celebration of the interconnectedness of the natural world.

I Took a Walk
Henry Cole (Greenwillow, 1998)

A child recounts a nature trek through woods, meadow, stream, and pond.

My First Nature Book
Angela Wilkes (Knopf, 1990)

Simple experiments provide an introduction to nature's wonders.

Me and My World (National Geographic) Video, 15 min. A young girl learns how things can be animals, vegetables, minerals, or all three.

Signs of Nature (National Geographic) Video, 20 min. An award-winning look at what nature's "signs" are and what we can learn from them.

Abdo & Daughters
4940 Viking Drive, Suite 622
Edina, MN 55435
(800) 458-8399 • www.abdopub.com

Aladdin Paperbacks
(Imprint of Simon & Schuster Children's Publishing)

Atheneum
(Imprint of Simon & Schuster Children's Publishing)

Bantam Doubleday Dell Books for Young Readers
(Imprint of Random House)

Blackbirch Press
1 Bradley Road, Suite 205
Woodbridge, CT 06525
(203) 387-7525 • (800) 831-9183

Blue Sky Press
(Imprint of Scholastic)

Boyds Mills Press
815 Church Street
Honesdale, PA 18431
(570) 253-1164 • Fax (570) 251-0179 •
(800) 949-7777

Bradbury Press
(Imprint of Simon & Schuster Children's Publishing)

BridgeWater Books
(Distributed by Penguin Putnam)

Candlewick Press
2067 Massachusetts Avenue
Cambridge, MA 02140
(617) 661-3330 • Fax (617) 661-0565

Carolrhoda Books
(Division of Lerner Publications Co.)

Charles Scribners's Sons
(Imprint of Simon & Schuster Children's Publishing)

Children's Press (Division of Grolier, Inc.)
P.O. Box 1796
Danbury, CT 06813-1333
(800) 621-1115 • www.grolier.com

Child's World
P.O. Box 326
Chanhassen, MN 55317-0326
(612) 906-3939 • (800) 599-READ •
www.childsworld.com

Chronicle Books
85 Second Street, Sixth Floor
San Francisco, CA 94105
(415) 537-3730 • (415) 537-4460 • (800) 722-6657 • www.chroniclebooks.com

Clarion Books
(Imprint of Houghton Mifflin, Inc.)
215 Park Avenue South
New York, NY 10003
(212) 420-5800 • (800) 726-0600 •
www.hmco.com/trade/childrens/
shelves.html

Crowell (Imprint of HarperCollins)

Crown Publishing Group
(Imprint of Random House)

Dial Books
(Imprint of Penguin Putnam Inc.)

Dorling Kindersley (DK Publishing)
95 Madison Avenue
New York, NY 10016
(212) 213-4800 • Fax (800) 774-6733 •
(888) 342-5357 • www.dk.com

Doubleday (Imprint of Random House)

E. P. Dutton Children's Books
(Imprint of Penguin Putnam Inc.)

Farrar Straus & Giroux
19 Union Square West
New York, NY 10003
(212) 741-6900 • Fax (212) 633-2427 •
(888) 330-8477

Four Winds Press
(Imprint of Macmillan, see Simon & Schuster Children's Publishing)

Greenwillow Books
(Imprint of William Morrow & Co, Inc.)

Grosset & Dunlap
(Imprint of Penguin Putnam, Inc.)

Harcourt Brace & Co.
525 "B" Street
San Diego, CA 92101
(619) 231-6616 • (800) 543-1918 •
www.harcourtbooks.com

Harper & Row (Imprint of HarperCollins)

HarperCollins Children's Books
10 East 53rd Street
New York, NY 10022
(212) 207-7000 • Fax (212) 202-7044 •
(800) 242-7737 •
www.harperchildrens.com

Henry Holt and Company
115 West 18th Street
New York, NY 10011
(212) 886-9200 • (212) 633-0748 • (888) 330-8477 • www.henryholt.com/byr/

Holiday House
425 Madison Avenue
New York, NY 10017
(212) 688-0085 • Fax (212) 421-6134

Houghton Mifflin
222 Berkeley Street
Boston, MA 02116
(617) 351-5000 • Fax (617) 351-1125 •
(800) 225-3362 • www.hmco.com/trade

Hyperion Books
(Imprint of Buena Vista Publishing Co.)
114 Fifth Avenue
New York, NY 10011
(212) 633-4400 • (800) 759-0190 •
www.disney.com

Ideals Children's Books
(Imprint of Hambleton-Hill Publishing, Inc.)
1501 County Hospital Road
Nashville, TN 37218
(615) 254-2480 • (800) 336-6438

Joy Street Books
(Imprint of Little, Brown & Co.)

Just Us Books
356 Glenwood Avenue
E. Orange, NJ 07017
(973) 672-0304 • Fax (973) 677-7570

Alfred A. Knopf
(Imprint of Random House)

Lee & Low Books
95 Madison Avenue
New York, NY 10016
(212) 779-4400 • Fax (212) 683-1894

Lerner Publications Co.
241 First Avenue North
Minneapolis, MN 55401
(612) 332-3344 • Fax (612) 332-7615 •
(800) 328-4929 • www.lernerbooks.com

Little, Brown & Co.
3 Center Plaza
Boston, MA 02108
(617) 227-0730 • Fax (617) 263-2864 •
(800) 343-9204 • www.littlebrown.com

Lothrop Lee & Shepard
(Imprint of William Morrow & Co.)

Macmillan
(Imprint of Simon & Schuster Children's Publishing)

Marshall Cavendish
99 White Plains Road
Tarrytown, NY 10591
(914) 332-8888 • Fax (914) 332-1082 •
(800) 821-9881 •
www.marshallcavendish.com

William Morrow & Co.
1350 Avenue of the Americas
New York, NY 10019
(212) 261-6500 • Fax (212) 261-6619 •
(800) 843-9389 •
www.williammorrow.com

Morrow Junior Books
(Imprint of William Morrow & Co.)

Mulberry Books
(Imprint of William Morrow & Co.)

National Geographic Society
1145 17th Street, NW
Washington, DC 20036
(202) 828-5667 • (800) 368-2728 •
www.nationalgeographic.com

Northland Publishing
(Division of Justin Industries)
P.O. Box 62
Flagstaff, AZ 86002
(520) 774-5251 • Fax (800) 257-9082 •
(800) 346-3257 • www.northlandpub.com

North-South Books
1123 Broadway, Suite 800
New York, NY 10010
(212) 463-9736 • Fax (212) 633-1004 •
(800) 722-6657 • www.northsouth.com

Orchard Books (A Grolier Company)
95 Madison Avenue
New York, NY 10016
(212) 951-2600 • Fax (212) 213-6435 •
(800) 621-1115 • www.grolier.com

Owlet (Imprint of Henry Holt & Co.)

Willa Perlman Books
(Imprint of Simon & Schuster Children's Publishing)

Philomel Books
(Imprint of Putnam Penguin, Inc.)

Puffin Books
(Imprint of Penguin Putnam, Inc.)

G.P. Putnam's Sons Publishing
(Imprint of Penguin Putnam, Inc.)

Penguin Putnam, Inc.
345 Hudson Street
New York, NY 10014
(212) 366-2000 • Fax (212) 366-2666 •
(800) 631-8571 •
www.penguinputnam.com

Random House
201 East 50th Street
New York, NY 10022
(212) 751-2600 • Fax (212) 572-2593 •
(800) 726-0600 • www.randomhouse/kids

Rourke Corporation
P.O. Box 3328
Vero Beach, FL 32964
(561) 234-6001 • (800) 394-7055 •
www.rourkepublishing.com

Scholastic
555 Broadway
New York, NY 10012
(212) 343-6100 • Fax (212) 343-6930 •
(800) SCHOLASTIC • www.scholastic.com

Sierra Junior Club
85 Second Street, Second Floor
San Francisco, CA 94105-3441
(415) 977-5500 • Fax (415) 977-5799 •
(800) 935-1056 • www.sierraclub.org

Simon & Schuster Children's Books
1230 Avenue of the Americas
New York, NY 10020
(212) 698-7200 • (800) 223-2336 •
www.simonsays.com/kidzone

Smith & Kraus
4 Lower Mill Road
N. Stratford, NH 03590
(603) 643-6431 • Fax (603) 643-1831 •
(800) 895-4331 • www.smithkraus.com

Teacher Ideas Press
(Division of Libraries Unlimited)
P.O. Box 6633
Englewood, CO 80155-6633
(303) 770-1220 • Fax (303) 220-8843 •
(800) 237-6124 • www.lu.com

Ticknor & Fields
(Imprint of Houghton Mifflin, Inc.)

Usborne (Imprint of EDC Publishing)
10302 E. 55th Place, Suite B
Tulsa, OK 74146-6515
(918) 622-4522 • (800) 475-4522 •
www.edcpub.com

Viking Children's Books
(Imprint of Penguin Putnam Inc.)

Watts Publishing
(Imprint of Grolier Publishing;
see Children's Press)

Walker & Co.
435 Hudson Street
New York, NY 10014
(212) 727-8300 • (212) 727-0984 • (800)
AT-WALKER

Whispering Coyote Press
300 Crescent Court, Suite 860
Dallas, TX 75201
(800) 929-6104 • Fax (214) 319-7298

Albert Whitman
6340 Oakton Street
Morton Grove, IL 60053-2723
(847) 581-0033 • Fax (847) 581-0039 •
(800) 255-7675 • www.awhitmanco.com

Workman Publishing Co., Inc.
708 Broadway
New York, NY 10003
(212) 254-5900 • Fax (800) 521-1832 •
(800) 722-7202 • www.workman.com

Multimedia Resources

AGC/United Learning
6633 West Howard Street
Niles, IL 60714-3389
(800) 424-0362 • www.unitedlearning.com

AIMS Multimedia
9710 DeSoto Avenue
Chatsworth, CA 91311-4409
(800) 367-2467 •
www.AIMS-multimedia.com

BFA Educational Media
(see Phoenix Learning Group)

Broderbund
(Parsons Technology;
also see The Learning Company)
500 Redwood Blvd
Novato, CA 94997
(800) 521-6263 • Fax (800) 474-8840 •
www.broderbund.com

Carousel Film and Video
260 Fifth Avenue, Suite 705
New York, NY 10001
(212) 683-1660 • e-mail:
carousel@pipeline.com

Cloud 9 Interactive
(888) 662-5683 • www.cloud9int.com

Computer Plus (see ESI)

Coronet/MTI
(see Phoenix Learning Group)

Davidson (see Knowledge Adventure)

Direct Cinema, Ltd.
P.O. Box 10003
Santa Monica, CA 90410-1003
(800) 525-0000

Disney Interactive
(800) 900-9234 •
www.disneyinteractive.com

DK Multimedia (Dorling Kindersley)
95 Madison Avenue
New York, NY 10016
(212) 213-4800 • Fax: (800) 774-6733 •
(888) 342-5357 • www.dk.com

Edmark Corp.
P.O. Box 97021
Redmond, CA 98073-9721
(800) 362-2890 • www.edmark.com

Encyclopaedia Britannica Educational Corp.
310 South Michigan Avenue
Chicago, IL 60604
(800) 554-9862 • www.eb.com

ESI/Educational Software
4213 S. 94th Street
Omaha, NE 68127
(800) 955-5570 • www.edsoft.com

GPN/Reading Rainbow
University of Nebraska-Lincoln
P.O. Box 80669
Lincoln, NE 68501-0669
(800) 228-4630 • www.gpn.unl.edu

Hasbro Interactive
(800) 683-5847 • www.hasbro.com

Humongous
13110 NE 177th Pl., Suite B101, Box 180
Woodenville, WA 98072
(800) 499-8386 • www.humongous.com

IBM Corp.
1133 Westchester Ave.
White Plains, NY 10604
(770) 863-1234 • Fax (770) 863-3030 •
(888) 411-1932 •
www.pc.ibm.com/multimedia/crayola

ICE, Inc.
(Distributed by Arch Publishing)
12B W. Main St.
Elmsford, NY 10523
(914) 347-2464 • (800) 843-9497 •
www.educorp.com

Knowledge Adventure
19840 Pioneer Avenue
Torrence, CA 90503
(800) 542-4240 • (800) 545-7677 •
www.knowledgeadventure.com

The Learning Company
6160 Summit Drive North
Minneapolis, MN 55430
(800) 685-6322 • www.learningco.com

Listening Library
One Park Avenue
Greenwich, CT 06870-1727
(800) 243-4504 • www.listeninglib.com

Macmillan/McGraw-Hill
(see SRA/McGraw-Hill)

Maxis
2121 N. California Blvd
Walnut Creek, CA 94596-3572
(925) 933-5630 • Fax (925) 927-3736 •
(800) 245-4525 • www.maxis.com

MECC
(see the Learning Company)

Microsoft
One Microsoft Way
Redmond, WA 98052-6399
(800) 426-9400 • www.microsoft.com/kids

National Geographic Society Educational Services
P.O. Box 10597
Des Moines, IA 50340-0597
(800) 368-2728 •
www.nationalgeographic.com

National School Products
101 East Broadway
Maryville, TN 37804
(800) 251-9124 • www.ierc.com

PBS Video
1320 Braddock Place
Alexandria, VA 22314
(800) 344-3337 • www.pbs.org

Phoenix Films
(see Phoenix Learning Group)

The Phoenix Learning Group
2348 Chaffee Drive
St. Louis, MO 63146
(800) 221-1274 • e-mail:
phoenixfilms@worldnet.att.net

Pied Piper (see AIMS Multimedia)

Scholastic New Media
555 Broadway
New York, NY 10003
(800) 724-6527 • www.scholastic.com

Simon & Schuster Interactive
(see Knowledge Adventure)

SRA/McGraw-Hill
220 Daniel Dale Road
De Soto, TX 75115
(800) 843-8855 • www.sra4kids.com

SVE/Churchill Media
6677 North Northwest Highway
Chicago, IL 60631
(800) 829-1900 •www.svemedia.com

Tom Snyder Productions (also see ESI)
80 Coolidge Hill Rd.
Watertown, MA 02472
(800) 342-0236 • www.teachtsp.com

Troll Associates
100 Corporate Drive
Mahwah, NJ 07430
(800) 929-8765 • Fax (800) 979-8765 •
www.troll.com

Voyager (see ESI)

Weston Woods
12 Oakwood Avenue
Norwalk, CT 06850
(800) 243-5020 • Fax (203) 845-0498

Zenger Media
10200 Jefferson Blvd., Room 94,
P.O. Box 802
Culver City, CA 90232-0802
(800) 421-4246 • (800) 944-5432 •
www.Zengermedia.com

Word List

UNIT 1

	Decodable Words				Vocabulary
THE HOUSE					**High-Frequency Words** the
A PRESENT					**High-Frequency Words** a
MY SCHOOL					**High-Frequency Words** my
NAN	an	**Nan**			**High-Frequency Words** that
THAT NAN!	Review				**High-Frequency Words** Review

UNIT 2

	Decodable Words				Vocabulary
DAN AND DAD	**Dad**	**Dan**			**High-Frequency Words** and
DAD, DAN, AND I	sad				**High-Frequency Words** I
I AM SAM!	**am** dam	mad	man	**Sam**	**High-Frequency Words** is
SID SAID	did dim	in	**Min**	**Sid**	**High-Frequency Words** said
IS SAM MAD?	Review				**High-Frequency Words** Review

Boldfaced words appear in the selection.

UNIT 3

	Decodable Words				Vocabulary
THAT TAM!	at	Nat	**Tam**	**Tim**	**High-Frequency Words**
	it	**sat**	tan	tin	we
	mat	**sit**			
NAT IS MY CAT	**can**	**cat**			**High-Frequency Words**
					are
ON THE DOT	cot	**dot**	**not**	**Tom**	**High-Frequency Words**
	Dom	**Mom**	**on**	tot	you
	Don				
WE FIT!	fan	fat	fin	**fit**	**High-Frequency Words**
					have
THE TAN CAT	Review				**High-Frequency Words**
					Review

UNIT 4

	Decodable Words				Vocabulary
YOU ARE IT!	**ran**	rod	**Ron**	rot	**High-Frequency Words**
	rat				**to**
TAP THE SAP	**cap**	pad	pod	**sip**	**High-Frequency Words**
	dip	**Pam**	**pot**	**tap**	me
	map	**pan**	rip	tip	
	mop	pat	**sap**	**top**	
	nap				
NAP IN A LAP	lad	lid	lit	lot	**High-Frequency Words**
	lap	lip			go
MUD FUN	**cup**	**mud**	run	sun	**High-Frequency Words**
	cut	nut	rut	up	do
	fun	pup			
FUN IN THE SUN	Review				**High-Frequency Words**
					Review

UNIT 5

	Decodable Words				**Vocabulary**
TOM IS SICK	dock	lock	**pick**	**sock**	**High-Frequency Words** **for**
	duck	luck	rack	tack	
	kid	Mack	rock	tick	
	Kim	Mick	sack	tock	
	kit	muck	**sick**	tuck	
	lick	pack			
PUG	dug	gum	**Pug**	tag	**High-Frequency Words** **he**
	fog	log	rag	tug	
	got	**mug**	rug		
A PET FOR KEN	den	leg	Ned	**red**	**High-Frequency Words** **she**
	fed	**let**	net	set	
	get	Meg	pen	Ted	
	Ken	men	**pet**	ten	
	led	met			
A BIG BUG	bad	bet	bog	cub	**High-Frequency Words** **has**
	bag	**big**	bud	Rob	
	bat	bin	**bug**	rub	
	bed	bit	but	tub	
	Ben				
A PUP AND A CAT	Review				**High-Frequency Words** Review

UNIT 6

	Decodable Words				Vocabulary
HOP WITH A HOG	had ham **hat** hen	him hip **hit**	**hog** **hop** hot	**hug** **hum** hut	**High-Frequency Words** **with**
WE WIN!	wag web	wed wet	wig	**win**	**High-Frequency Words** **was**
THE VET VAN	ax box **fix**	fox **Max** mix	ox **Rex** six	**van** **vet** wax	**High-Frequency Words** **not**
JEN AND YIP	jam Jan **Jen** jet jig Jim	job **jog** jot jug **quack** **quick**	quit yam yet **Yip** yuck	yum Zack Zeb **zigzag** zip	**High-Frequency Words** **of**
ZACK AND JAN	Review				**High-Frequency Words** Review

Listening, Speaking, Viewing, Representing

☑ Tested Skill

Tinted panels show skills, strategies, and other teaching opportunities

	K	1	2	3	4	5	6
LISTENING							
Learn the vocabulary of school (numbers, shapes, colors, directions, and categories)							
Identify the musical elements of literary language, such as rhymes, repeated sounds, onomatopoeia							
Determine purposes for listening (get information, solve problems, enjoy and appreciate)							
Listen critically and responsively							
Ask and answer relevant questions							
Listen critically to interpret and evaluate							
Listen responsively to stories and other texts read aloud, including selections from classic and contemporary works							
Connect own experiences, ideas, and traditions with those of others							
Apply comprehension strategies in listening activities							
Understand the major ideas and supporting evidence in spoken messages							
Participate in listening activities related to reading and writing (such as discussions, group activities, conferences)							
Listen to learn by taking notes, organizing, and summarizing spoken ideas							
SPEAKING							
Learn the vocabulary of school (numbers, shapes, colors, directions, and categories)							
Use appropriate language and vocabulary learned to describe ideas, feelings, and experiences							
Ask and answer relevant questions							
Communicate effectively in everyday situations (such as discussions, group activities, conferences)							
Demonstrate speaking skills (audience, purpose, occasion, volume, pitch, tone, rate, fluency)							
Clarify and support spoken messages and ideas with objects, charts, evidence, elaboration, examples							
Use verbal and nonverbal communication in effective ways when, for example, making announcements, giving directions, or making introductions							
Retell a spoken message by summarizing or clarifying							
Connect own experiences, ideas, and traditions with those of others							
Determine purposes for speaking (inform, entertain, give directions, persuade, express personal feelings and opinions)							
Demonstrate skills of reporting and providing information							
Demonstrate skills of interviewing, requesting and providing information							
Apply composition strategies in speaking activities							
Monitor own understanding of spoken message and seek clarification as needed							
VIEWING							
Demonstrate viewing skills (focus attention, organize information)							
Respond to audiovisual media in a variety of ways							
Participate in viewing activities related to reading and writing							
Apply comprehension strategies in viewing activities							
Recognize artists' craft and techniques for conveying meaning							
Interpret information from various formats such as maps, charts, graphics, video segments, technology							
Evaluate purposes of various media (information, appreciation, entertainment, directions, persuasion)							
Use media to compare ideas and points of view							
REPRESENTING							
Select, organize, or produce visuals to complement or extend meanings							
Produce communication using appropriate media to develop a class paper, multimedia or video reports							
Show how language, medium, and presentation contribute to the message							

Reading: Alphabetic Principle, Sounds/Symbols

☑ Tested Skill

☐ Tinted panels show skills, strategies, and other teaching opportunities

PRINT AWARENESS	K	1	2	3	4	5	6
Know the order of the alphabet							
Recognize that print represents spoken language and conveys meaning							
Understand directionality (tracking print from left to right; return sweep)							
Understand that written words are separated by spaces							
Know the difference between individual letters and printed words							
Understand that spoken words are represented in written language by specific sequence of letters							
Recognize that there are correct spellings for words							
Know the difference between capital and lowercase letters							
Recognize how readers use capitalization and punctuation to comprehend							
Recognize the distinguishing features of a paragraph							
Recognize that parts of a book (such as cover/title page and table of contents) offer information							

PHONOLOGICAL AWARENESS	K	1	2	3	4	5	6
Identify letters, words, sentences							
Divide spoken sentence into individual words							
Produce rhyming words and distinguish rhyming words from nonrhyming words							
Identify, segment, and combine syllables within spoken words							
Identify and isolate the initial and final sound of a spoken word							
Add, delete, or change sounds to change words (such as *cow* to *how*, *pan* to *fan*)							
Blend sounds to make spoken words							
Segment one-syllable spoken words into individual phonemes							

PHONICS AND DECODING	K	1	2	3	4	5	6
Alphabetic principle: Letter/sound correspondence	☑	☑	☑				
Blending CVC words	☑						
Segmenting CVC words	☑						
Blending CVC, CVCe, CCVC, CVCC, CVVC words	☑	☑	☑				
Segmenting CVC, CVCe, CCVC, CVCC, CVVC words	☑	☑	☑				
Initial and final consonants: /n/n, /d/d, /s/s, /m/m, /t/t, /k/c, /f/f, /r/r, /p/p, /l/l, /k/k, /g/g, /b/b, /h/h, /w/w, /v/v, /ks/x, /kw/qu, /j/j, /y/y, /z/z	☑	☑					
Initial and medial short vowels: *a, i, u, o, e*	☑	☑	☑				
Long vowels: *a-e, i-e, o-e, u-e* (vowel-consonant-e)		☑	☑				
Long vowels, including *ay, ai; e, ee, ie, ea, o, oa, oe, ow; i, y, igh*		☑	☑				
Consonant Digraphs: *sh, th, ch, wh*		☑					
Consonant Blends: continuant/continuant, including *sl, sm, sn, fl, fr, ll, ss, ff*		☑					
Consonant Blends: continuant/stop, including *st, sk, sp, ng, nt, nd, mp, ft*		☑					
Consonant Blends: stop/continuant, including *tr, pr, pl, cr, tw*		☑					
Variant vowels: including /u/oo; /ô/a, aw, au; /ü/ue, ew		☑	☑				
Diphthongs, including /ou/ou, ow; /oi/oi, oy		☑	☑				
r-controlled vowels, including /âr/are; /ôr/or, ore; /îr/ear		☑					
Soft *c* and soft *g*		☑					
nk		☑	☑				
Consonant Digraphs: *ck*	☑	☑					
Consonant Digraphs: *ph, tch, ch*			☑				
Short *e: ea*			☑				
Long *e: y, ey*			☑				
/ü/oo		☑	☑				
/är/ar; /ûr/ir, ur, er		☑	☑				
Silent letters: including *l, b, k, w, g, h, gh*			☑				
Schwa: /ər/er; /ən/en; /əl/le;			☑				
Reading/identifying multisyllabic words		☑	☑				

Reading: Vocabulary/Word Identification

WORD STRUCTURE	K	1	2	3	4	5	6
Common spelling patterns							
Syllable patterns							
Plurals							
Possessives							
Contractions							
Root, or base, words and inflectional endings (-s, -es, -ed, -ing)							
Compound Words							
Prefixes and suffixes (such as un-, re-, dis-, non-; -ly, -y, -ful, -able, -tion)							
Root words and derivational endings							

WORD MEANING	K	1	2	3	4	5	6
Develop vocabulary through concrete experiences							
Develop vocabulary through selections read aloud							
Develop vocabulary through reading							
Cueing systems: syntactic, semantic, phonetic							
Context clues, including semantic clues (word meaning), syntactical clues (word order), and phonetic clues	☑	☑	☑	☑	☑	☑	☑
High-frequency words (such as the, a, an, and, said, was, where, is)							
Identify words that name persons, places, things, and actions							
Automatic reading of regular and irregular words							
Use resources and references dictionary, glossary, thesaurus, synonym finder, technology and software, and context)							
Synonyms and antonyms							
Multiple-meaning words							
Figurative language							
Decode derivatives (root words, such as like, pay, happy with affixes, such as dis-, pre-, -un)							
Systematic study of words across content areas and in current events							
Locate meanings, pronunciations, and derivations (including dictionaries, glossaries, and other sources)							
Denotation and connotation							
Word origins as aid to understanding historical influences on English word meanings							
Homophones, homographs							
Analogies							
Idioms							

Reading: Comprehension

PREREADING STRATEGIES	K	1	2	3	4	5	6
Preview and Predict							
Use prior knowledge							
Establish and adjust purposes for reading							
Build background							

MONITORING STRATEGIES	K	1	2	3	4	5	6
Adjust reading rate							
Reread, search for clues, ask questions, ask for help							
Visualize							
Read a portion aloud, use reference aids							
Use decoding and vocabulary strategies							
Paraphrase							
Create story maps, diagrams, charts, story props to help comprehend, analyze, synthesize and evaluate texts							

(continued on next page)

✓ Tested Skill

Tinted panels show skills, strategies, and other teaching opportunities

SKILLS AND STRATEGIES

Skill	K	1	2	3	4	5	6
Story details	✓						
Use illustrations	✓	✓					
Reality and fantasy	✓	✓	✓	✓			
Classify and categorize	✓						
Make predictions	✓	✓	✓	✓	✓	✓	✓
Sequence of events (tell or act out)	✓	✓	✓	✓	✓	✓	✓
Cause and effect		✓	✓	✓	✓	✓	✓
Compare and contrast	✓	✓	✓	✓	✓	✓	✓
Summarize	✓	✓	✓	✓	✓	✓	✓
Make and explain inferences		✓	✓	✓	✓	✓	✓
Draw conclusions		✓	✓	✓	✓	✓	✓
Important and unimportant information					✓	✓	✓
Main idea and supporting details	✓	✓	✓	✓	✓	✓	✓
Form conclusions or generalizations and support with evidence from text				✓	✓	✓	✓
Fact and opinion (including news stories and advertisements)				✓	✓	✓	✓
Problem and solution				✓	✓	✓	✓
Steps in a process		✓	✓	✓	✓	✓	✓
Make judgments and decisions				✓	✓	✓	✓
Fact and nonfact				✓	✓	✓	✓
Recognize techniques of persuasion and propaganda					✓	✓	✓
Evaluate evidence and sources of information					✓	✓	✓
Identify similarities and differences across texts (including topics, characters, problems, themes, treatment, scope, or organization)							
Practice various questions and tasks (test-like comprehension questions)							
Paraphrase and summarize to recall, inform, and organize							
Answer various types of questions (open-ended, literal, interpretative, test-like such as true-false, multiple choice, short-answer)							
Use study strategies to learn and recall (preview, question, reread, and record)							

LITERARY RESPONSE

Skill	K	1	2	3	4	5	6
Listen to stories being read aloud							
React, speculate, join in, read along when predictable and patterned selections are read aloud							
Respond through talk, movement, music, art, drama, and writing to a variety of stories and poems							
Show understanding through writing, illustrating, developing demonstrations, and using technology							
Connect ideas and themes across texts							
Support responses by referring to relevant aspects of text and own experiences							
Offer observations, make connections, speculate, interpret, and raise questions in response to texts							
Interpret text ideas through journal writing, discussion, enactment, and media							

TEXT STRUCTURE/LITERARY CONCEPTS

Skill	K	1	2	3	4	5	6
Distinguish forms of texts and the functions they serve (lists, newsletters, signs)							
Understand story structure							
Identify narrative (for entertainment) and expository (for information)							
Distinguish fiction from nonfiction, including fact and fantasy							
Understand literary forms (stories, poems, plays, and informational books)							
Understand literary terms by distinguishing between roles of author and illustrator							
Understand title, author, and illustrator across a variety of texts							
Analyze character, character's point of view, plot, setting, style, tone, mood		✓	✓	✓	✓	✓	✓
Compare communication in different forms							
Understand terms such as title, author, illustrator, playwright, theater, stage, act, dialogue, and scene							
Recognize stories, poems, myths, folktales, fables, tall tales, limericks, plays, biographies, and autobiographies							
Judge internal logic of story text							
Recognize that authors organize information in specific ways							
Identify texts to inform, influence, express, or entertain							
Describe how author's point of view affects text							
Recognize biography, historical fiction, realistic fiction, modern fantasy, informational texts, and poetry							
Analyze ways authors present ideas (cause/effect, compare/contrast, inductively, deductively, chronologically)							
Recognize flashback, foreshadowing, symbolism							

(continued on next page)

(Reading: Comprehension continued)

VARIETY OF TEXT	K	1	2	3	4	5	6
Read a variety of genres							
Use informational texts to acquire information							
Read for a variety of purposes							
Select varied sources when reading for information or pleasure							
FLUENCY							
Read regularly in independent-level and instructional-level materials							
Read orally with fluency from familiar texts							
Self-select independent-level reading							
Read silently for increasing periods of time							
Demonstrate characteristics of fluent and effective reading							
Adjust reading rate to purpose							
Read aloud in selected texts, showing understanding of text and engaging the listener							
CULTURES							
Connect own experience with culture of others							
Compare experiences of characters across cultures							
Articulate and discuss themes and connections that cross cultures							
CRITICAL THINKING							
Experiences (comprehend, apply, analyze, synthesize, evaluate)							
Make connections (comprehend, apply, analyze, synthesize, evaluate)							
Expression (comprehend, apply, analyze, synthesize, evaluate)							
Inquiry (comprehend, apply, analyze, synthesize, evaluate)							
Problem solving (comprehend, apply, analyze, synthesize, evaluate)							
Making decisions (comprehend, apply, analyze, synthesize, evaluate)							

Study Skills

INQUIRY/RESEARCH	K	1	2	3	4	5	6
Follow directions							
Use alphabetical order							
Identify/frame questions for research							
Obtain, organize, and summarize information: classify, take notes, outline							
Evaluate research and raise new questions							
Use technology to present information in various formats							
Follow accepted formats for writing research, including documenting sources							
Use test-taking strategies							
Use text organizers (book cover; title page—title, author, illustrator; contents; headings; glossary; index)		☑	☑	☑	☑	☑	☑
Use graphic aids, including maps, diagrams, charts, graphs		☑	☑	☑	☑	☑	☑
Read and interpret varied texts including environmental print, signs, lists, encyclopedia, dictionary, glossary, newspaper, advertisement, magazine, calendar, directions, floor plans		☑	☑	☑	☑	☑	☑
Use reference sources, such as glossary, dictionary, encyclopedia, telephone directory, technology resources		☑	☑	☑	☑	☑	☑
Recognize Library/Media center resources, such as computerized references; catalog search—subject, author, title; encyclopedia index		☑	☑	☑	☑	☑	☑

Writing

MODES AND FORMS	K	1	2	3	4	5	6
Interactive writing							
Personal narrative (Expressive narrative)			☑	☑	☑	☑	☑
Writing that compares (Informative classificatory)			☑	☑	☑	☑	☑
Explanatory writing (Informative narrative)		☑	☑	☑	☑	☑	☑
Persuasive writing (Persuasive descriptive)			☑	☑	☑	☑	☑
Writing a story		☑	☑	☑	☑	☑	☑
Expository writing	☑	☑	☑	☑	☑	☑	☑
Write using a variety of formats, such as advertisement, autobiography, biography, book report/report, comparison-contrast, critique/review/editorial, description, essay, how-to, interview, invitation, journal/log/notes, message/list, paragraph/multi-paragraph composition, picture book, play (scene), poem/rhyme, story, summary, note, letter							

PURPOSES/AUDIENCES	K	1	2	3	4	5	6
Dictate messages such as news and stories for others to write							
Write labels, notes, and captions for illustrations, possessions, charts, and centers							
Write to record, to discover and develop ideas, to inform, to influence, to entertain							
Exhibit an identifiable voice in personal narratives and stories							
Use literary devices (suspense, dialogue, and figurative language)							
Produce written texts by organizing ideas, using effective transitions, and choosing precise wording							

PROCESSES	K	1	2	3	4	5	6
Generate ideas for self-selected and assigned topics using prewriting strategies							
Develop drafts							
Revise drafts for varied purposes							
Edit for appropriate grammar, spelling, punctuation, and features of polished writings							
Proofread own writing and that of others							
Bring pieces to final form and "publish" them for audiences							
Use technology to compose text							
Select and use reference materials and resources for writing, revising, and editing final drafts							

SPELLING	K	1	2	3	4	5	6
Spell own name and write high-frequency words							
Words with short vowels (including CVC and one-syllable words with blends CCVC, CVCC, CCVCC)							
Words with long vowels (including CVCe)							
Words with digraphs, blends, consonant clusters, double consonants							
Words with diphthongs							
Words with variant vowels							
Words with r-controlled vowels							
Words with /ər/, /əl/, and /ən/							
Words with silent letters							
Words with soft c and soft g							
Inflectional endings (including plurals and past tense and words that drop the final e when adding -ing, -ed)							
Compound words							
Contractions							
Homonyms							
Suffixes including -able, -ly, or -less, and prefixes including dis-, re-, pre-, or un-							
Spell words ending in -tion and -sion, such as station and procession							
Accurate spelling of root or base words							
Orthographic patterns and rules such as keep/can; sack/book; out/now; oil/toy; match/speech; ledge/cage; consonant doubling, dropping e, changing y to i							
Multisyllabic words using regularly spelled phonogram patterns							
Syllable patterns (including closed, open, syllable boundary patterns)							
Synonyms and antonyms							
Words from Social Studies, Science, Math, and Physical Education							
Words derived from other languages and cultures							
Use resources to find correct spellings, synonyms, and replacement words							
Use conventional spelling of familiar words in writing assignments							
Spell accurately in final drafts							

(continued on next page)

☑ Tested Skill

Tinted panels show skills, strategies, and other teaching opportunities

GRAMMAR AND USAGE

	K	1	2	3	4	5	6
Understand sentence concepts (word order, statements, questions, exclamations, commands)							
Recognize complete and incomplete sentences							
Nouns (common; proper; singular; plural; irregular plural; possessives)							
Verbs (action; helping; linking; irregular)							
Verb tense (present, past, future, perfect, and progressive)							
Pronouns (possessive, subject and object, pronoun-verb agreement)							
Use objective case pronouns accurately							
Adjectives							
Adverbs that tell how, when, where							
Subjects, predicates							
Subject-verb agreement							
Sentence combining							
Recognize sentence structure (simple, compound, complex)							
Synonyms and antonyms							
Contractions							
Conjunctions							
Prepositions and prepositional phrases							

PENMANSHIP

	K	1	2	3	4	5	6
Write each letter of alphabet (capital and lowercase) using correct formation, appropriate size and spacing							
Write own name and other important words							
Use phonological knowledge to map sounds to letters to write messages							
Write messages that move left to right, top to bottom							
Gain increasing control of penmanship, pencil grip, paper position, beginning stroke							
Use word and letter spacing and margins to make messages readable							
Write legibly by selecting cursive or manuscript as appropriate							

MECHANICS

	K	1	2	3	4	5	6
Use capitalization in sentences, proper nouns, titles, abbreviations and the pronoun I							
Use end marks correctly (period, question mark, exclamation point)							
Use commas (in dates, in addresses, in a series, in letters, in direct address)							
Use apostrophes in contractions and possessives							
Use quotation marks							
Use hyphens, semicolons, colons							

EVALUATION

	K	1	2	3	4	5	6
Identify the most effective features of a piece of writing using class/teacher generated criteria							
Respond constructively to others' writing							
Determine how his/her own writing achieves its purpose							
Use published pieces as models for writing							
Review own written work to monitor growth as writer							

For more detailed scope and sequence including page numbers and additional phonics information, see McGraw-Hill Reading Program scope and sequence (K-6)

Scoring Chart

The Scoring Chart is provided for your convenience in grading your students' work.

- Find the column that shows the total number of items.
- Find the row that matches the number of items answered correctly.
- The intersection of the two rows provides the percentage score.

TOTAL NUMBER OF ITEMS

NUMBER CORRECT

N.C. \ Items	1	2	3	4	5	6	7	8	9	10	11	12	13	14	15	16	17	18	19	20	21	22	23	24	25	26	27	28	29	30
1	100	50	33	25	20	17	14	13	11	10	9	8	8	7	7	6	6	6	5	5	5	5	4	4	4	4	4	4	3	3
2		100	66	50	40	33	29	25	22	20	18	17	15	14	13	13	12	11	11	10	10	9	9	8	8	8	7	7	7	7
3			100	75	60	50	43	38	33	30	27	25	23	21	20	19	18	17	16	15	14	14	13	13	12	12	11	11	10	10
4				100	80	67	57	50	44	40	36	33	31	29	27	25	24	22	21	20	19	18	17	17	16	15	15	14	14	13
5					100	83	71	63	56	50	45	42	38	36	33	31	29	28	26	25	24	23	22	21	20	19	19	18	17	17
6						100	86	75	67	60	55	50	46	43	40	38	35	33	32	30	29	27	26	25	24	23	22	21	21	20
7							100	88	78	70	64	58	54	50	47	44	41	39	37	35	33	32	30	29	28	27	26	25	24	23
8								100	89	80	73	67	62	57	53	50	47	44	42	40	38	36	35	33	32	31	30	29	28	27
9									100	90	82	75	69	64	60	56	53	50	47	45	43	41	39	38	36	35	33	32	31	30
10										100	91	83	77	71	67	63	59	56	53	50	48	45	43	42	40	38	37	36	34	33
11											100	92	85	79	73	69	65	61	58	55	52	50	48	46	44	42	41	39	38	37
12												100	92	86	80	75	71	67	63	60	57	55	52	50	48	46	44	43	41	40
13													100	93	87	81	76	72	68	65	62	59	57	54	52	50	48	46	45	43
14														100	93	88	82	78	74	70	67	64	61	58	56	54	52	50	48	47
15															100	94	88	83	79	75	71	68	65	63	60	58	56	54	52	50
16																100	94	89	84	80	76	73	70	67	64	62	59	57	55	53
17																	100	94	89	85	81	77	74	71	68	65	63	61	59	57
18																		100	95	90	86	82	78	75	72	69	67	64	62	60
19																			100	95	90	86	83	79	76	73	70	68	66	63
20																				100	95	91	87	83	80	77	74	71	69	67
21																					100	95	91	88	84	81	78	75	72	70
22																						100	96	92	88	85	81	79	76	73
23																							100	96	92	88	85	82	79	77
24																								100	96	92	89	86	83	80
25																									100	96	93	89	86	83
26																										100	96	93	90	87
27																											100	96	93	90
28																												100	97	93
29																													100	97
30																														100

Notes

Notes

Notes

Notes